GREEN ARROW

THE ARCHER'S QUEST

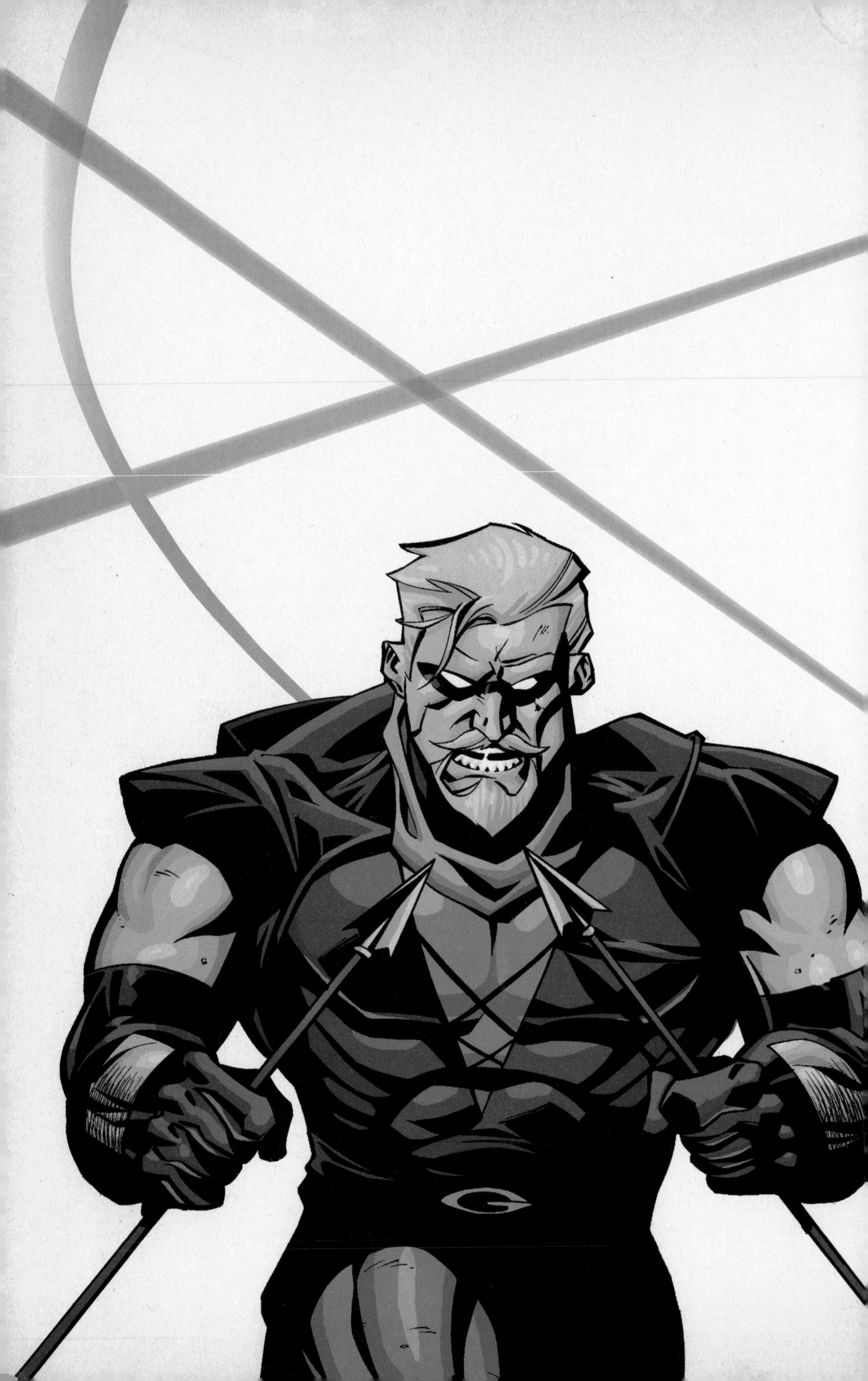

BRAD MELTZER
Writer

PHIL HESTER
Penciller

ANDE PARKS
Inker

JAMES SINCLAIR
Colorist

SEAN KONOT
Letterer

MATT WAGNER
Original Covers

GREEN ARROW

THE ARCHER'S QUEST

DAN DIDIO
VP-Editorial

BOB SCHRECK
Editor-original series

BOB GREENBERGER
Senior Editor-collected edition

ROBBIN BROSTERMAN
Senior Art Director

PAUL LEVITZ
President & Publisher

GEORG BREWER
VP-Design & Retail Product Development

RICHARD BRUNING
Senior VP-Creative Director

PATRICK CALDON
Senior VP-Finance & Operations

CHRIS CARAMALIS
VP-Finance

TERRI CUNNINGHAM
VP-Managing Editor

ALISON GILL
VP-Manufacturing

LILLIAN LASERSON
Senior VP & General Counsel

JIM LEE
Editorial Director-WildStorm

DAVID MCKILLIPS
VP-Advertising & Custom Publishing

JOHN NEE
VP-Business Development

CHERYL RUBIN
VP-Brand Management

BOB WAYNE
VP-Sales & Marketing

For my Dad,

who bought me comics all those years,

even when he would've rather been buying baseballs

GREEN ARROW: THE ARCHER'S QUEST
Published by DC Comics. Cover, introduction and compilation copyright
© 2003 DC Comics. All Rights Reserved.

Originally published in single magazine form in GREEN ARROW 16-21.
Copyright © 2002, 2003 DC Comics. All Rights Reserved.
All characters, their distinctive likenesses and related indicia featured in
this publication are trademarks of DC Comics. The stories, characters and
incidents featured in this publication are entirely fictional.
DC Comics does not read or accept unsolicited submissions of ideas,
stories or artwork.

DC Comics, 1700 Broadway, New York, NY 10019
A Warner Bros. Entertainment Company
Printed in Canada. First Printing.
ISBN: 1-4012-0010-9
Cover illustration by Phil Hester and Ande Parks
Cover color by Richard and Tanya Horie

GREEN ARROW: THE ARCHER'S QUEST

INTRODUCTION by PATRICK LEAHY

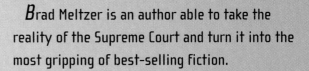

*B*rad Meltzer is an author able to take the reality of the Supreme Court and turn it into the most gripping of best-selling fiction.

In *The Archer's Quest*, he draws together threads of the decades-old legend of Green Arrow and weaves it anew into a contemporary epic. It is a literary exercise worth doing, and one that is worthy of Brad Meltzer's talent.

Through the years, Green Arrow has evolved from a wisecracking archer, with arrows equipped with everything from boxing gloves to handcuffs, to a member of the Justice League, to finally his own funeral.

In *The Archer's Quest*, Oliver Queen comes back to life. His evolution from an early, roughhewn character to a complex baby-boomer is masterfully and delicately achieved. Brad Meltzer stays true throughout to the story arc of Green Arrow and the Justice League of America, weaving together mortals and immortals, humans and mutants, Earth-born and alien alike.

New readers get a fascinating history and older readers are rewarded by snippets they recall from youth, like the memories of Ollie driving cross-country with Hal in an old pickup truck.

In the earliest of Green Arrows, it was a simpler but enjoyable storyline that echoed the times. Today we live in a far more complex world, and Green Arrow's life reflects that. It is not just the battling evil, in its sometimes ambiguous forms, but coming to grips with his love of Dinah, acceptance of his son Connor, understanding the relationship with Roy, and even though he is just returned from the grave, making plans for his own final end.

The author knows he is writing both for a generation just discovering these books and for those a generation or more older. He has Green Arrow evaluating where he is now: "I was dead. I came back to life." He hunts for those most cherished parts of his past left behind, he debates what his life should be in the present and he faces the possibility of a future death. In this the author goes way beyond our childhood days when no hero died. Oliver Queen knows how many of his fellow heroes died and that life forever is no longer the rule. He emphasizes this when he tells Roy: "Batman's going to die, Roy. He refuses to believe it but it is true."

If all this was not enough in one storyline, the author skillfully tosses in references for longtime readers, like the splitting of arrows in a security camera; the dark humor of the Dark Knight showing Green Arrow's access code listing him as deceased, while keeping the code obviously active; adding Flash and Green Lantern, past and present; deflating Superman's superiority; and even arranging a key alliance with the Injustice League. It is hard to think of another author who could do all this and keep it true to the tradition of Green Arrow.

Maybe Brad Meltzer next can turn his talents to deciphering the intricacies of the 100 mortals and those who consider themselves immortals in the United States Senate, picking up where Robert Caro left off. I could assure him that the first hundred copies would zip off the shelves.

In this book, we have an author who doesn't just tell of Oliver Queen, Roy Harper, and the others, but writes them in all their complexities, weaknesses and strengths, and who reminds us that even such heroes are mortals and have doubts, and fears, about the future. He takes a timeless character and remolds him as a perfect reflection of our time.

—Patrick Leahy
United States Senator
Vermont
July, 2003

GREEN ARROW

While stranded on a desert island, millionaire Oliver Queen developed amazing archery skills. After his rescue, he used those abilities to fight for the weak and defenseless. Formerly a member of the Justice League, Green Arrow has not always seen eye-to-eye with the group's mission. Queen sacrificed his life to save Metropolis, but strange events and powers conspired to bring him back from the dead. His body and soul have recently been reunited, and he is now readjusting to a world that has moved on without him.

ARSENAL

Idolizing Green Arrow, orphan Roy Harper had mastered archery when he was a teenager on a Navajo reservation. Harper became billionaire Oliver Queen's ward, and his guardian later named him Speedy because of the quickness he exhibited with his bow. The partners had a falling-out, and, as the distance grew, Speedy turned to heroin for the comfort he could not find elsewhere. With the help of Black Canary and the Teen Titans, Speedy entered rehab and kicked the habit. Renaming himself Arsenal, Harper went on to work for the U.S. government, lead the Titans, and fall in love with the assassin Cheshire, fathering a child, Lian, with her.

BLACK CANARY

Dinah Lance grew up in the shadow of the legendary Justice Society of America, inheriting the role of Black Canary from her well-intentioned but domineering mother. Armed with a super-powered sonic cry and a mastery of several martial arts, Dinah helped found the JSA's successor, the Justice League of America. When her relationship with Oliver Queen soured, Dinah left the Emerald Archer to blaze her own path. She currently operates out of Gotham City, partnered with Oracle.

GREEN ARROW II

The unknown son of Oliver Queen, Connor Hawke entered the same ashram monastery that Queen had sought asylum in years earlier. Raised as a Buddhist monk under the tutelage of Master Jansen, Hawke trained extensively in the martial arts. Though he sought inner peace, he also yearned for adventure, spurred by the adoration he held for the father who never knew him. When Queen died, Connor became the new Green Arrow, even serving for a time with the JLA. Today, father and son protect Star City together.

THE SHADE

In 1838, the man who was later called the Shade received his power over shadow from something called The Dark Zone. Since then he has traveled the world — adventuring, gaining wealth, and gradually shedding his morals as he realized that he no longer aged and was therefore perhaps above the morality of mere "mortals." The Shade has acted the roles of super-villain and champion for justice, depending on his whim. As a result, he has a complex relationship with many of today's super-heroes.

SOLOMON GRUNDY

In 1894, millionaire Cyrus Gold was attacked and robbed, his dying body thrown into Gotham City's Slaughter Swamp. Over the next half-century, the muck and plant life congealed and grew around Gold's skeleton — and a dark and twisted miracle gave life to the creature who, though almost mindless, was drven by the emotions of Gold's violent death to rage, death, and destruction. Over the years, Solomon Grundy has been destroyed and reborn many times, more often than not in combat against Earth's costumed crimefighters.

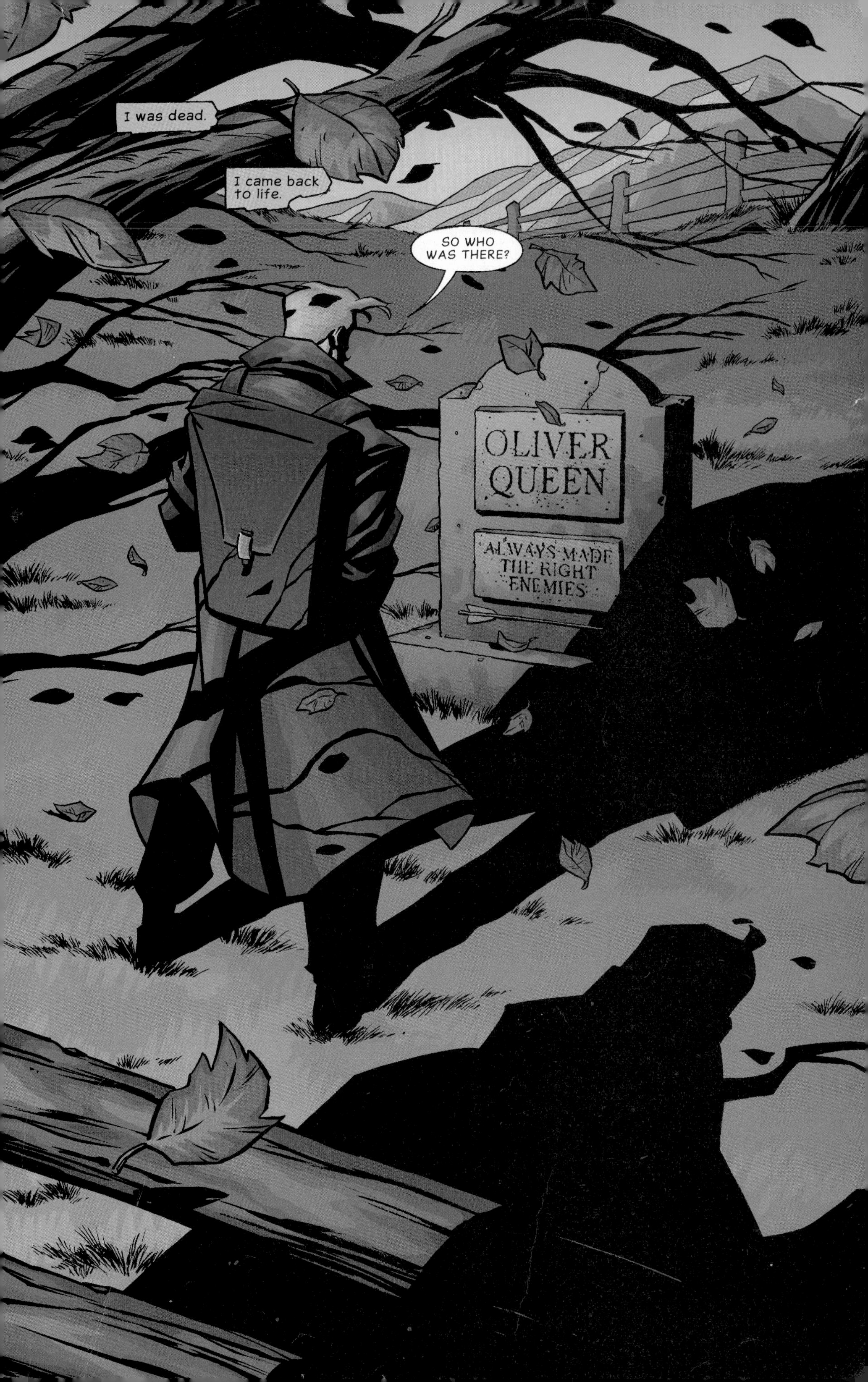
I was dead.
I came back to life.
SO WHO WAS THERE?
OLIVER QUEEN
ALWAYS MADE THE RIGHT ENEMIES

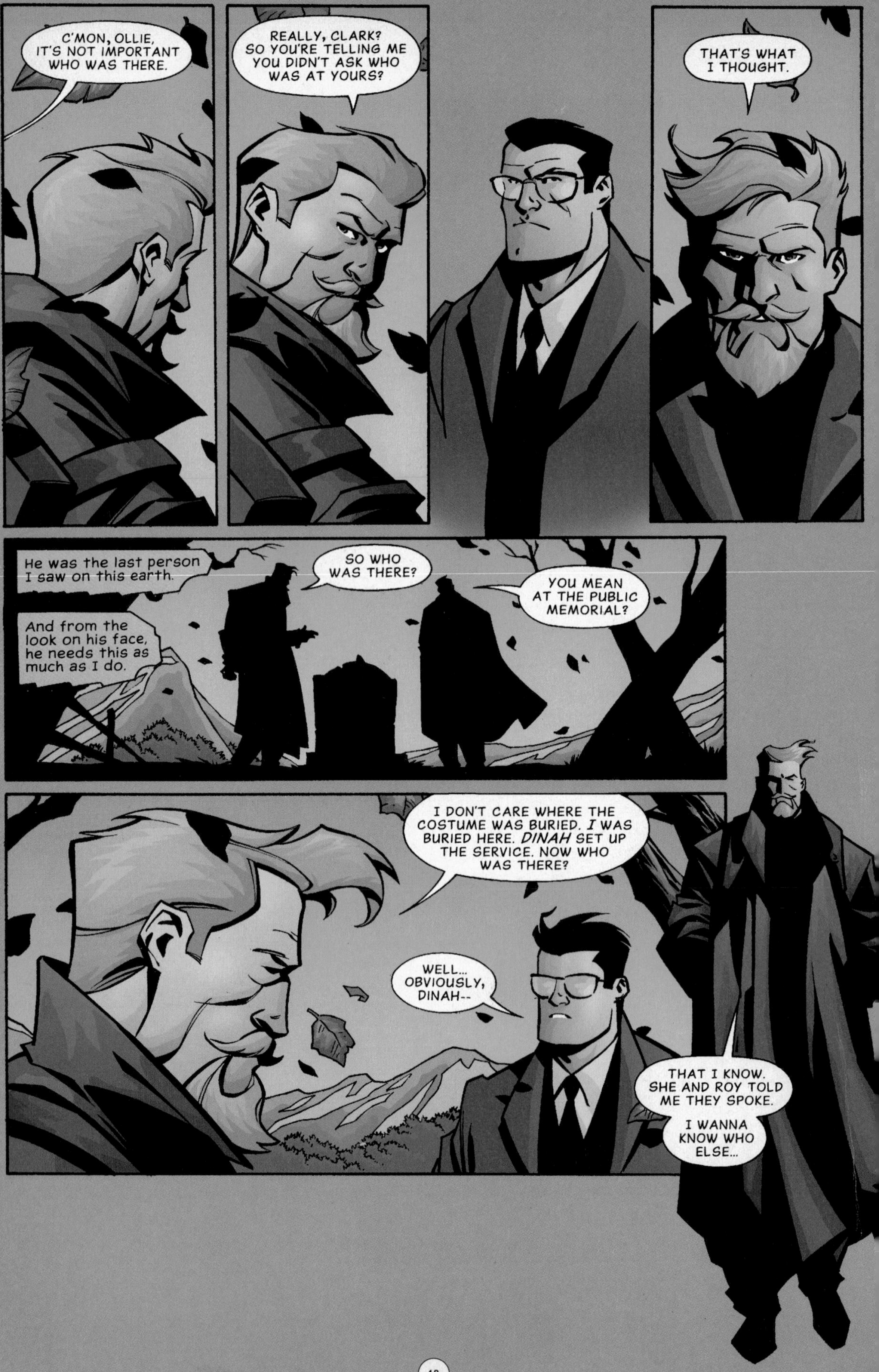
C'MON, OLLIE, IT'S NOT IMPORTANT WHO WAS THERE.
REALLY, CLARK? SO YOU'RE TELLING ME YOU DIDN'T ASK WHO WAS AT YOURS?
THAT'S WHAT I THOUGHT.
He was the last person I saw on this earth.
And from the look on his face, he needs this as much as I do.
SO WHO WAS THERE?
YOU MEAN AT THE PUBLIC MEMORIAL?
I DON'T CARE WHERE THE COSTUME WAS BURIED. *I* WAS BURIED HERE. *DINAH* SET UP THE SERVICE. NOW WHO WAS THERE?
WELL... OBVIOUSLY, DINAH--
THAT I KNOW. SHE AND ROY TOLD ME THEY SPOKE.
I WANNA KNOW WHO ELSE...

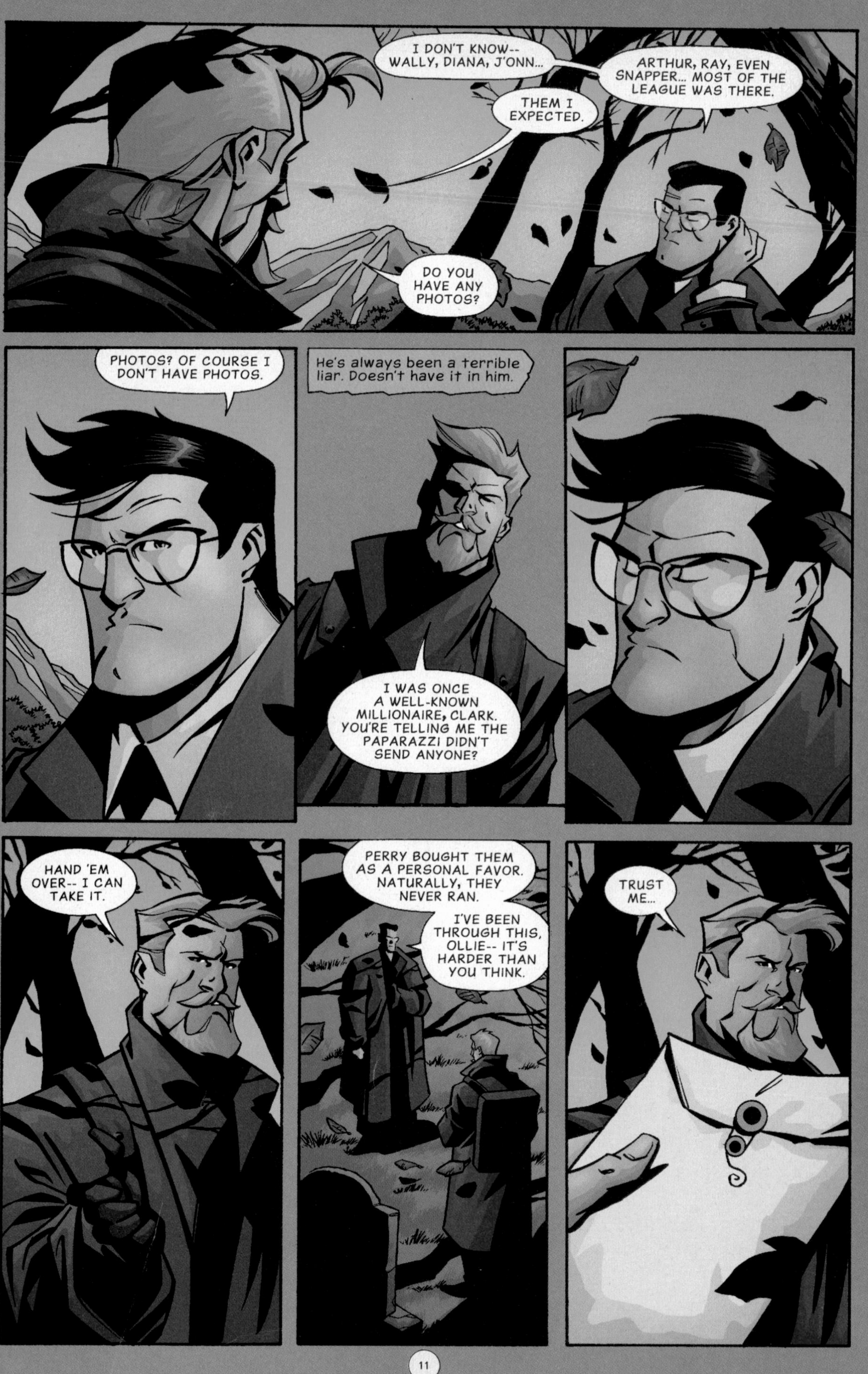
I DON'T KNOW-- WALLY, DIANA, J'ONN...
ARTHUR, RAY, EVEN SNAPPER... MOST OF THE LEAGUE WAS THERE.
THEM I EXPECTED.
DO YOU HAVE ANY PHOTOS?
PHOTOS? OF COURSE I DON'T HAVE PHOTOS.
He's always been a terrible liar. Doesn't have it in him.
I WAS ONCE A WELL-KNOWN MILLIONAIRE, CLARK. YOU'RE TELLING ME THE PAPARAZZI DIDN'T SEND ANYONE?
HAND 'EM OVER-- I CAN TAKE IT.
PERRY BOUGHT THEM AS A PERSONAL FAVOR. NATURALLY, THEY NEVER RAN.
I'VE BEEN THROUGH THIS, OLLIE-- IT'S HARDER THAN YOU THINK.
TRUST ME...

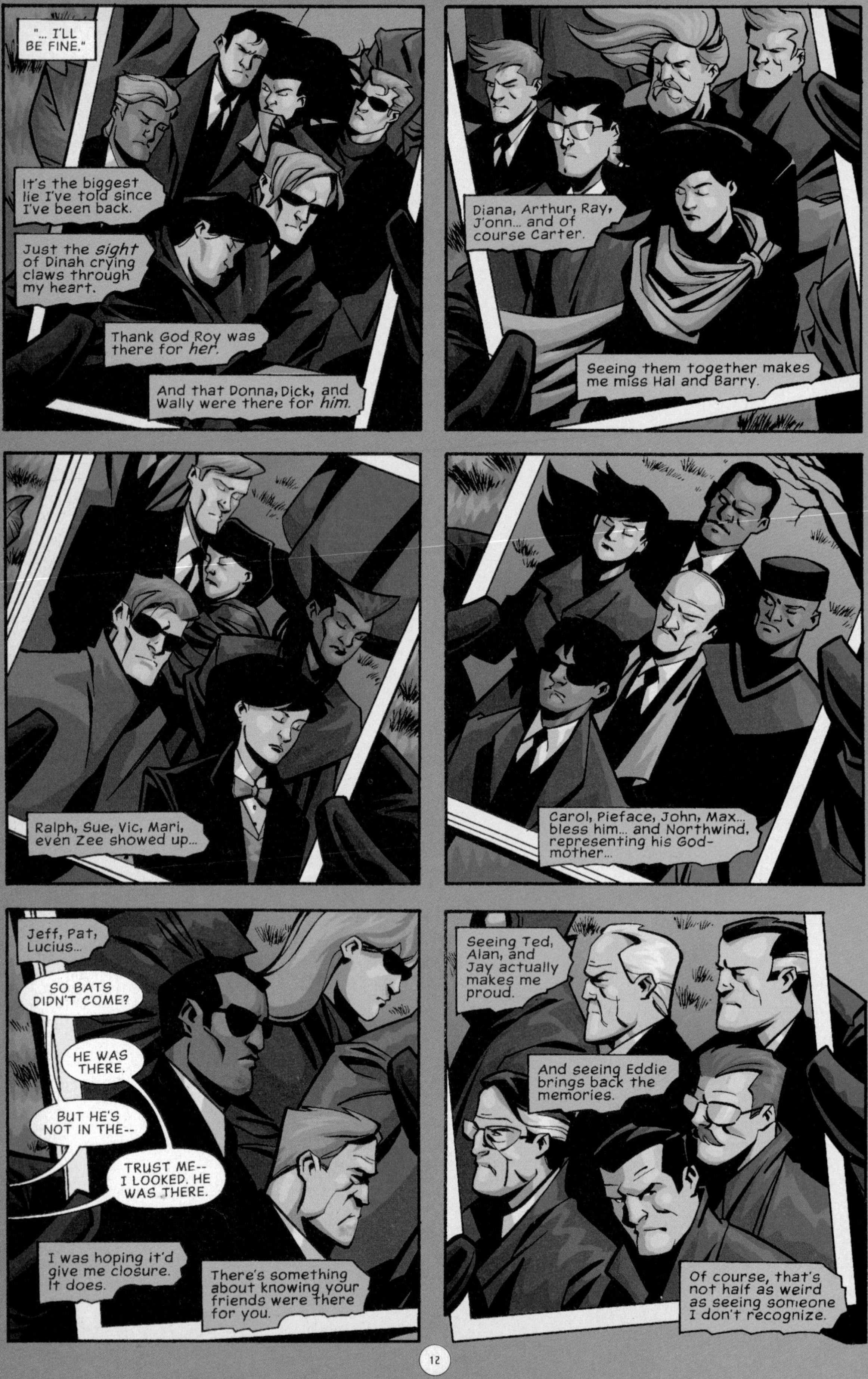
"... I'LL BE FINE."
It's the biggest lie I've told since I've been back.
Just the *sight* of Dinah crying claws through my heart.
Thank God Roy was there for *her.*
And that Donna, Dick, and Wally were there for *him.*
Diana, Arthur, Ray, J'onn... and of course Carter.
Seeing them together makes me miss Hal and Barry.
Ralph, Sue, Vic, Mari, even Zee showed up...
Carol, Pieface, John, Max... bless him... and Northwind, representing his God-mother...
Jeff, Pat, Lucius...
SO BATS DIDN'T COME?
HE WAS THERE.
BUT HE'S NOT IN THE--
TRUST ME-- I LOOKED. HE WAS THERE.
I was hoping it'd give me closure. It does.
There's something about knowing your friends were there for you.
Seeing Ted, Alan, and Jay actually makes me proud.
And seeing Eddie brings back the memories.
Of course, that's not half as weird as seeing someone I don't recognize.

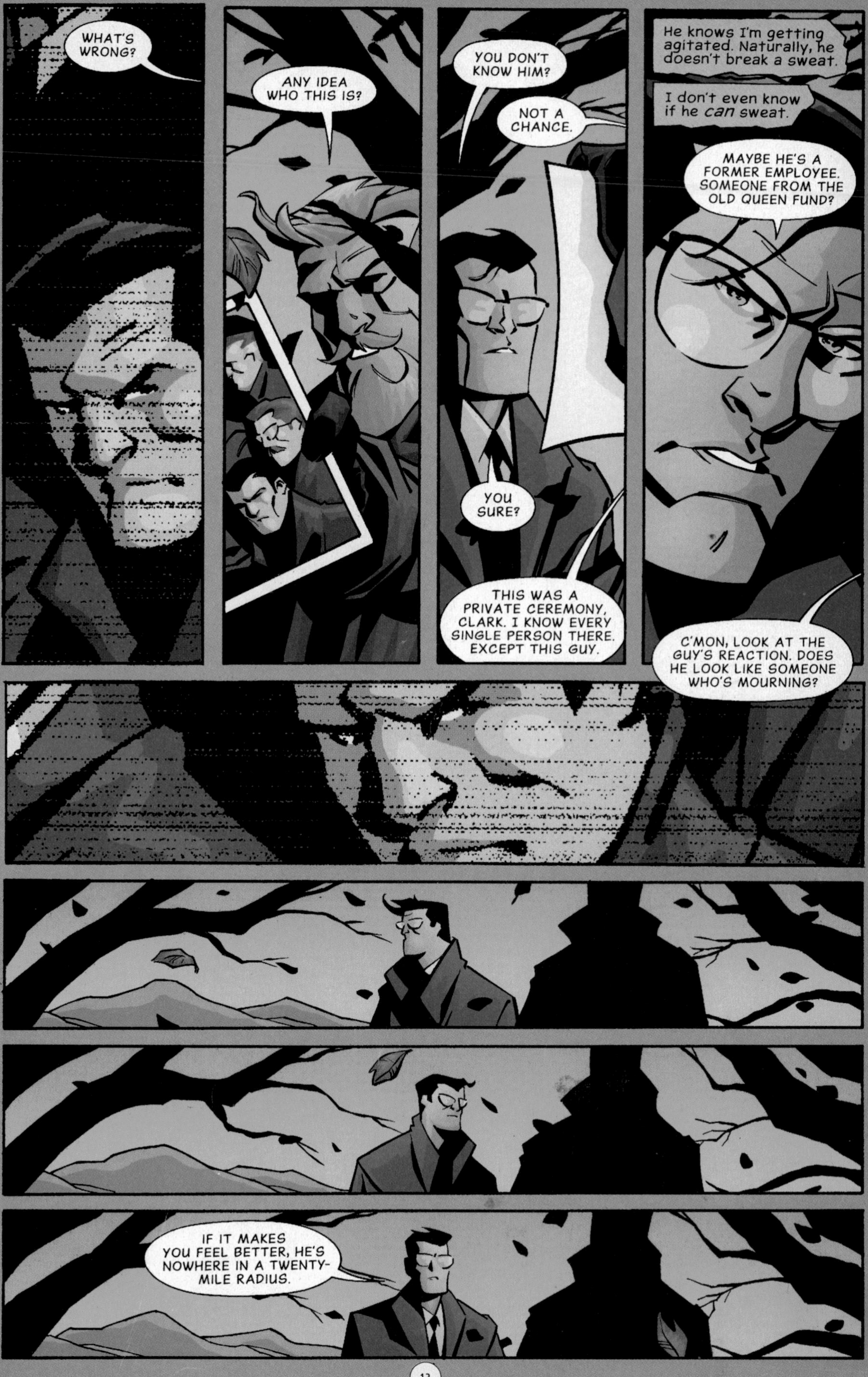
WHAT'S WRONG?
ANY IDEA WHO THIS IS?
YOU DON'T KNOW HIM?
NOT A CHANCE.
YOU SURE?
THIS WAS A PRIVATE CEREMONY, CLARK. I KNOW EVERY SINGLE PERSON THERE. EXCEPT THIS GUY.
He knows I'm getting agitated. Naturally, he doesn't break a sweat.
I don't even know if he *can* sweat.
MAYBE HE'S A FORMER EMPLOYEE. SOMEONE FROM THE OLD QUEEN FUND?
C'MON, LOOK AT THE GUY'S REACTION. DOES HE LOOK LIKE SOMEONE WHO'S MOURNING?
IF IT MAKES YOU FEEL BETTER, HE'S NOWHERE IN A TWENTY-MILE RADIUS.

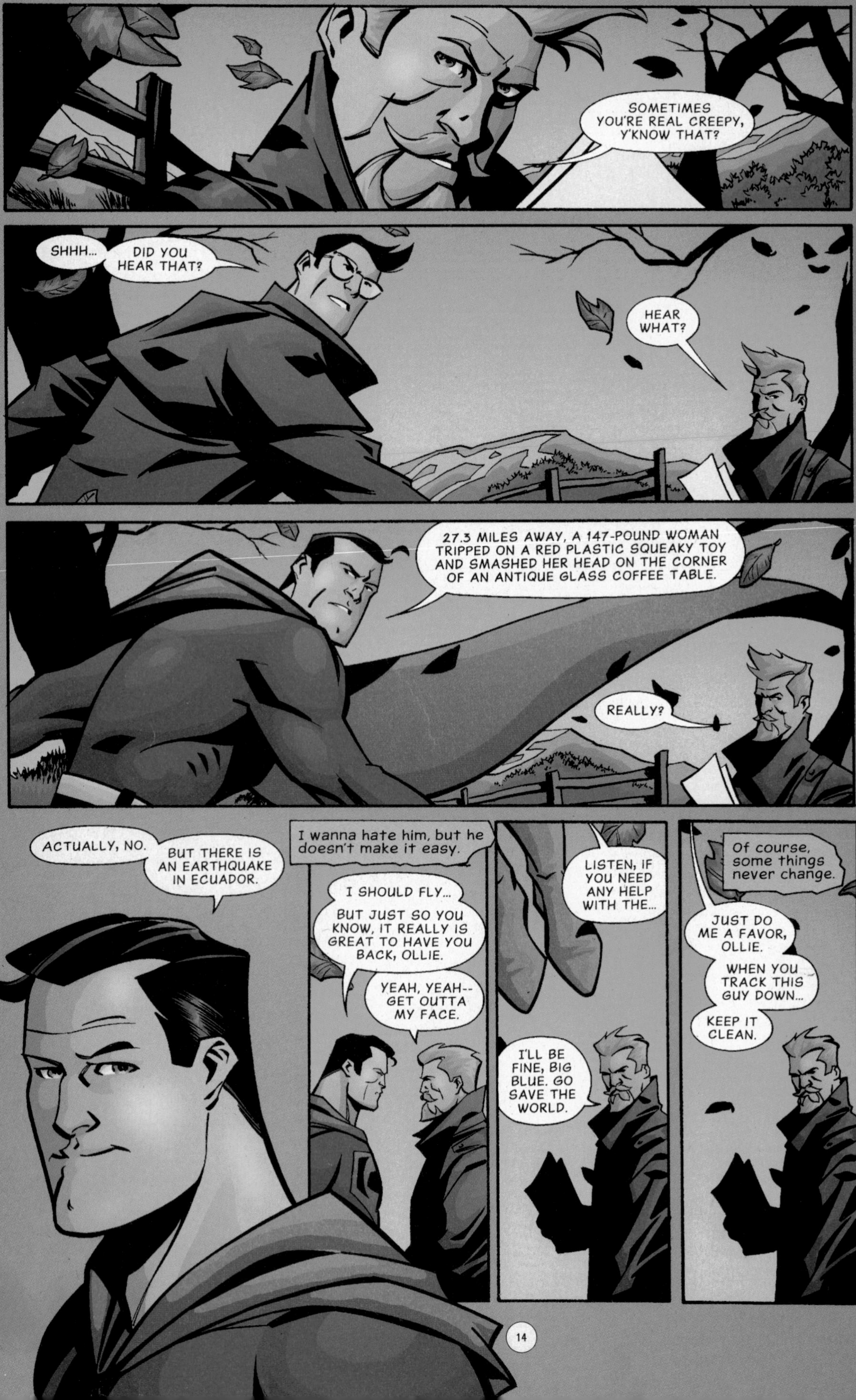
SOMETIMES YOU'RE REAL CREEPY, Y'KNOW THAT?
SHHH...
DID YOU HEAR THAT?
HEAR WHAT?
27.3 MILES AWAY, A 147-POUND WOMAN TRIPPED ON A RED PLASTIC SQUEAKY TOY AND SMASHED HER HEAD ON THE CORNER OF AN ANTIQUE GLASS COFFEE TABLE.
REALLY?
ACTUALLY, NO.
BUT THERE IS AN EARTHQUAKE IN ECUADOR.
I wanna hate him, but he doesn't make it easy.
I SHOULD FLY...
BUT JUST SO YOU KNOW, IT REALLY IS GREAT TO HAVE YOU BACK, OLLIE.
YEAH, YEAH-- GET OUTTA MY FACE.
LISTEN, IF YOU NEED ANY HELP WITH THE...
I'LL BE FINE, BIG BLUE. GO SAVE THE WORLD.
Of course, some things never change.
JUST DO ME A FAVOR, OLLIE.
WHEN YOU TRACK THIS GUY DOWN...
KEEP IT CLEAN.

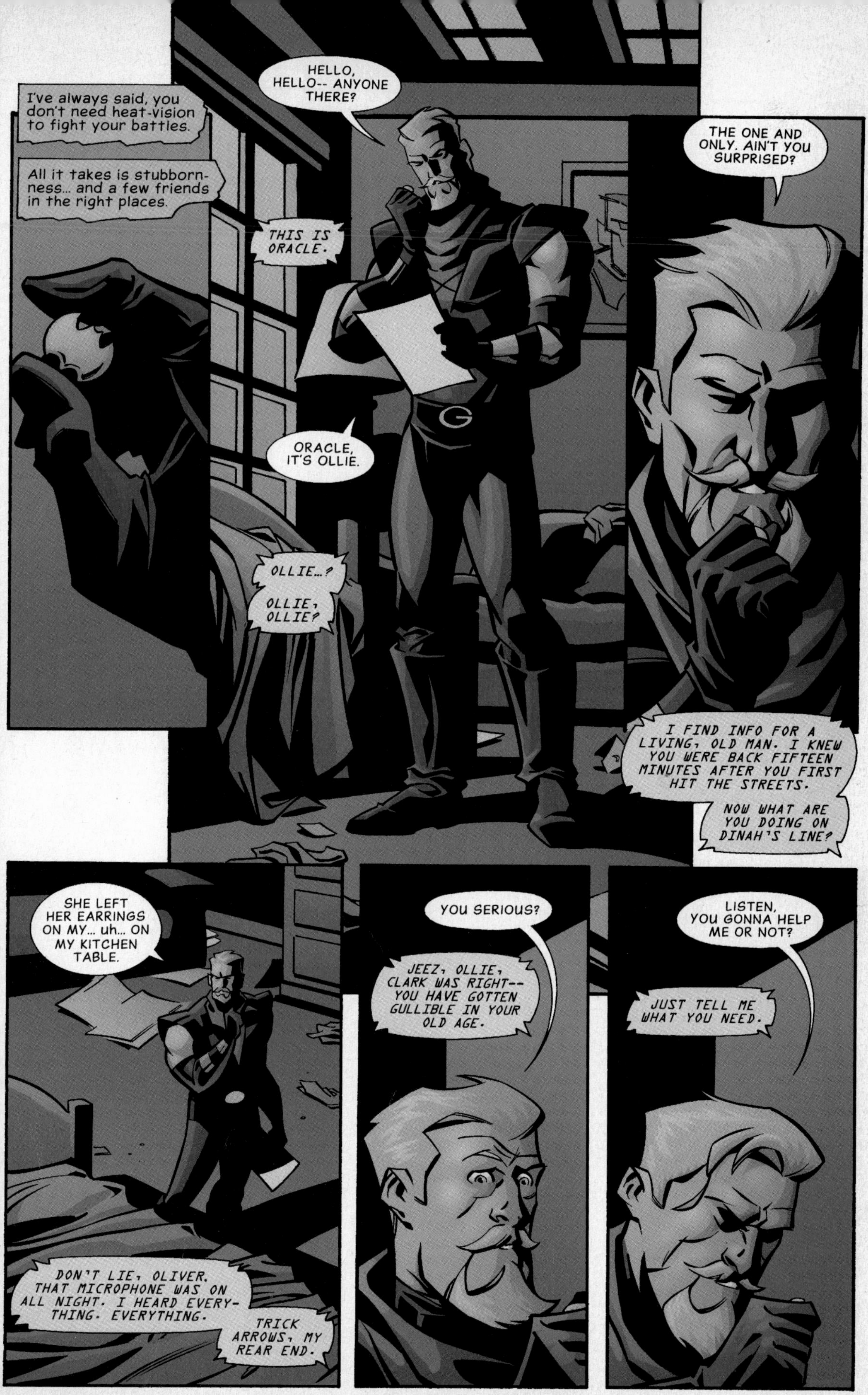
I've always said, you don't need heat-vision to fight your battles.
All it takes is stubbornness... and a few friends in the right places.
HELLO, HELLO-- ANYONE THERE?
THIS IS ORACLE.
ORACLE, IT'S OLLIE.
OLLIE...?
OLLIE, OLLIE?
THE ONE AND ONLY. AIN'T YOU SURPRISED?
I FIND INFO FOR A LIVING, OLD MAN. I KNEW YOU WERE BACK FIFTEEN MINUTES AFTER YOU FIRST HIT THE STREETS.
NOW WHAT ARE YOU DOING ON DINAH'S LINE?
SHE LEFT HER EARRINGS ON MY... uh... ON MY KITCHEN TABLE.
DON'T LIE, OLIVER. THAT MICROPHONE WAS ON ALL NIGHT. I HEARD EVERYTHING. EVERYTHING.
TRICK ARROWS, MY REAR END.
YOU SERIOUS?
JEEZ, OLLIE, CLARK WAS RIGHT-- YOU HAVE GOTTEN GULLIBLE IN YOUR OLD AGE.
LISTEN, YOU GONNA HELP ME OR NOT?
JUST TELL ME WHAT YOU NEED.

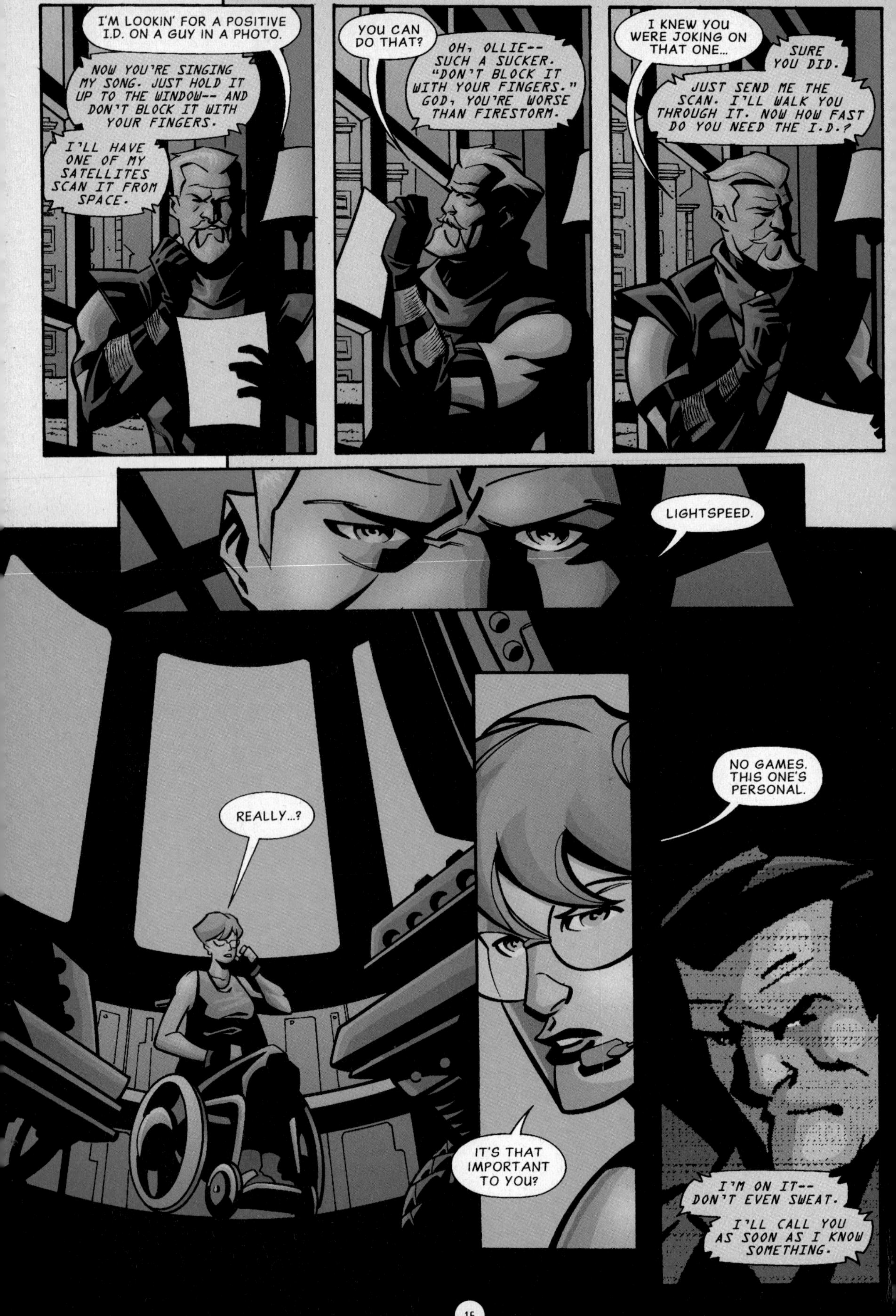
I'M LOOKIN' FOR A POSITIVE I.D. ON A GUY IN A PHOTO.
NOW YOU'RE SINGING MY SONG. JUST HOLD IT UP TO THE WINDOW-- AND DON'T BLOCK IT WITH YOUR FINGERS.
I'LL HAVE ONE OF MY SATELLITES SCAN IT FROM SPACE.
YOU CAN DO THAT?
OH, OLLIE-- SUCH A SUCKER. "DON'T BLOCK IT WITH YOUR FINGERS." GOD, YOU'RE WORSE THAN FIRESTORM.
I KNEW YOU WERE JOKING ON THAT ONE...
SURE YOU DID.
JUST SEND ME THE SCAN. I'LL WALK YOU THROUGH IT. NOW HOW FAST DO YOU NEED THE I.D.?
LIGHTSPEED.
REALLY...?
NO GAMES. THIS ONE'S PERSONAL.
IT'S THAT IMPORTANT TO YOU?
I'M ON IT-- DON'T EVEN SWEAT.
I'LL CALL YOU AS SOON AS I KNOW SOMETHING.

Nothing.

Nothing.

Nothing.

Nothing.

Nothing.

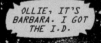

OLLIE, IT'S BARBARA. I GOT THE I.D.

Gratification.

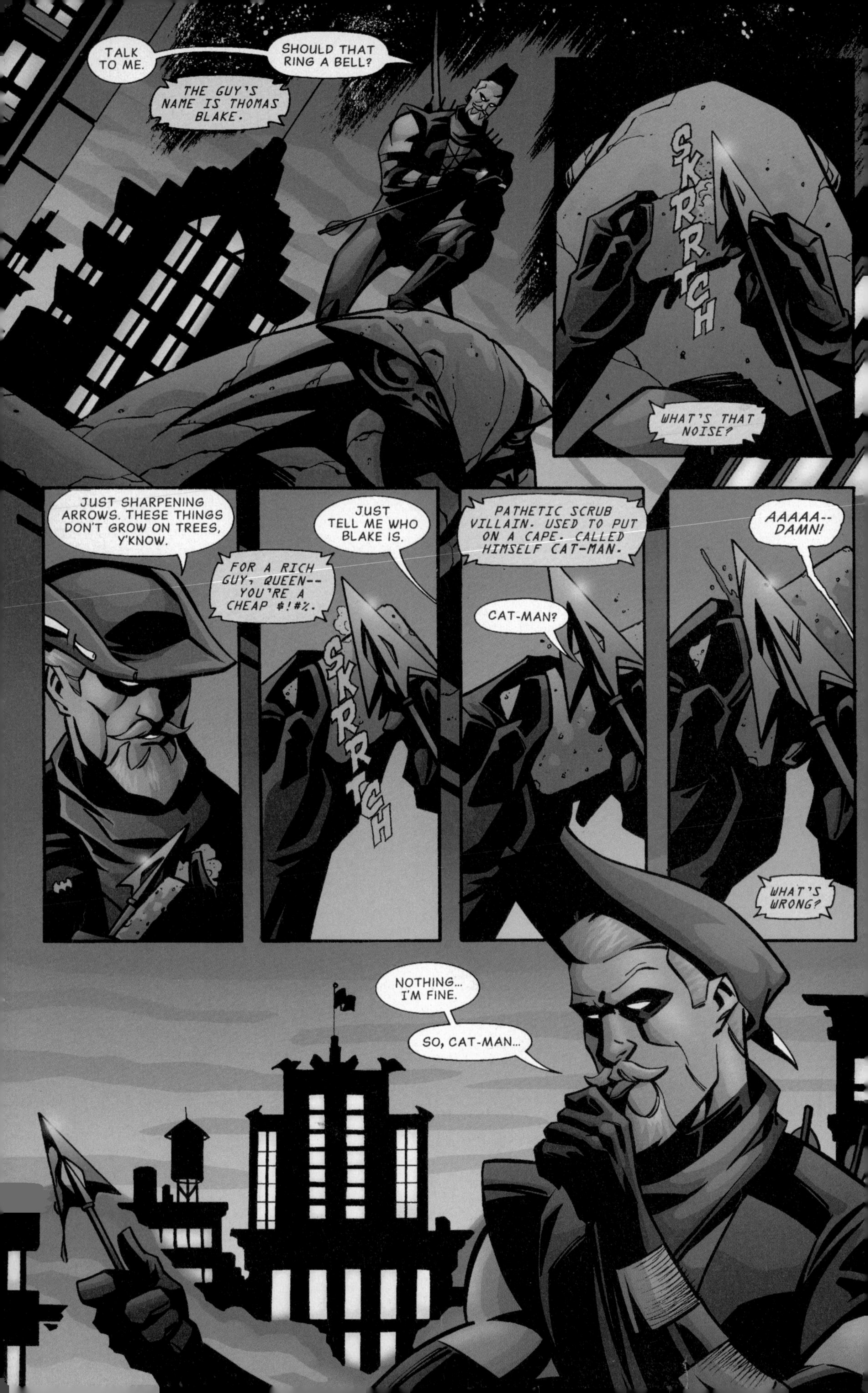
TALK TO ME.
SHOULD THAT RING A BELL?
THE GUY'S NAME IS THOMAS BLAKE.
SKRRTCH
WHAT'S THAT NOISE?
JUST SHARPENING ARROWS. THESE THINGS DON'T GROW ON TREES, Y'KNOW.
FOR A RICH GUY, QUEEN-- YOU'RE A CHEAP $!#%.
JUST TELL ME WHO BLAKE IS.
SKRRTCH
PATHETIC SCRUB VILLAIN. USED TO PUT ON A CAPE. CALLED HIMSELF CAT-MAN.
CAT-MAN?
AAAAA-- DAMN!
WHAT'S WRONG?
NOTHING... I'M FINE.
SO, CAT-MAN...

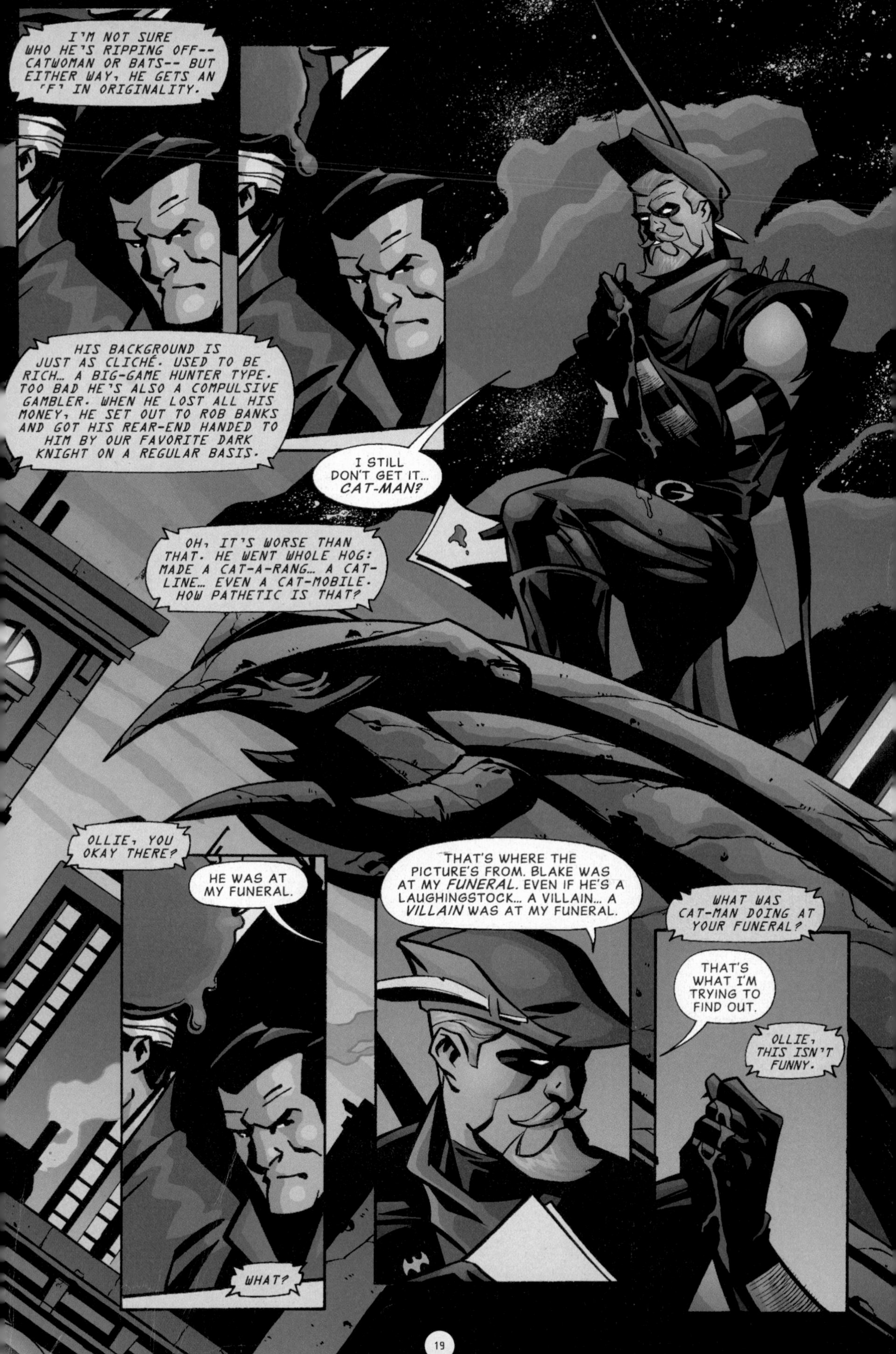
I'M NOT SURE WHO HE'S RIPPING OFF-- CATWOMAN OR BATS-- BUT EITHER WAY, HE GETS AN 'F' IN ORIGINALITY.
HIS BACKGROUND IS JUST AS CLICHÉ. USED TO BE RICH... A BIG-GAME HUNTER TYPE. TOO BAD HE'S ALSO A COMPULSIVE GAMBLER. WHEN HE LOST ALL HIS MONEY, HE SET OUT TO ROB BANKS AND GOT HIS REAR-END HANDED TO HIM BY OUR FAVORITE DARK KNIGHT ON A REGULAR BASIS.
I STILL DON'T GET IT... CAT-MAN?
OH, IT'S WORSE THAN THAT. HE WENT WHOLE HOG: MADE A CAT-A-RANG... A CAT-LINE... EVEN A CAT-MOBILE. HOW PATHETIC IS THAT?
OLLIE, YOU OKAY THERE?
HE WAS AT MY FUNERAL.
WHAT?
THAT'S WHERE THE PICTURE'S FROM. BLAKE WAS AT MY FUNERAL. EVEN IF HE'S A LAUGHINGSTOCK... A VILLAIN... A VILLAIN WAS AT MY FUNERAL.
WHAT WAS CAT-MAN DOING AT YOUR FUNERAL?
THAT'S WHAT I'M TRYING TO FIND OUT.
OLLIE, THIS ISN'T FUNNY.

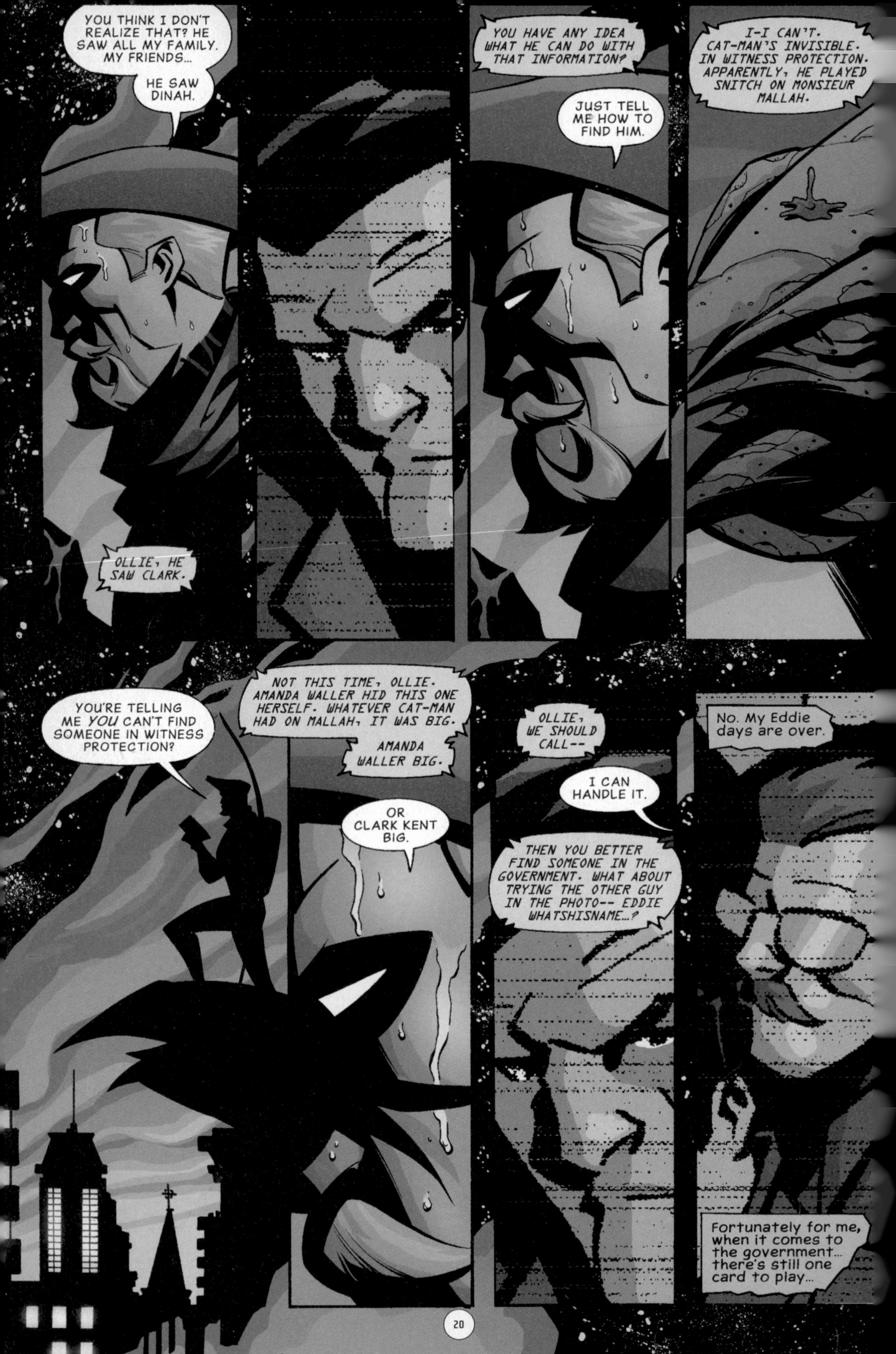
YOU THINK I DON'T REALIZE THAT? HE SAW ALL MY FAMILY. MY FRIENDS...
HE SAW DINAH.
OLLIE, HE SAW CLARK.
YOU HAVE ANY IDEA WHAT HE CAN DO WITH THAT INFORMATION?
JUST TELL ME HOW TO FIND HIM.
I-I CAN'T. CAT-MAN'S INVISIBLE. IN WITNESS PROTECTION. APPARENTLY, HE PLAYED SNITCH ON MONSIEUR MALLAH.
YOU'RE TELLING ME *YOU* CAN'T FIND SOMEONE IN WITNESS PROTECTION?
NOT THIS TIME, OLLIE. AMANDA WALLER HID THIS ONE HERSELF. WHATEVER CAT-MAN HAD ON MALLAH, IT WAS BIG.
AMANDA WALLER BIG.
OR CLARK KENT BIG.
OLLIE, WE SHOULD CALL--
I CAN HANDLE IT.
THEN YOU BETTER FIND SOMEONE IN THE GOVERNMENT. WHAT ABOUT TRYING THE OTHER GUY IN THE PHOTO-- EDDIE WHATSHISNAME...?
No. My Eddie days are over.
Fortunately for me, when it comes to the government... there's still one card to play...

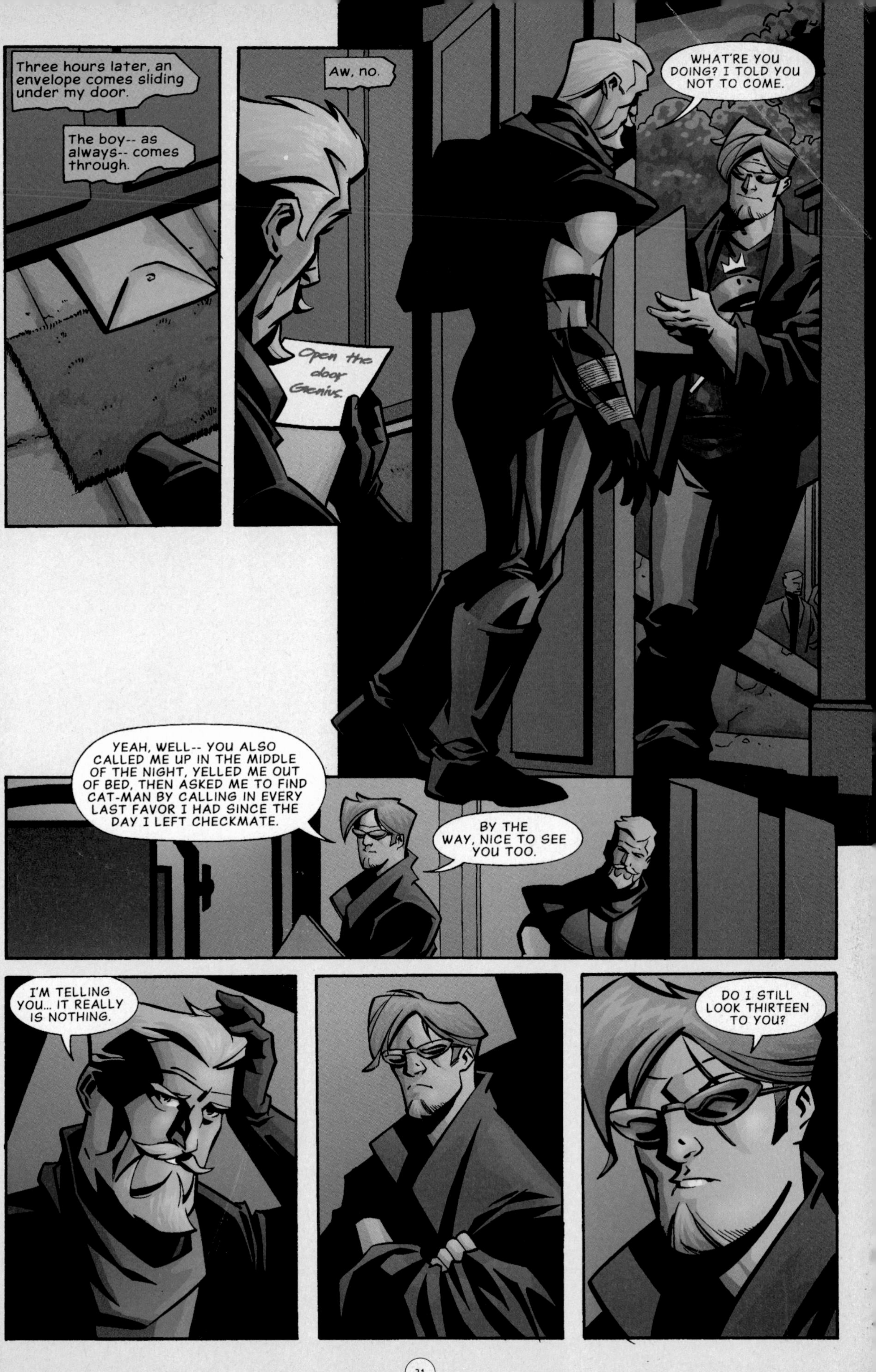

Three hours later, an envelope comes sliding under my door.
The boy-- as always-- comes through.
Aw, no.
Open the door Genius.
WHAT'RE YOU DOING? I TOLD YOU NOT TO COME.
YEAH, WELL-- YOU ALSO CALLED ME UP IN THE MIDDLE OF THE NIGHT, YELLED ME OUT OF BED, THEN ASKED ME TO FIND CAT-MAN BY CALLING IN EVERY LAST FAVOR I HAD SINCE THE DAY I LEFT CHECKMATE.
BY THE WAY, NICE TO SEE YOU TOO.
I'M TELLING YOU... IT REALLY IS NOTHING.
DO I STILL LOOK THIRTEEN TO YOU?

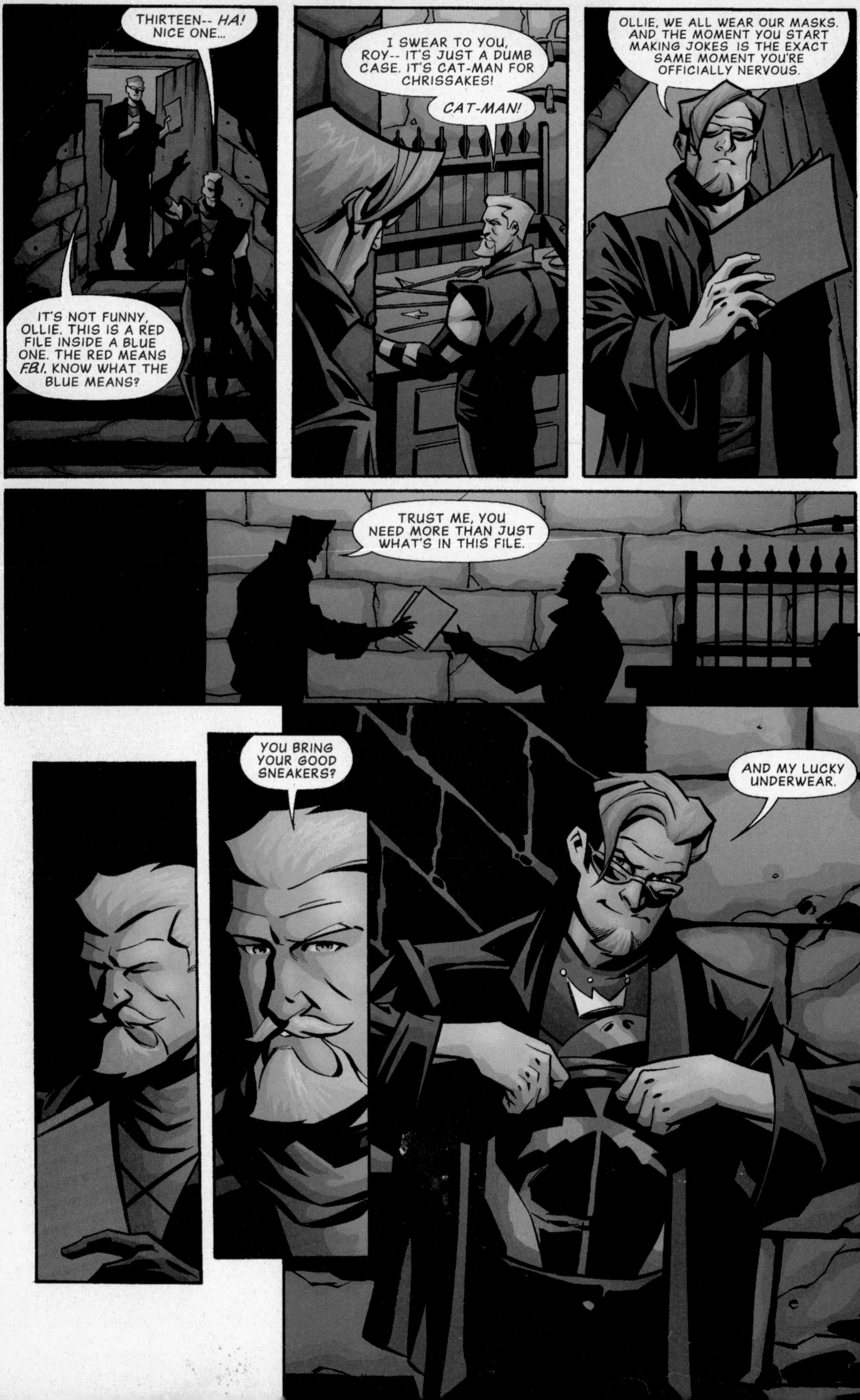
THIRTEEN-- HA! NICE ONE...
IT'S NOT FUNNY, OLLIE. THIS IS A RED FILE INSIDE A BLUE ONE. THE RED MEANS F.B.I. KNOW WHAT THE BLUE MEANS?
I SWEAR TO YOU, ROY-- IT'S JUST A DUMB CASE. IT'S CAT-MAN FOR CHRISSAKES!
CAT-MAN!
OLLIE, WE ALL WEAR OUR MASKS. AND THE MOMENT YOU START MAKING JOKES IS THE EXACT SAME MOMENT YOU'RE OFFICIALLY NERVOUS.
TRUST ME, YOU NEED MORE THAN JUST WHAT'S IN THIS FILE.
YOU BRING YOUR GOOD SNEAKERS?
AND MY LUCKY UNDERWEAR.

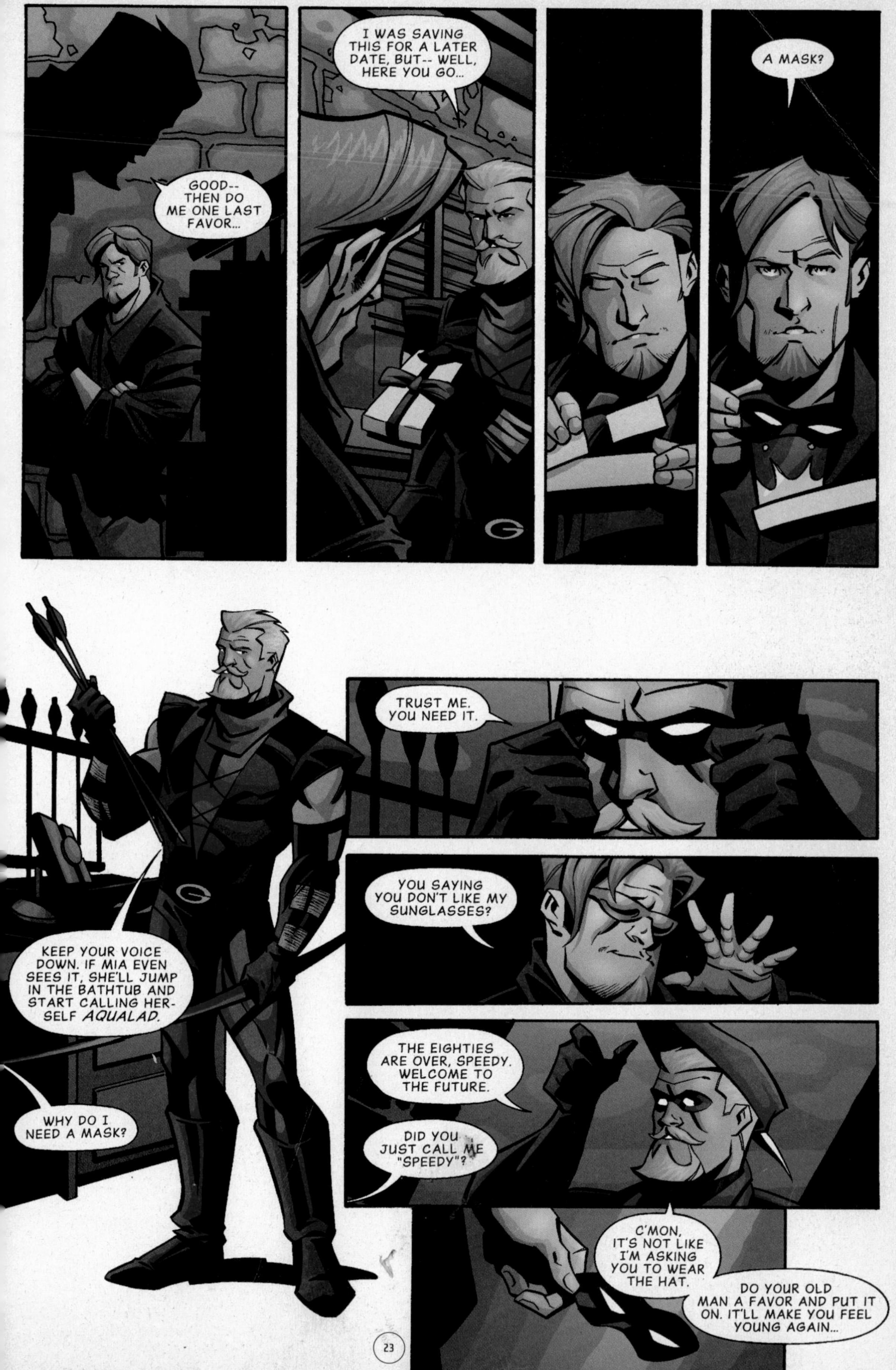

GOOD-- THEN DO ME ONE LAST FAVOR...
I WAS SAVING THIS FOR A LATER DATE, BUT-- WELL, HERE YOU GO...
A MASK?
WHY DO I NEED A MASK?
KEEP YOUR VOICE DOWN. IF MIA EVEN SEES IT, SHE'LL JUMP IN THE BATHTUB AND START CALLING HER-SELF AQUALAD.
TRUST ME. YOU NEED IT.
YOU SAYING YOU DON'T LIKE MY SUNGLASSES?
THE EIGHTIES ARE OVER, SPEEDY. WELCOME TO THE FUTURE.
DID YOU JUST CALL ME "SPEEDY"?
C'MON, IT'S NOT LIKE I'M ASKING YOU TO WEAR THE HAT.
DO YOUR OLD MAN A FAVOR AND PUT IT ON. IT'LL MAKE YOU FEEL YOUNG AGAIN...

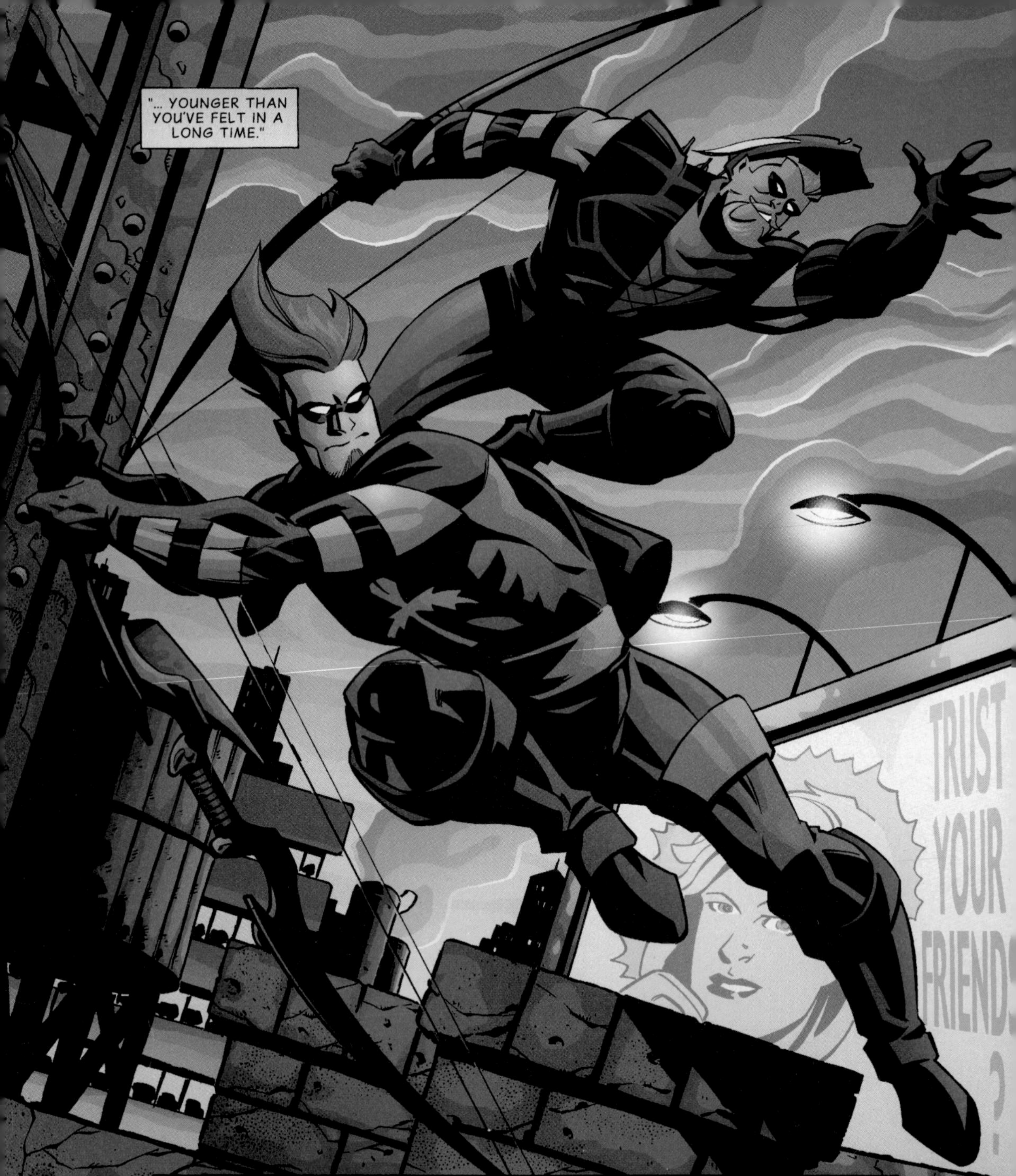
"... YOUNGER THAN YOU'VE FELT IN A LONG TIME."
TRUST YOUR FRIENDS ?
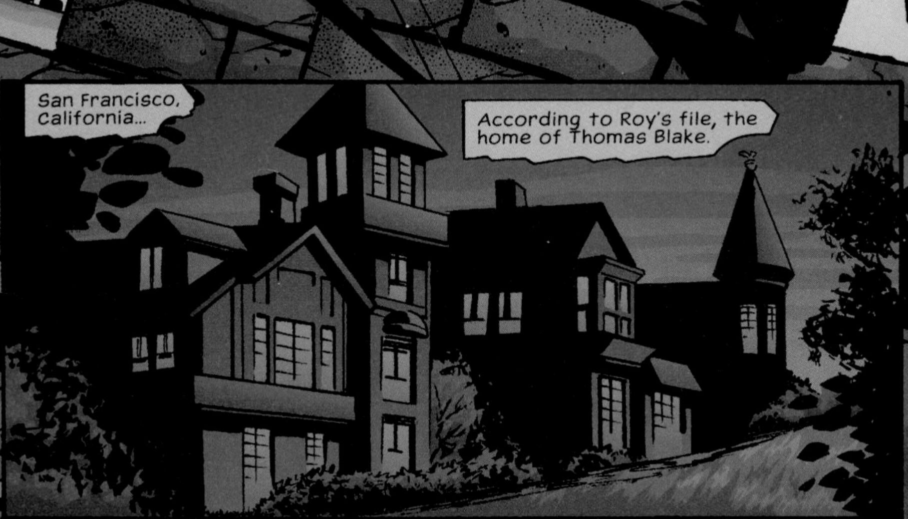
San Francisco, California...
According to Roy's file, the home of Thomas Blake.

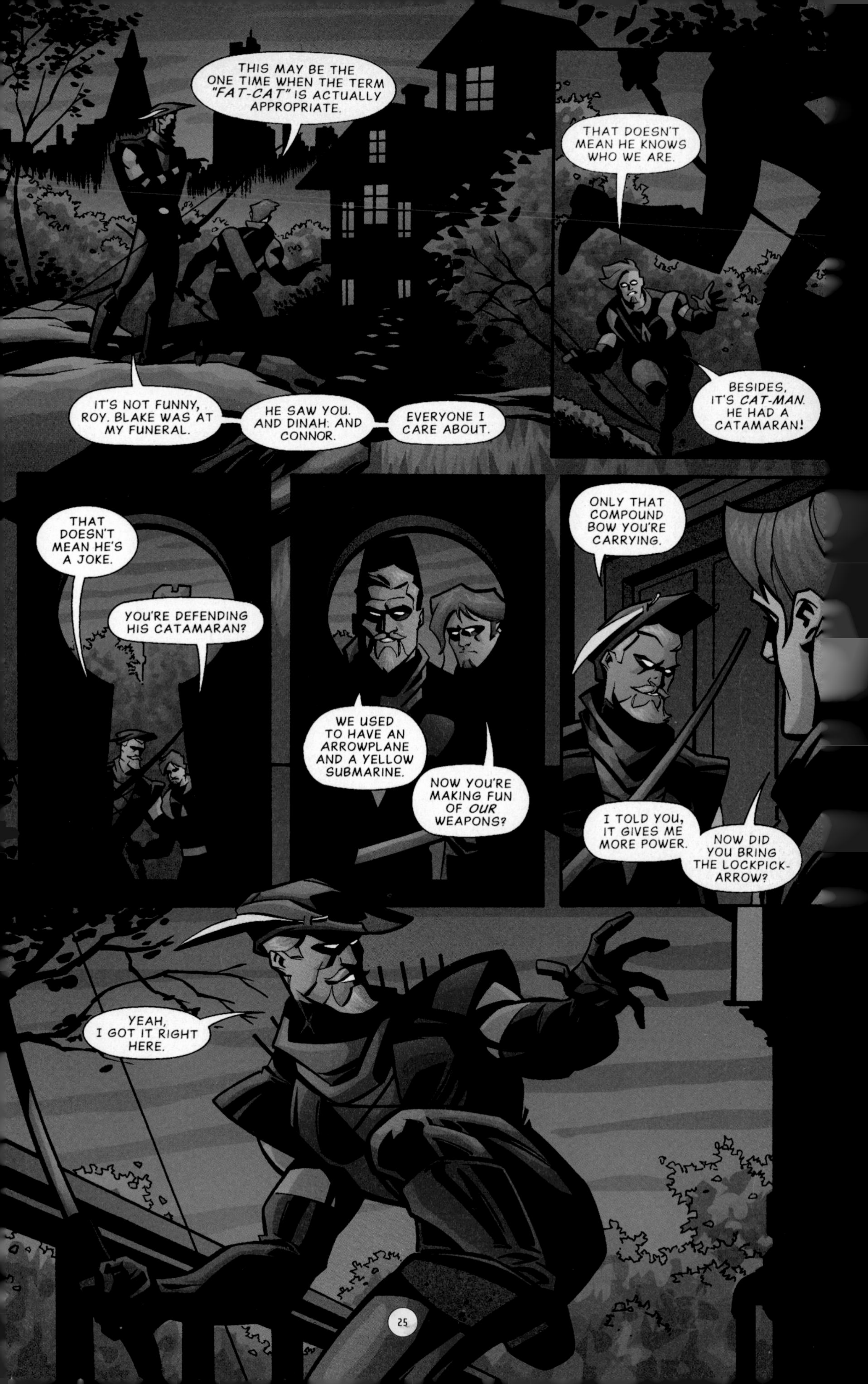
THIS MAY BE THE ONE TIME WHEN THE TERM "FAT-CAT" IS ACTUALLY APPROPRIATE.
IT'S NOT FUNNY, ROY. BLAKE WAS AT MY FUNERAL.
HE SAW YOU. AND DINAH. AND CONNOR.
EVERYONE I CARE ABOUT.
THAT DOESN'T MEAN HE KNOWS WHO WE ARE.
BESIDES, IT'S CAT-MAN. HE HAD A CATAMARAN!
THAT DOESN'T MEAN HE'S A JOKE.
YOU'RE DEFENDING HIS CATAMARAN?
WE USED TO HAVE AN ARROWPLANE AND A YELLOW SUBMARINE.
NOW YOU'RE MAKING FUN OF OUR WEAPONS?
ONLY THAT COMPOUND BOW YOU'RE CARRYING.
I TOLD YOU, IT GIVES ME MORE POWER.
NOW DID YOU BRING THE LOCKPICK-ARROW?
YEAH, I GOT IT RIGHT HERE.

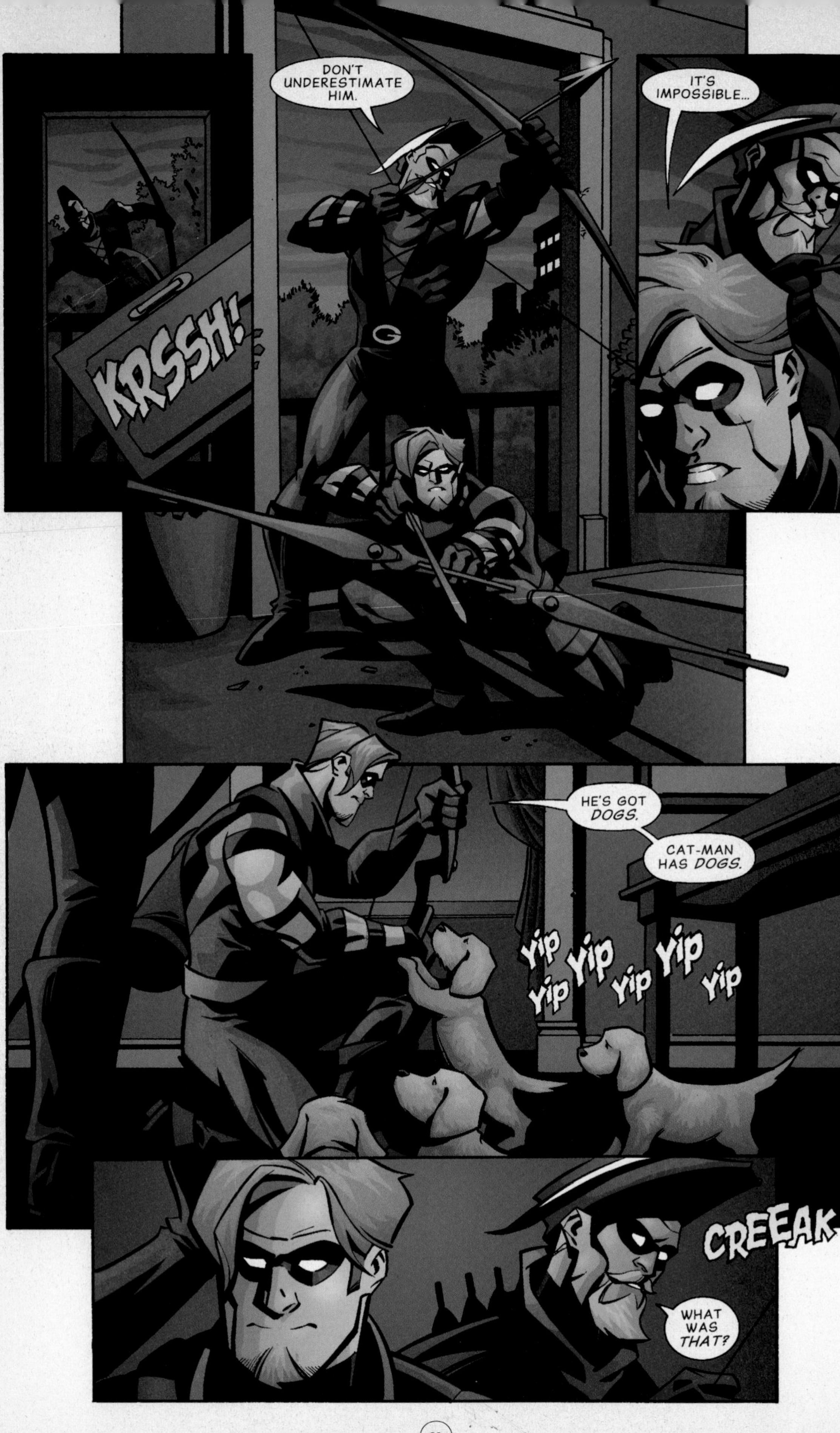
KRSSH!
DON'T UNDERESTIMATE HIM.
IT'S IMPOSSIBLE...
HE'S GOT *DOGS.*
CAT-MAN HAS *DOGS.*
YIP YIP YIP YIP YIP YIP YIP
CREEAK
WHAT WAS *THAT?*

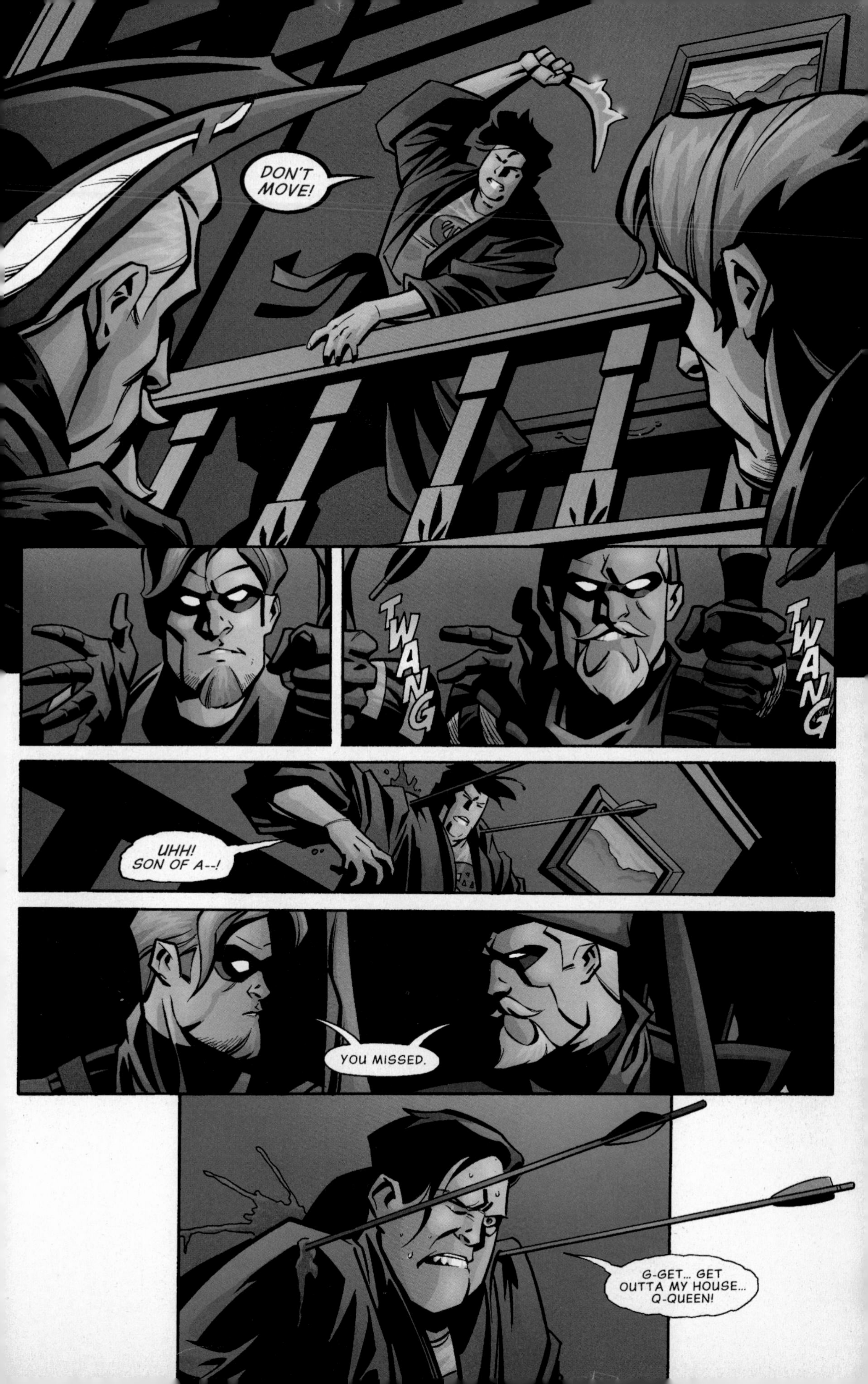
DON'T MOVE!
TWANG
TWANG
UHH! SON OF A--!
YOU MISSED.
G-GET... GET OUTTA MY HOUSE... Q-QUEEN!

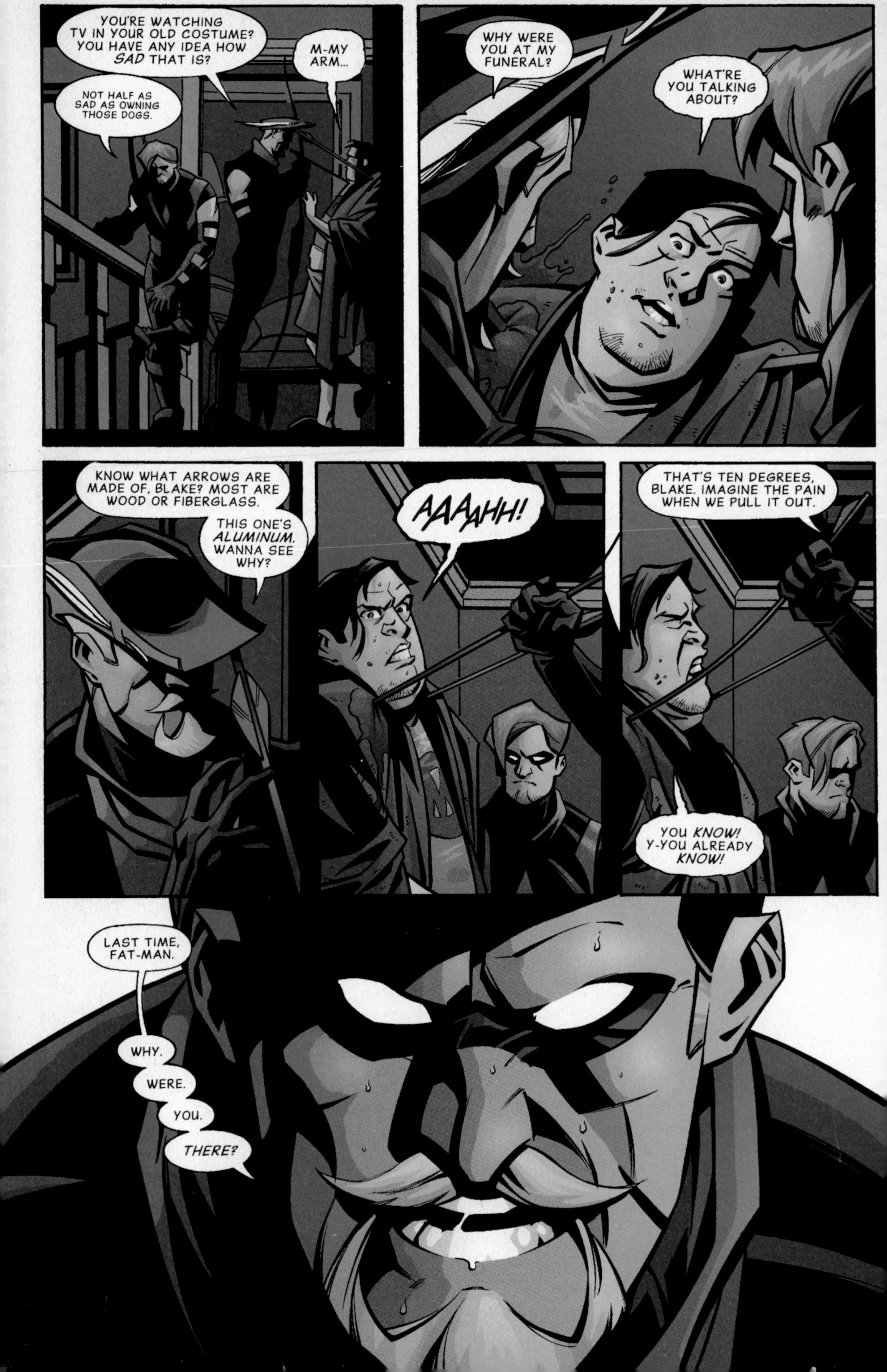
YOU'RE WATCHING TV IN YOUR OLD COSTUME? YOU HAVE ANY IDEA HOW *SAD* THAT IS?
NOT HALF AS SAD AS OWNING THOSE DOGS.
M-MY ARM...
WHY WERE YOU AT MY FUNERAL?
WHAT'RE YOU TALKING ABOUT?
KNOW WHAT ARROWS ARE MADE OF, BLAKE? MOST ARE WOOD OR FIBERGLASS.
THIS ONE'S *ALUMINUM.* WANNA SEE WHY?
AAAAHH!
THAT'S TEN DEGREES, BLAKE. IMAGINE THE PAIN WHEN WE PULL IT OUT.
YOU *KNOW!* Y-YOU ALREADY *KNOW!*
LAST TIME, FAT-MAN.
WHY.
WERE.
YOU.
THERE?

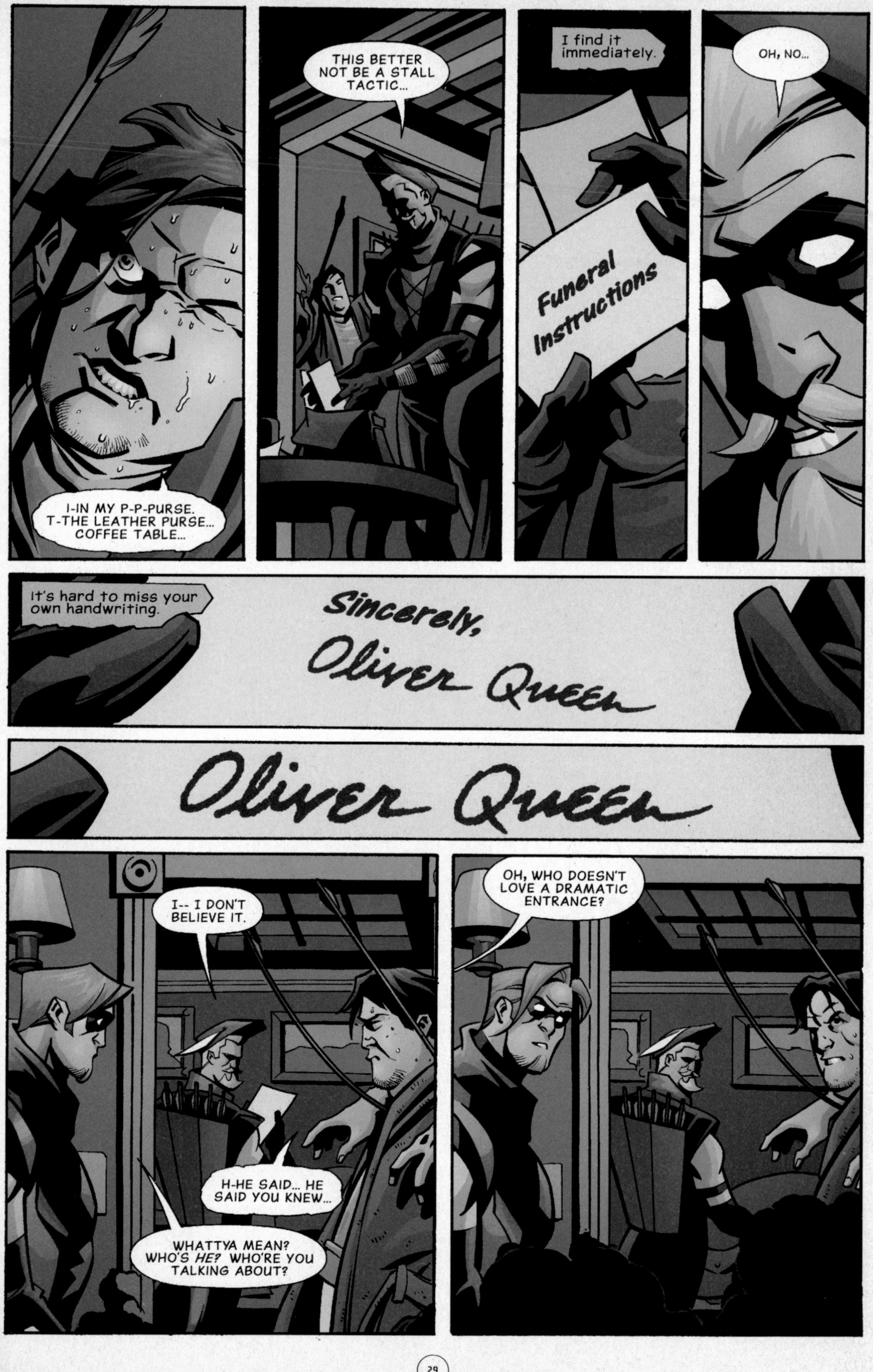
I-IN MY P-P-PURSE. T-THE LEATHER PURSE... COFFEE TABLE...
THIS BETTER NOT BE A STALL TACTIC...
I find it immediately.
Funeral Instructions
OH, NO...
It's hard to miss your own handwriting.
Sincerely, Oliver Queen
Oliver Queen
I-- I DON'T BELIEVE IT.
H-HE SAID... HE SAID YOU KNEW...
WHATTYA MEAN? WHO'S HE? WHO'RE YOU TALKING ABOUT?
OH, WHO DOESN'T LOVE A DRAMATIC ENTRANCE?

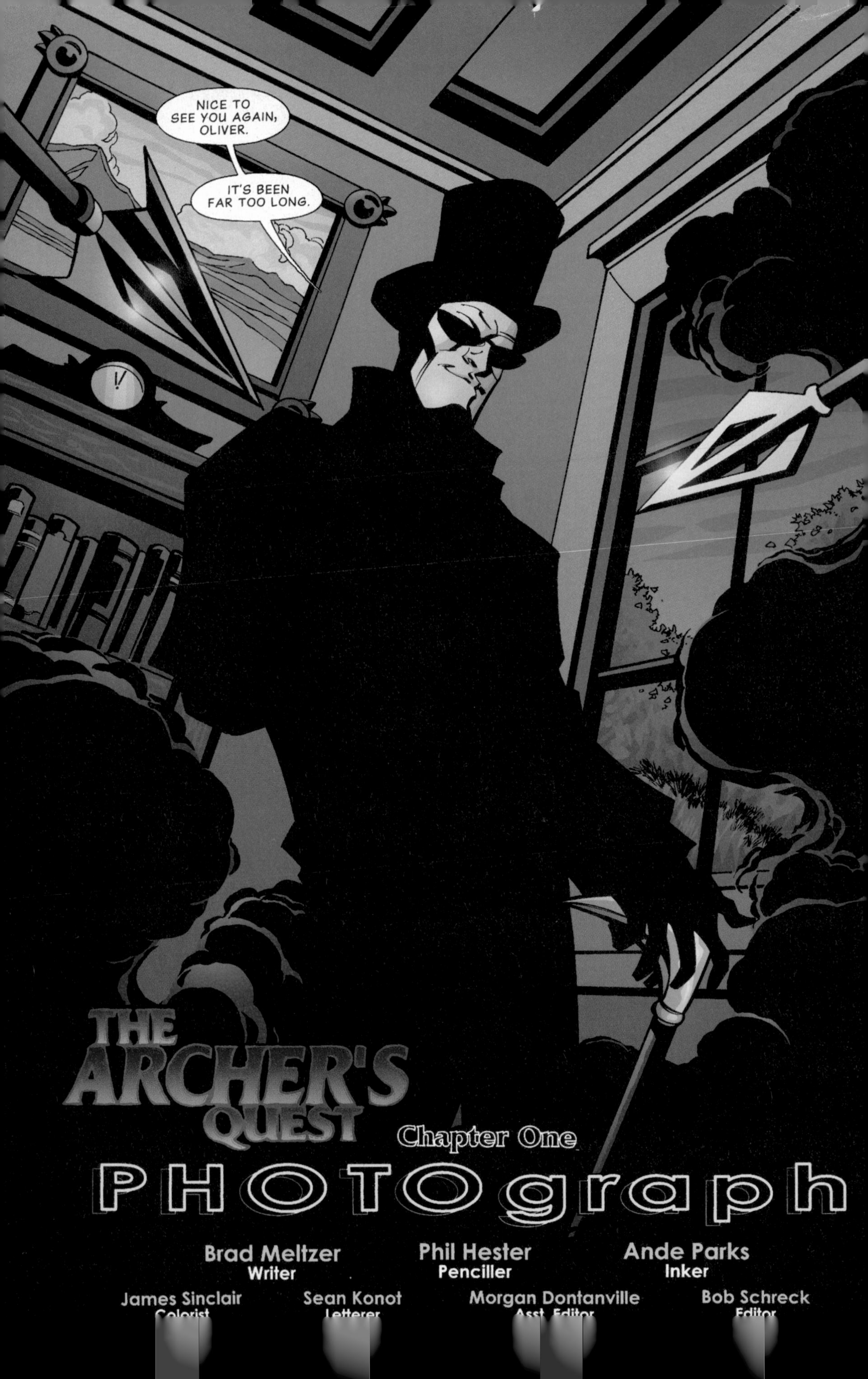
NICE TO SEE YOU AGAIN, OLIVER.
IT'S BEEN FAR TOO LONG.
THE ARCHER'S QUEST
Chapter One
PHOTOgraph
Brad Meltzer Writer
Phil Hester Penciller
Ande Parks Inker
James Sinclair Colorist
Sean Konot Letterer
Morgan Dontanville Asst. Editor
Bob Schreck Editor

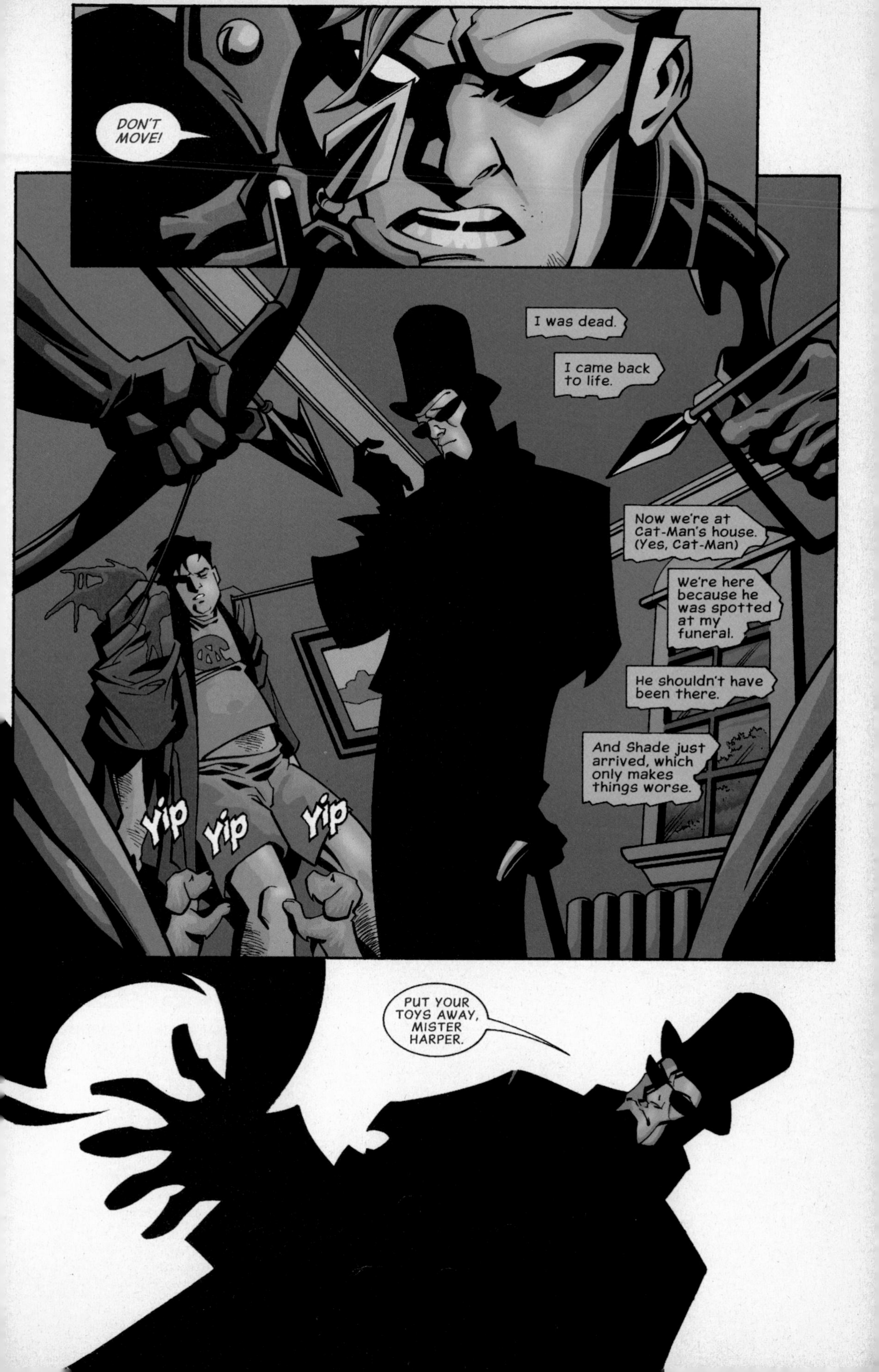
DON'T MOVE!
I was dead.
I came back to life.
Now we're at Cat-Man's house. (Yes, Cat-Man)
We're here because he was spotted at my funeral.
He shouldn't have been there.
And Shade just arrived, which only makes things worse.
YIP
YIP
YIP
PUT YOUR TOYS AWAY, MISTER HARPER.

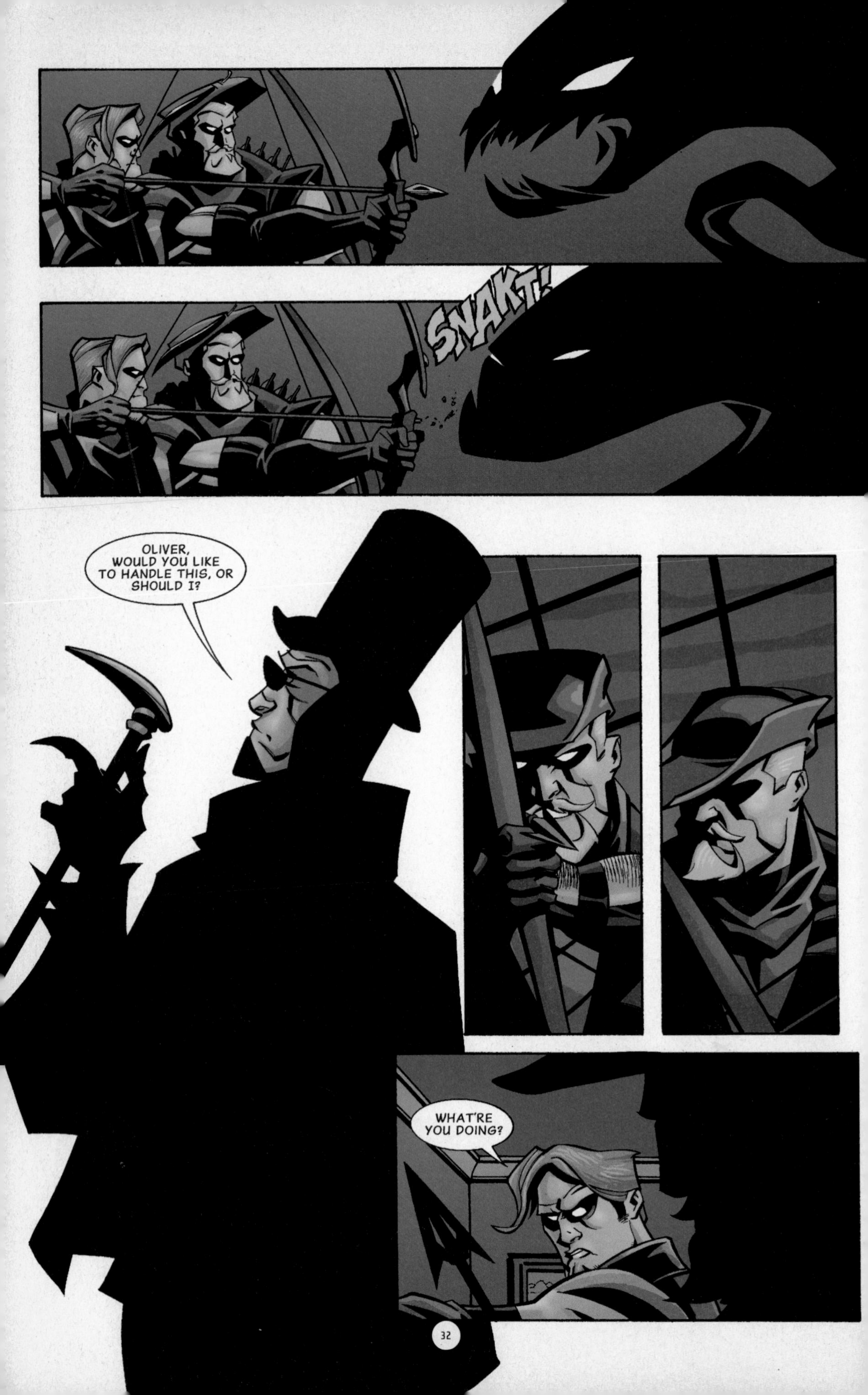
SNAKT!
OLIVER, WOULD YOU LIKE TO HANDLE THIS, OR SHOULD I?
WHAT'RE YOU DOING?

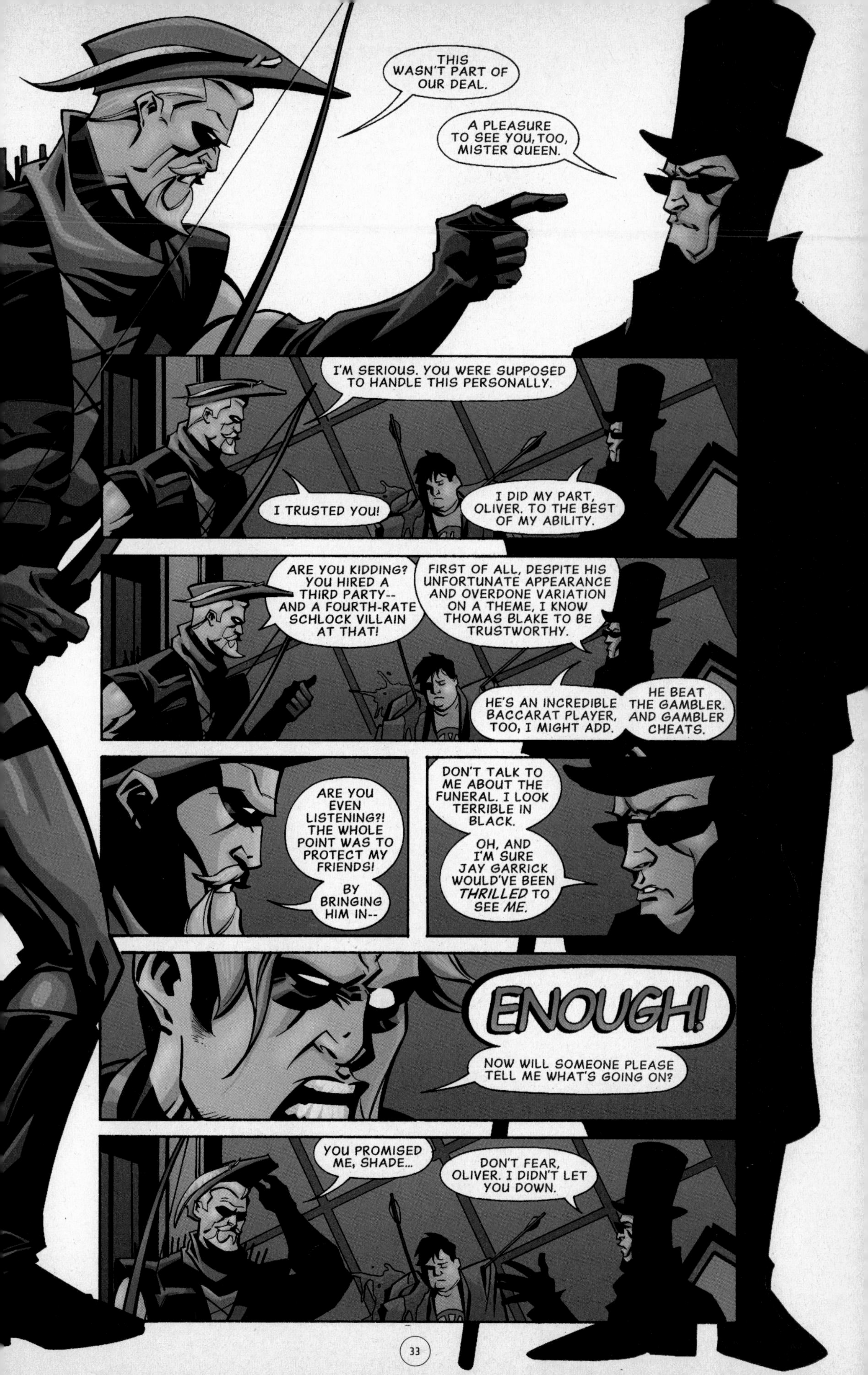
THIS WASN'T PART OF OUR DEAL.
A PLEASURE TO SEE YOU, TOO, MISTER QUEEN.
I'M SERIOUS. YOU WERE SUPPOSED TO HANDLE THIS PERSONALLY.
I TRUSTED YOU!
I DID MY PART, OLIVER. TO THE BEST OF MY ABILITY.
ARE YOU KIDDING? YOU HIRED A THIRD PARTY-- AND A FOURTH-RATE SCHLOCK VILLAIN AT THAT!
FIRST OF ALL, DESPITE HIS UNFORTUNATE APPEARANCE AND OVERDONE VARIATION ON A THEME, I KNOW THOMAS BLAKE TO BE TRUSTWORTHY.
HE'S AN INCREDIBLE BACCARAT PLAYER, TOO, I MIGHT ADD.
HE BEAT THE GAMBLER. AND GAMBLER CHEATS.
ARE YOU EVEN LISTENING?! THE WHOLE POINT WAS TO PROTECT MY FRIENDS!
BY BRINGING HIM IN--
DON'T TALK TO ME ABOUT THE FUNERAL. I LOOK TERRIBLE IN BLACK.
OH, AND I'M SURE JAY GARRICK WOULD'VE BEEN *THRILLED* TO SEE *ME*.
ENOUGH!
NOW WILL SOMEONE PLEASE TELL ME WHAT'S GOING ON?
YOU PROMISED ME, SHADE...
DON'T FEAR, OLIVER. I DIDN'T LET YOU DOWN.

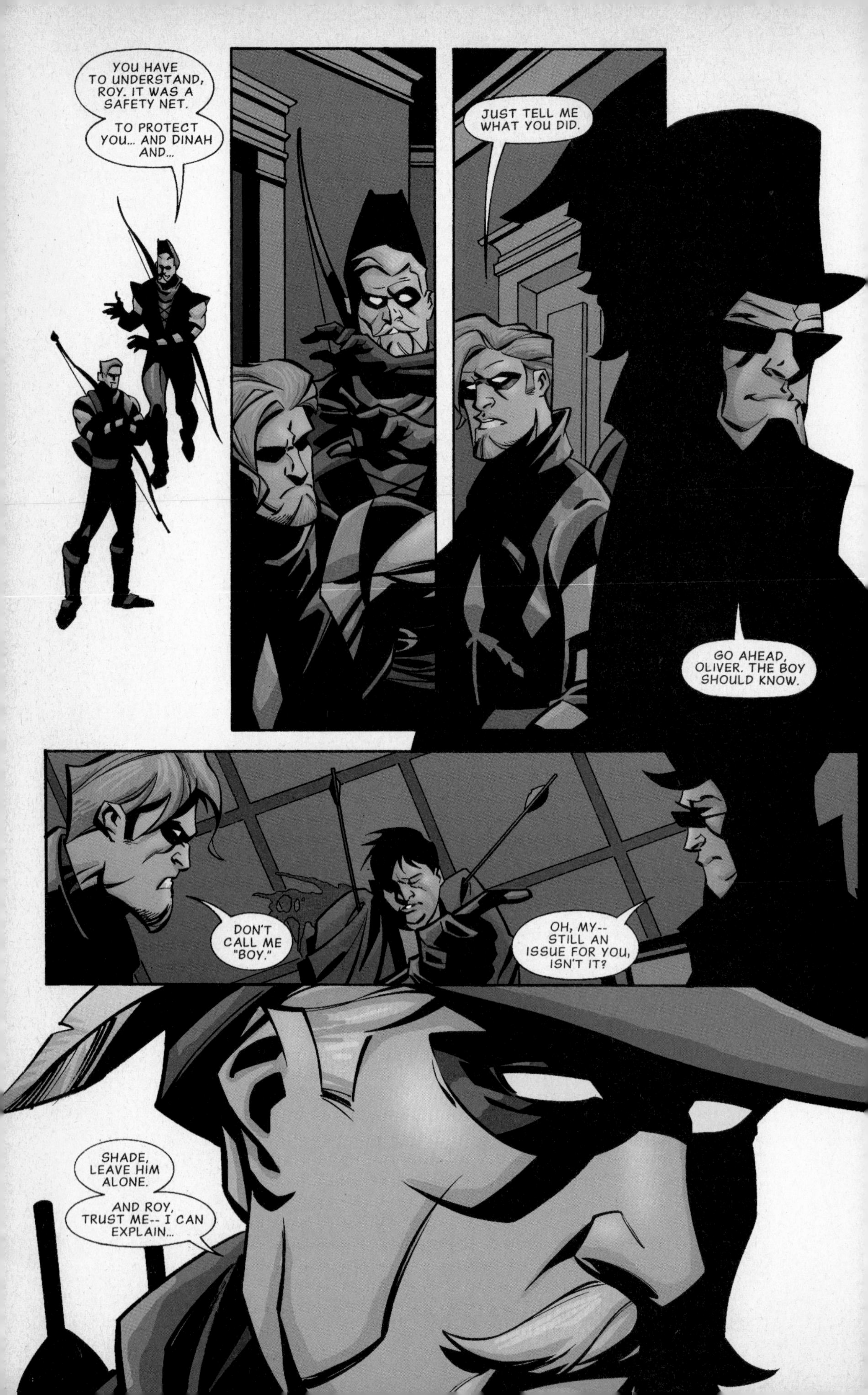
YOU HAVE TO UNDERSTAND, ROY. IT WAS A SAFETY NET.
TO PROTECT YOU... AND DINAH AND...
JUST TELL ME WHAT YOU DID.
GO AHEAD, OLIVER. THE BOY SHOULD KNOW.
DON'T CALL ME "BOY."
OH, MY-- STILL AN ISSUE FOR YOU, ISN'T IT?
SHADE, LEAVE HIM ALONE.
AND ROY, TRUST ME-- I CAN EXPLAIN...

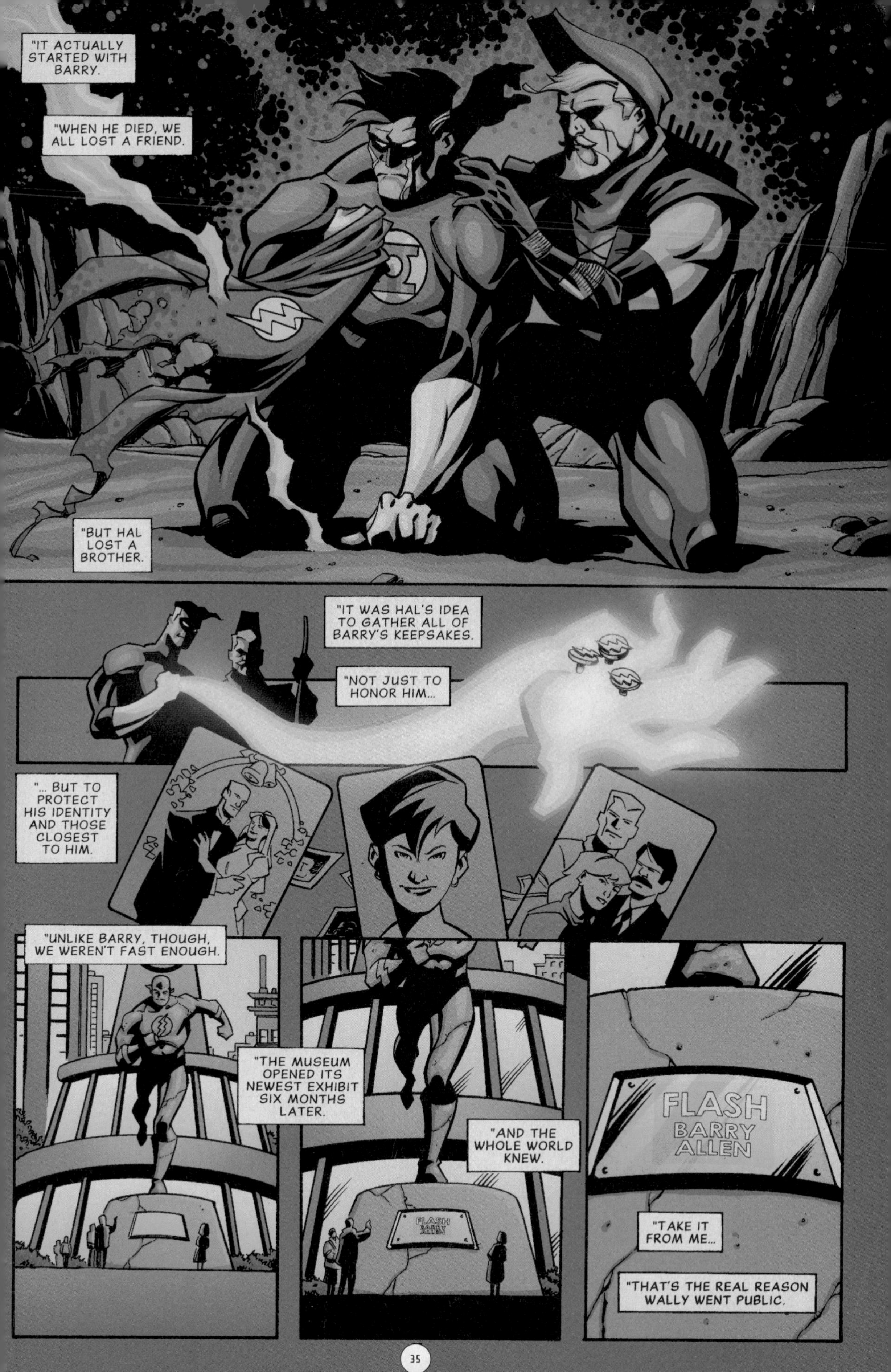
"IT ACTUALLY STARTED WITH BARRY.
"WHEN HE DIED, WE ALL LOST A FRIEND.
"BUT HAL LOST A BROTHER.
"IT WAS HAL'S IDEA TO GATHER ALL OF BARRY'S KEEPSAKES.
"NOT JUST TO HONOR HIM...
"... BUT TO PROTECT HIS IDENTITY AND THOSE CLOSEST TO HIM.
"UNLIKE BARRY, THOUGH, WE WEREN'T FAST ENOUGH.
"THE MUSEUM OPENED ITS NEWEST EXHIBIT SIX MONTHS LATER.
"AND THE WHOLE WORLD KNEW.
FLASH
BARRY ALLEN
FLASH
BARRY ALLEN
"TAKE IT FROM ME...
"THAT'S THE REAL REASON WALLY WENT PUBLIC.

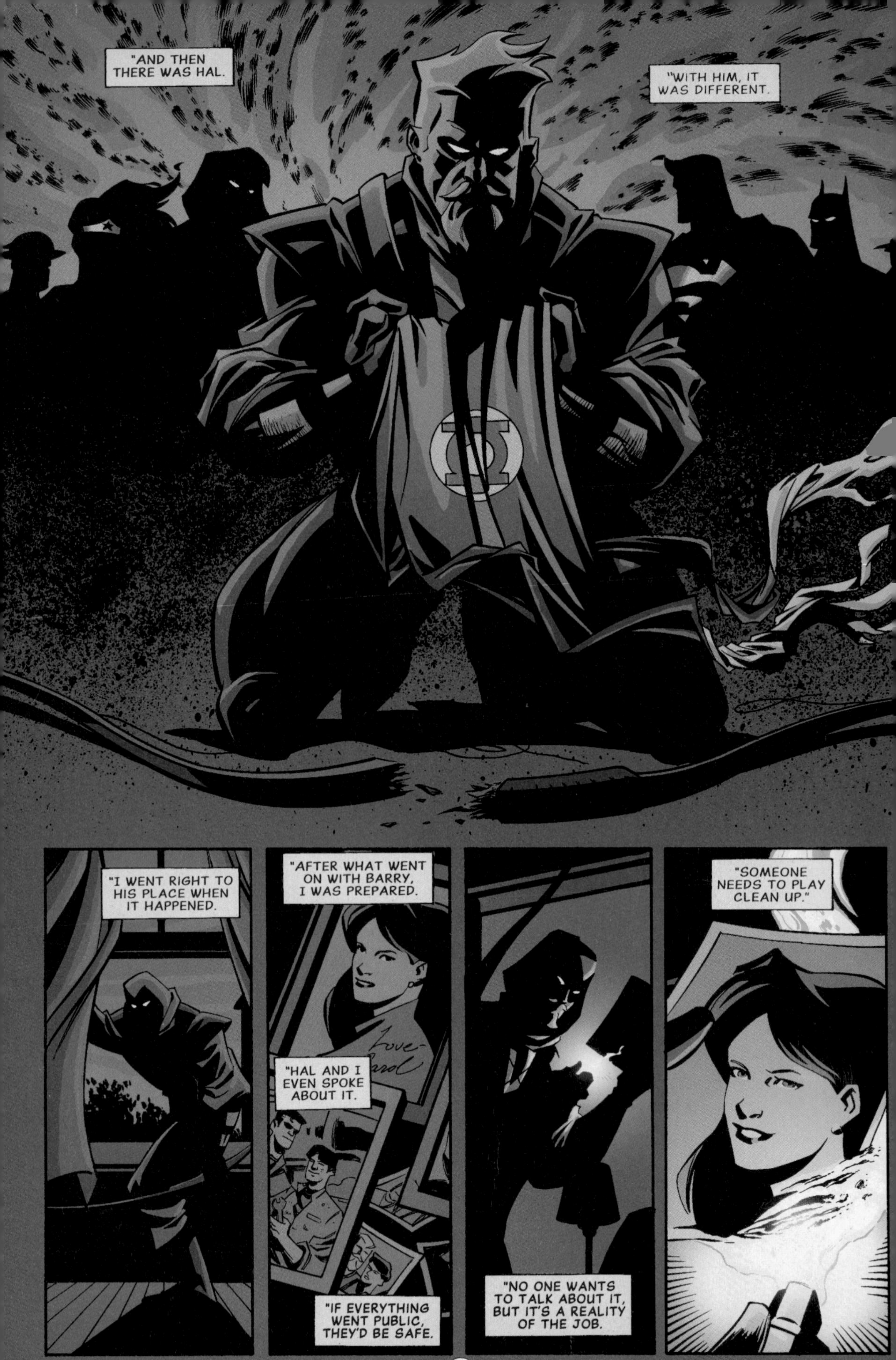
"AND THEN THERE WAS HAL.
"WITH HIM, IT WAS DIFFERENT.
"I WENT RIGHT TO HIS PLACE WHEN IT HAPPENED.
"AFTER WHAT WENT ON WITH BARRY, I WAS PREPARED.
"HAL AND I EVEN SPOKE ABOUT IT.
"IF EVERYTHING WENT PUBLIC, THEY'D BE SAFE.
"NO ONE WANTS TO TALK ABOUT IT, BUT IT'S A REALITY OF THE JOB.
"SOMEONE NEEDS TO PLAY CLEAN UP."

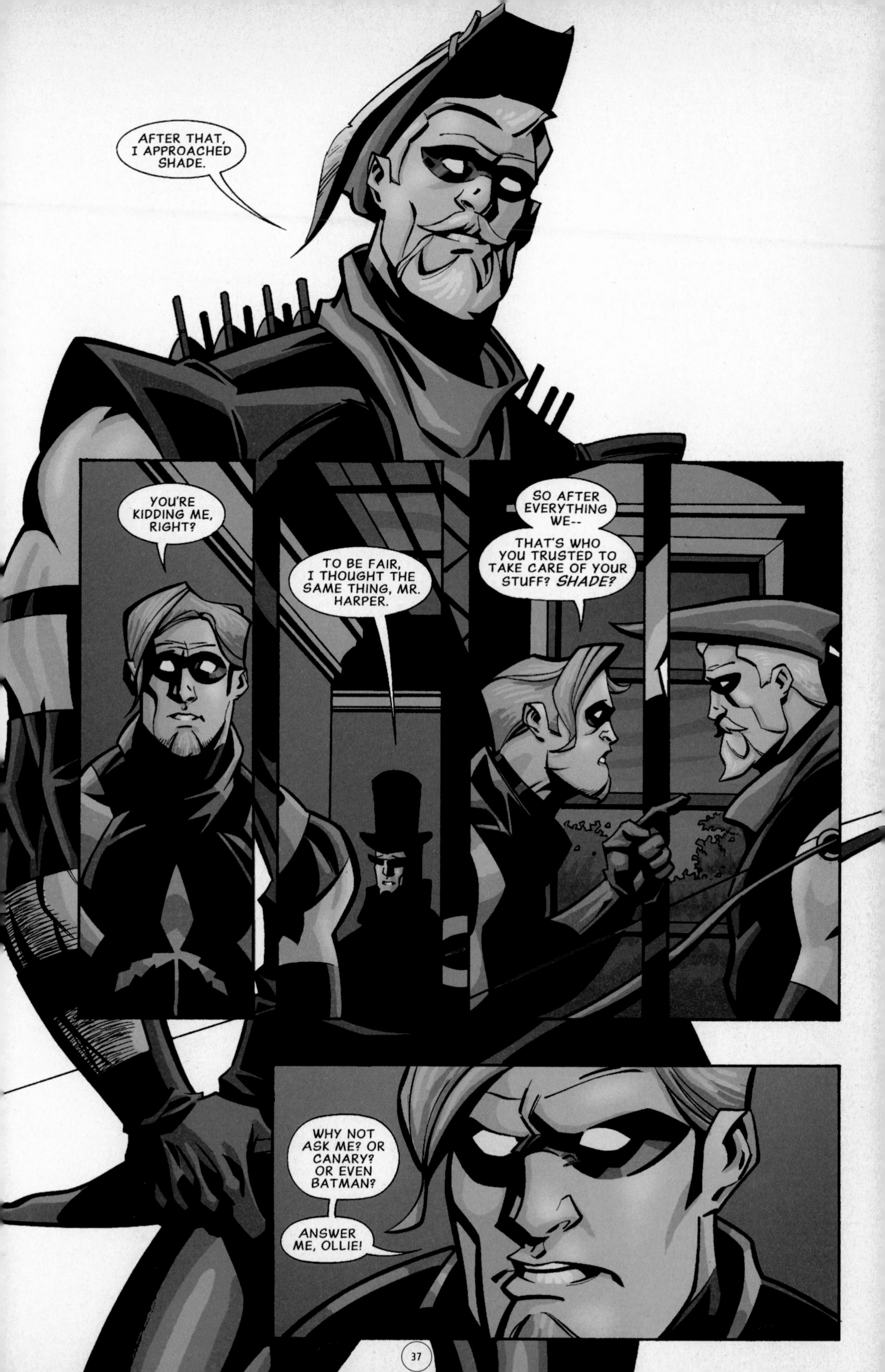
AFTER THAT, I APPROACHED SHADE.
YOU'RE KIDDING ME, RIGHT?
TO BE FAIR, I THOUGHT THE SAME THING, MR. HARPER.
SO AFTER EVERYTHING WE--
THAT'S WHO YOU TRUSTED TO TAKE CARE OF YOUR STUFF? *SHADE?*
WHY NOT ASK ME? OR CANARY? OR EVEN BATMAN?
ANSWER ME, OLLIE!

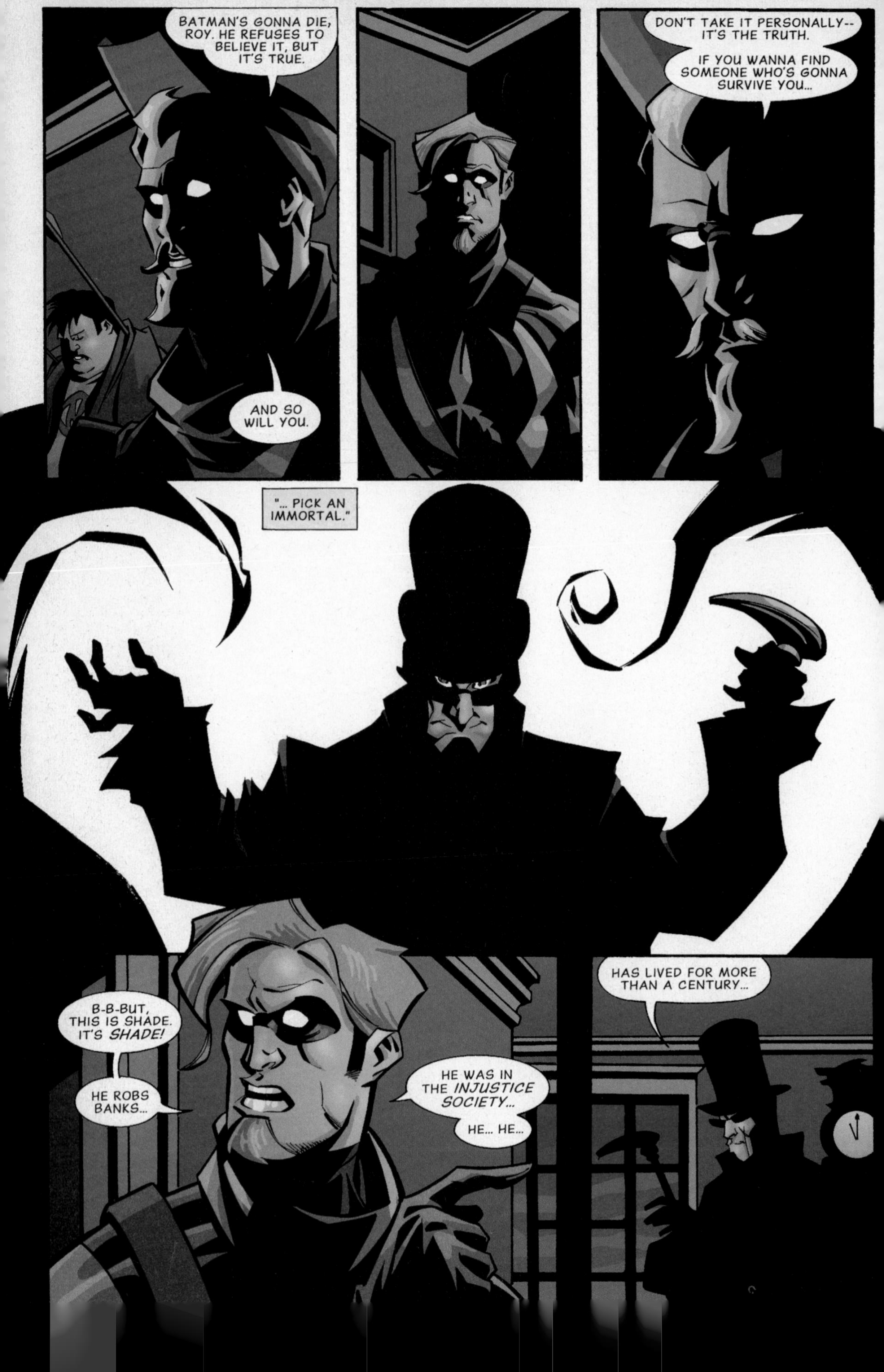
BATMAN'S GONNA DIE, ROY. HE REFUSES TO BELIEVE IT, BUT IT'S TRUE.
AND SO WILL YOU.
DON'T TAKE IT PERSONALLY-- IT'S THE TRUTH.
IF YOU WANNA FIND SOMEONE WHO'S GONNA SURVIVE YOU...
"... PICK AN IMMORTAL."
B-B-BUT, THIS IS SHADE. IT'S *SHADE!*
HE ROBS BANKS...
HE WAS IN THE *INJUSTICE SOCIETY*...
HE... HE...
HAS LIVED FOR MORE THAN A CENTURY...

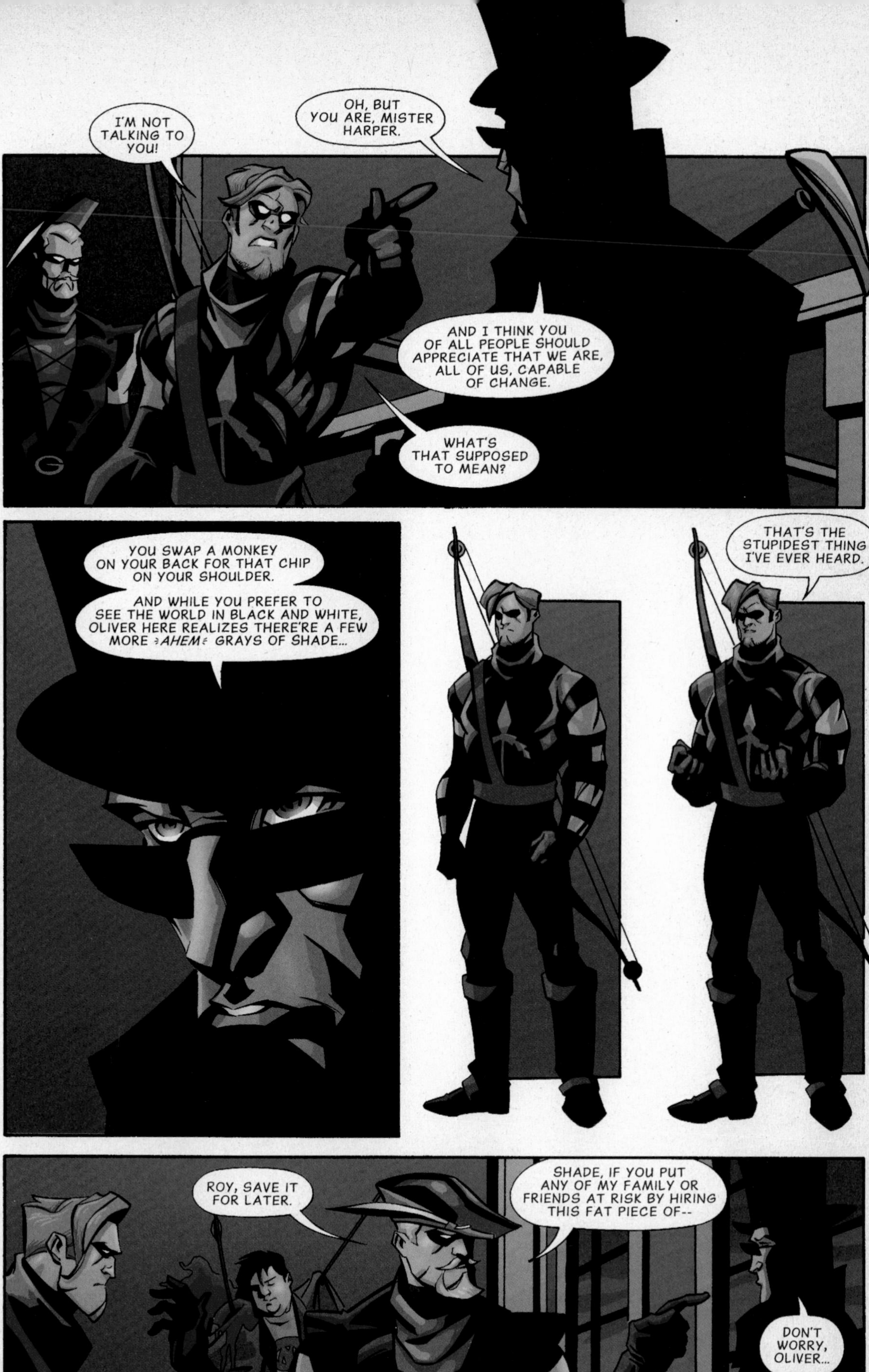
I'M NOT TALKING TO YOU!
OH, BUT YOU ARE, MISTER HARPER.
AND I THINK YOU OF ALL PEOPLE SHOULD APPRECIATE THAT WE ARE, ALL OF US, CAPABLE OF CHANGE.
WHAT'S THAT SUPPOSED TO MEAN?
YOU SWAP A MONKEY ON YOUR BACK FOR THAT CHIP ON YOUR SHOULDER.
AND WHILE YOU PREFER TO SEE THE WORLD IN BLACK AND WHITE, OLIVER HERE REALIZES THERE'RE A FEW MORE *AHEM* GRAYS OF SHADE...
THAT'S THE STUPIDEST THING I'VE EVER HEARD.
ROY, SAVE IT FOR LATER.
SHADE, IF YOU PUT ANY OF MY FAMILY OR FRIENDS AT RISK BY HIRING THIS FAT PIECE OF--
DON'T WORRY, OLIVER...

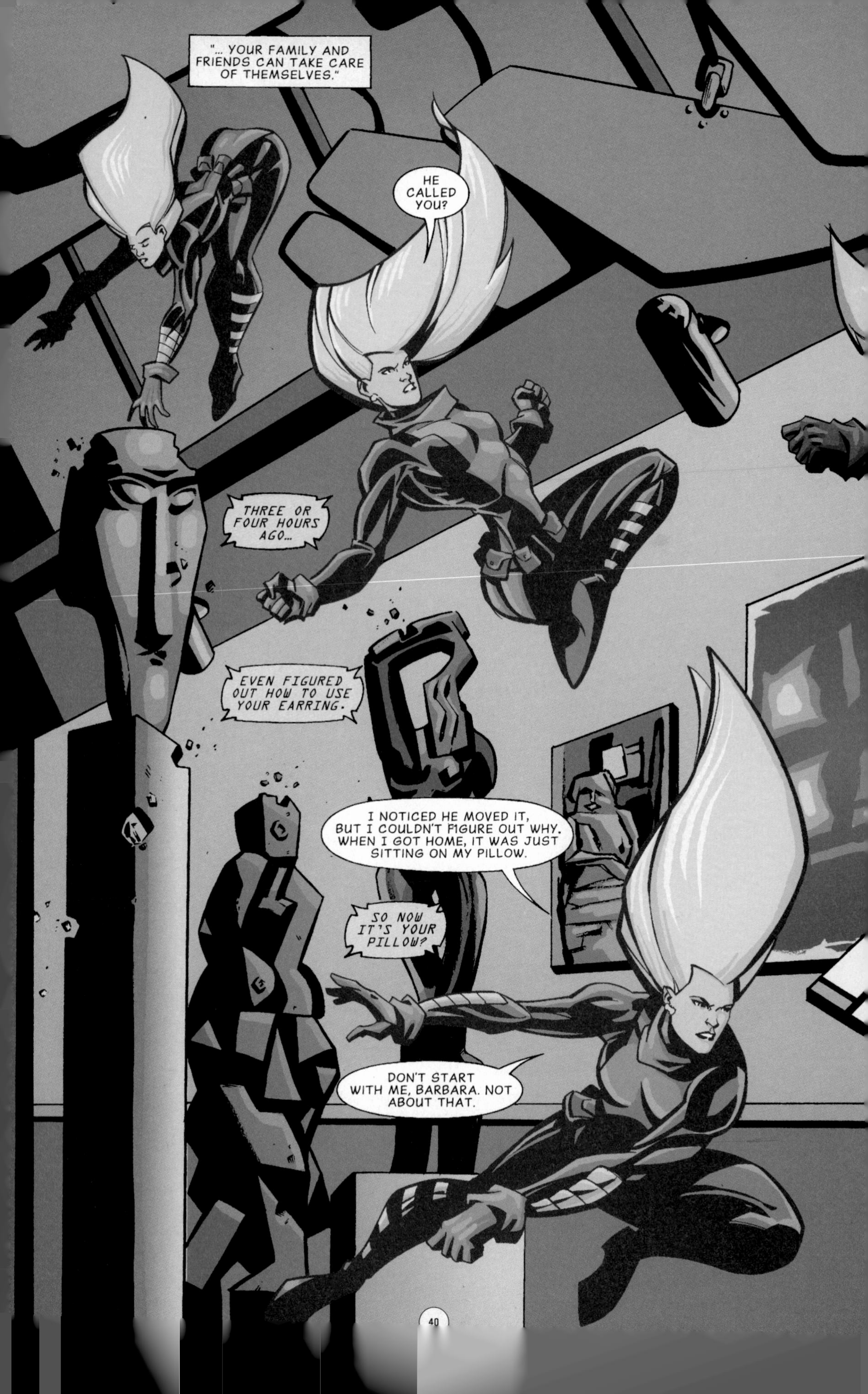
"... YOUR FAMILY AND FRIENDS CAN TAKE CARE OF THEMSELVES."
HE CALLED YOU?
THREE OR FOUR HOURS AGO...
EVEN FIGURED OUT HOW TO USE YOUR EARRING.
I NOTICED HE MOVED IT, BUT I COULDN'T FIGURE OUT WHY. WHEN I GOT HOME, IT WAS JUST SITTING ON MY PILLOW.
SO NOW IT'S YOUR PILLOW?
DON'T START WITH ME, BARBARA. NOT ABOUT THAT.

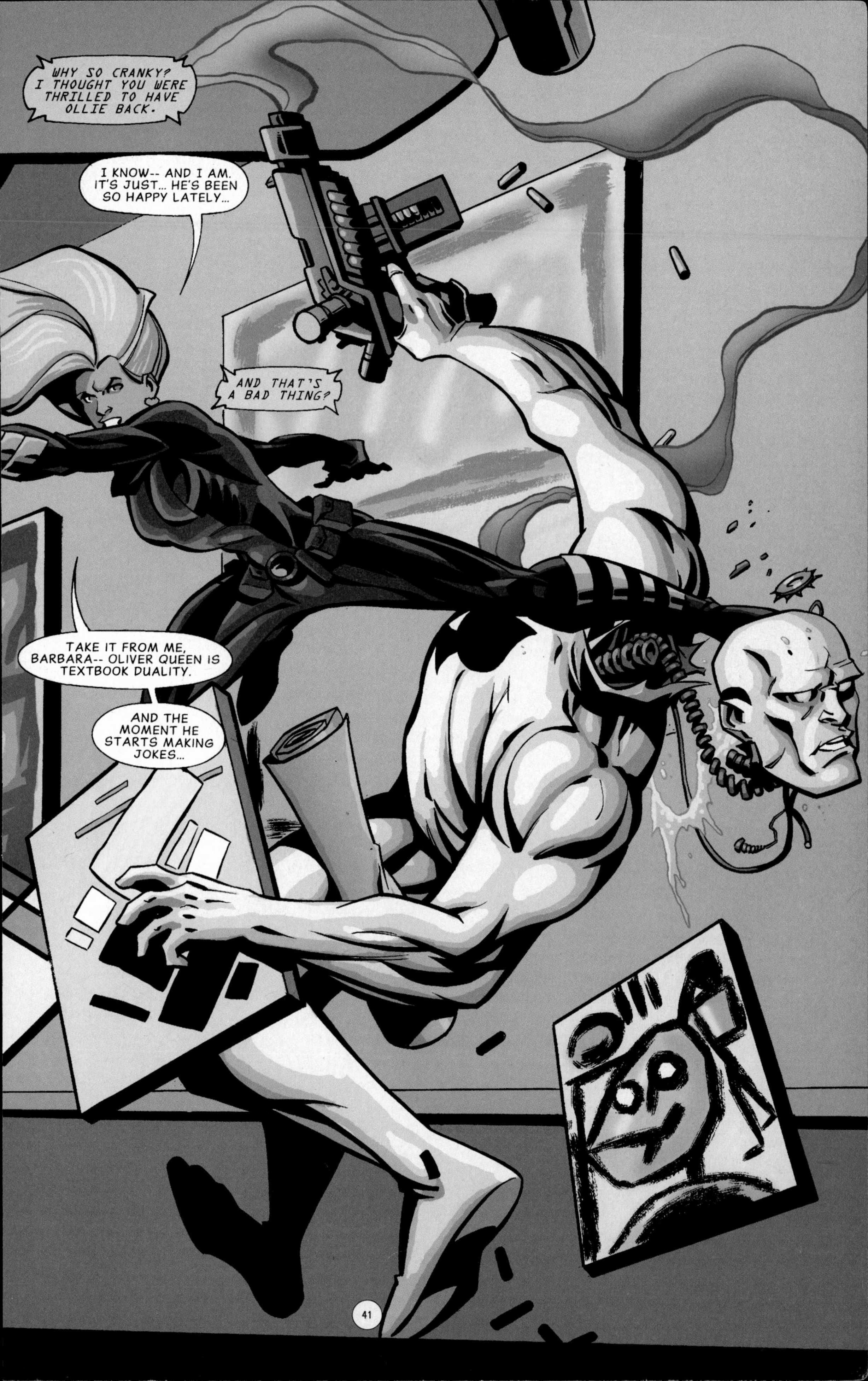
WHY SO CRANKY? I THOUGHT YOU WERE THRILLED TO HAVE OLLIE BACK.
I KNOW-- AND I AM. IT'S JUST... HE'S BEEN SO HAPPY LATELY...
AND THAT'S A BAD THING?
TAKE IT FROM ME, BARBARA-- OLIVER QUEEN IS TEXTBOOK DUALITY.
AND THE MOMENT HE STARTS MAKING JOKES...

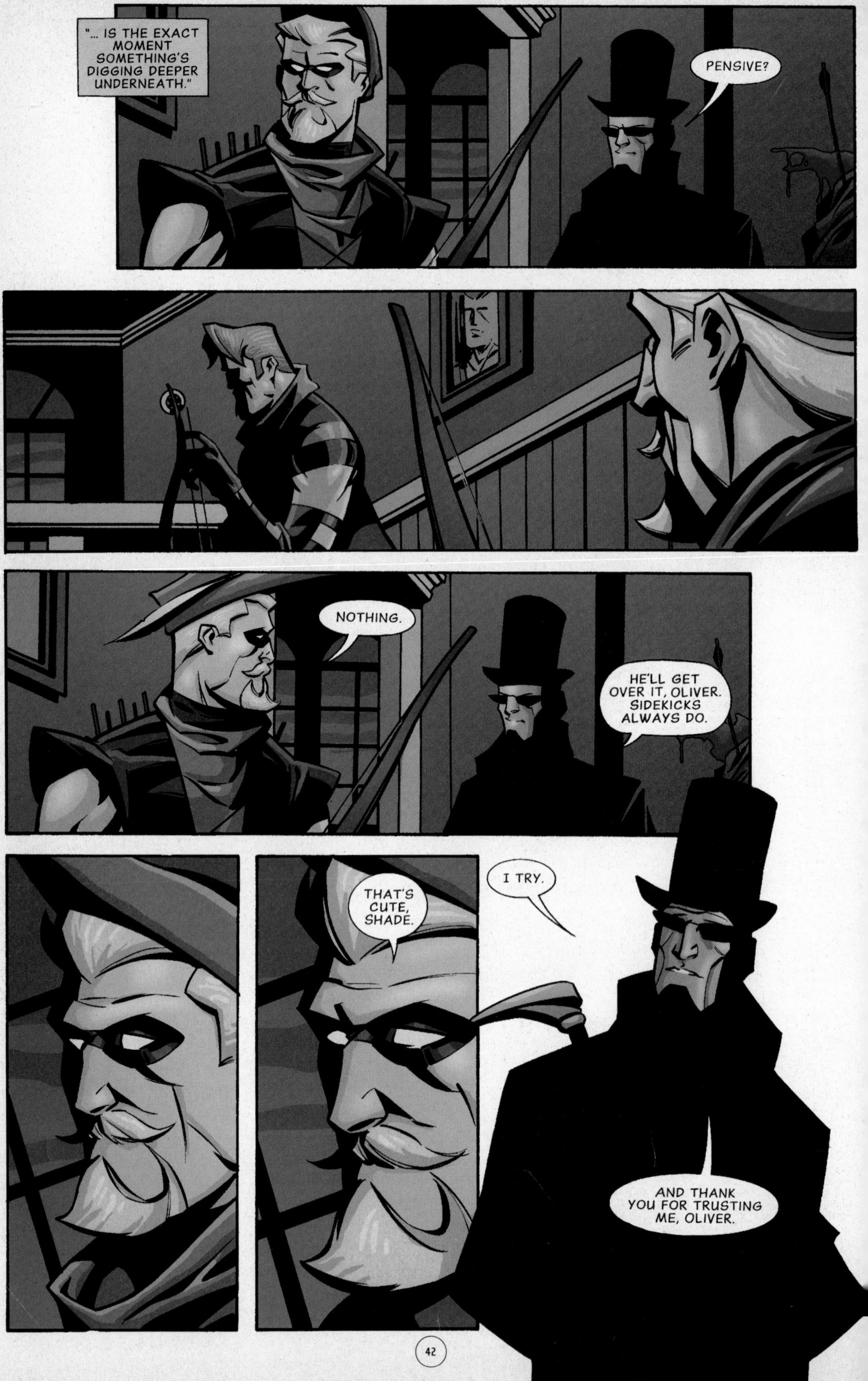
"... IS THE EXACT MOMENT SOMETHING'S DIGGING DEEPER UNDERNEATH."
PENSIVE?
NOTHING.
HE'LL GET OVER IT, OLIVER. SIDEKICKS ALWAYS DO.
THAT'S CUTE, SHADE.
I TRY.
AND THANK YOU FOR TRUSTING ME, OLIVER.

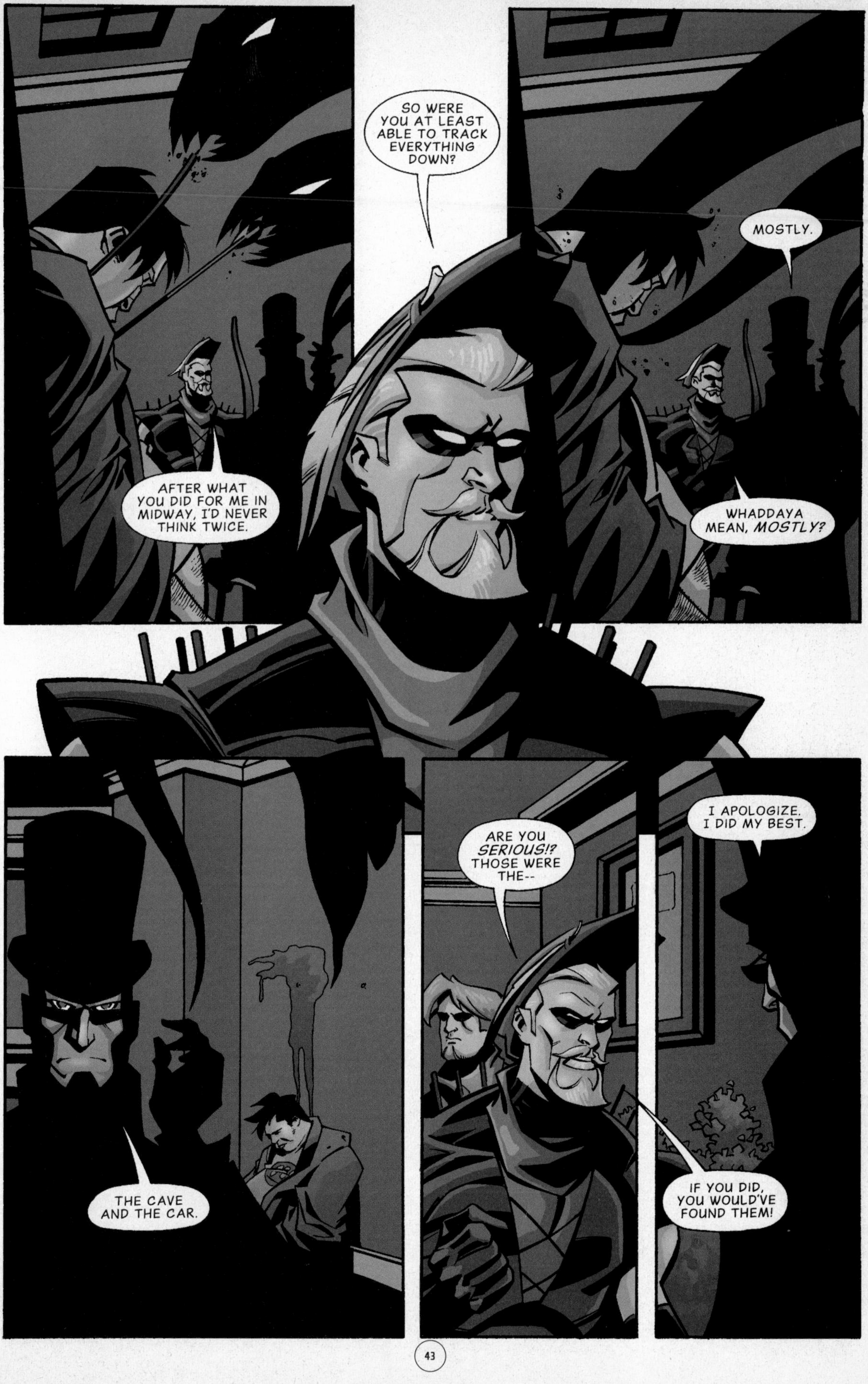
SO WERE YOU AT LEAST ABLE TO TRACK EVERYTHING DOWN?
AFTER WHAT YOU DID FOR ME IN MIDWAY, I'D NEVER THINK TWICE.
MOSTLY.
WHADDAYA MEAN, *MOSTLY?*
THE CAVE AND THE CAR.
ARE YOU *SERIOUS!?* THOSE WERE THE--
I APOLOGIZE. I DID MY BEST.
IF YOU DID, YOU WOULD'VE FOUND THEM!

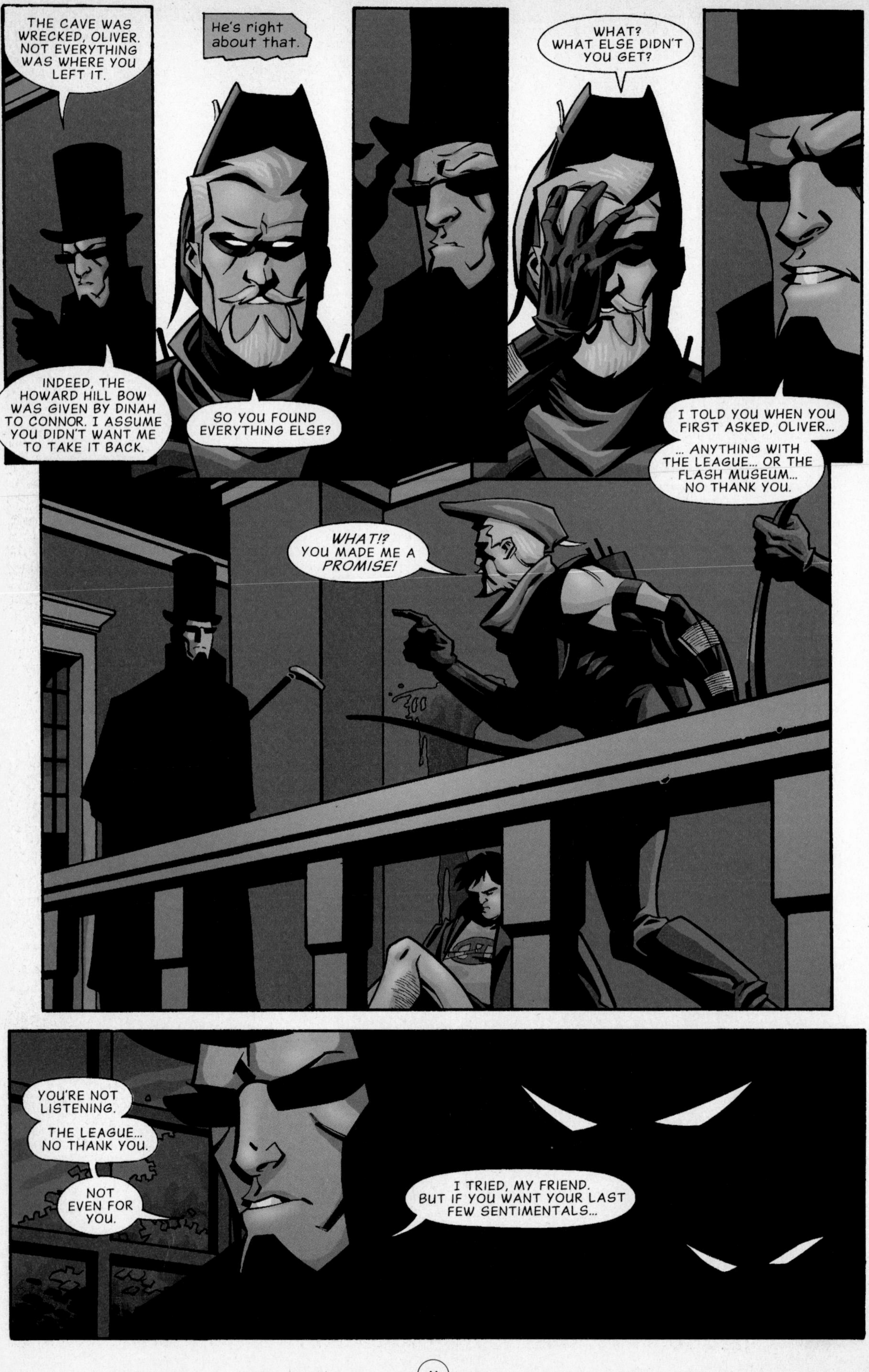
THE CAVE WAS WRECKED, OLIVER. NOT EVERYTHING WAS WHERE YOU LEFT IT.
INDEED, THE HOWARD HILL BOW WAS GIVEN BY DINAH TO CONNOR. I ASSUME YOU DIDN'T WANT ME TO TAKE IT BACK.
He's right about that.
SO YOU FOUND EVERYTHING ELSE?
WHAT? WHAT ELSE DIDN'T YOU GET?
I TOLD YOU WHEN YOU FIRST ASKED, OLIVER...
... ANYTHING WITH THE LEAGUE... OR THE FLASH MUSEUM... NO THANK YOU.
WHAT!? YOU MADE ME A PROMISE!
YOU'RE NOT LISTENING.
THE LEAGUE... NO THANK YOU.
NOT EVEN FOR YOU.
I TRIED, MY FRIEND. BUT IF YOU WANT YOUR LAST FEW SENTIMENTALS...

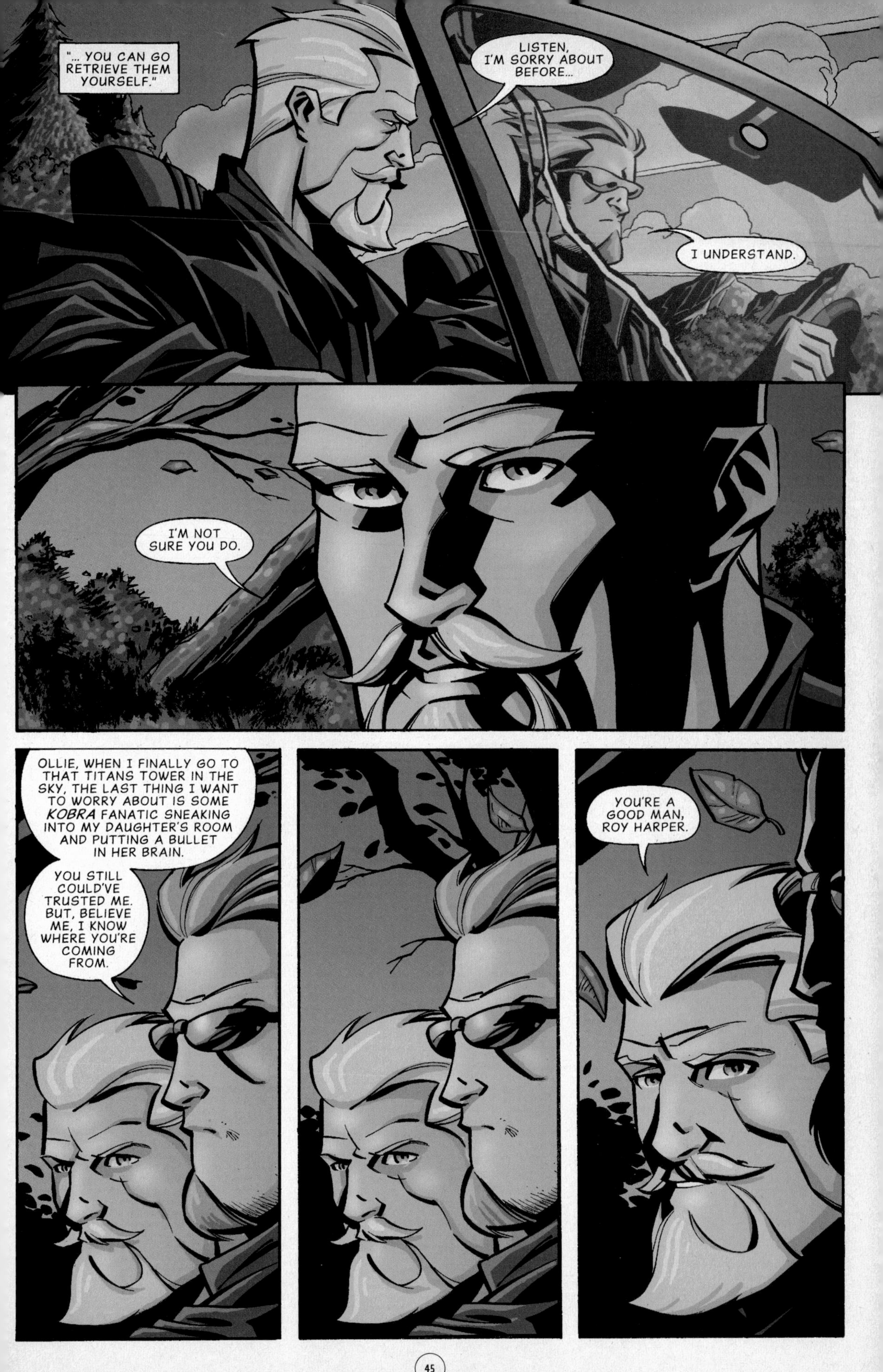
"... YOU CAN GO RETRIEVE THEM YOURSELF."
LISTEN, I'M SORRY ABOUT BEFORE...
I UNDERSTAND.
I'M NOT SURE YOU DO.
OLLIE, WHEN I FINALLY GO TO THAT TITANS TOWER IN THE SKY, THE LAST THING I WANT TO WORRY ABOUT IS SOME *KOBRA* FANATIC SNEAKING INTO MY DAUGHTER'S ROOM AND PUTTING A BULLET IN HER BRAIN.
YOU STILL COULD'VE TRUSTED ME. BUT, BELIEVE ME, I KNOW WHERE YOU'RE COMING FROM.
YOU'RE A GOOD MAN, ROY HARPER.

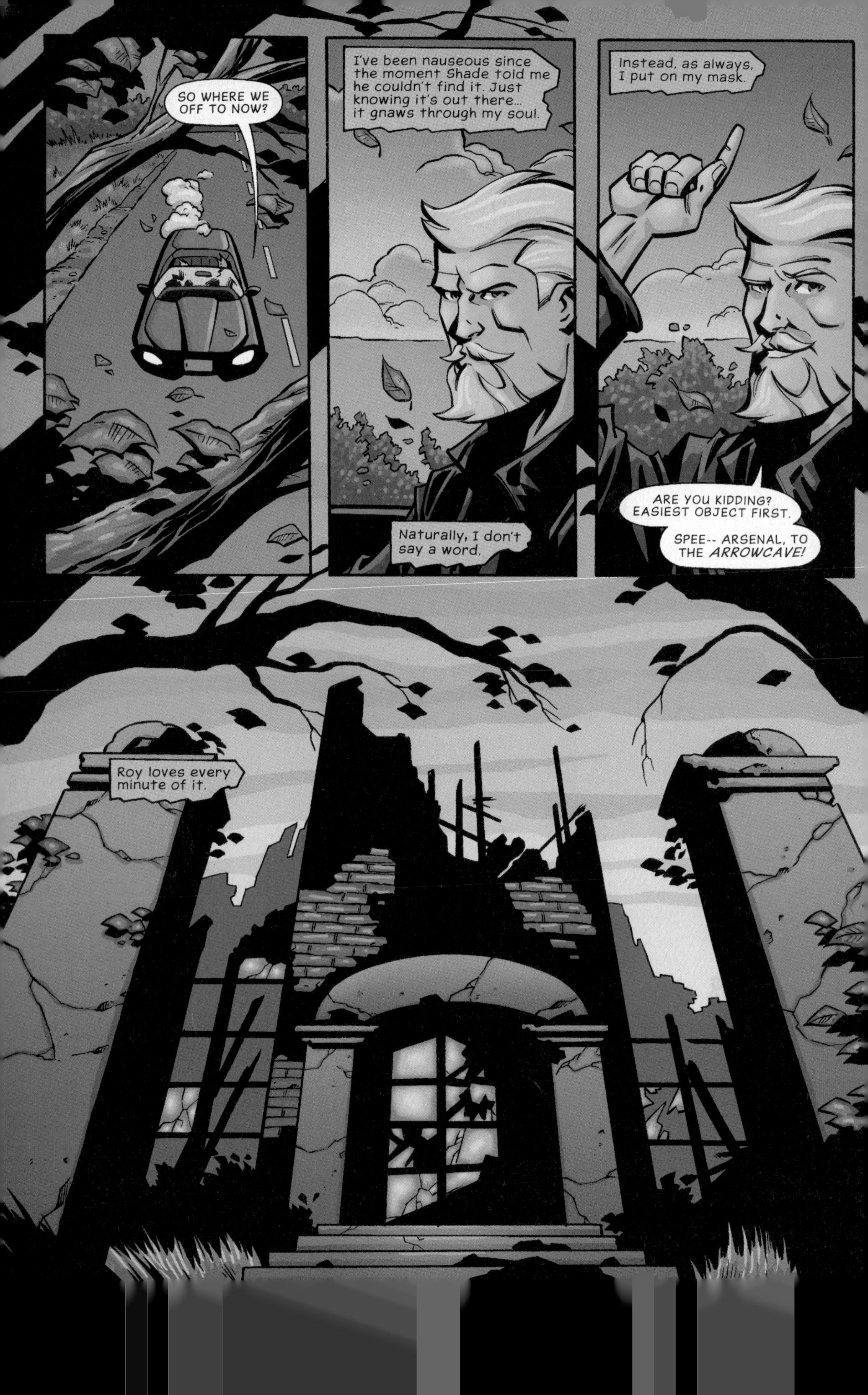
SO WHERE WE OFF TO NOW?
I've been nauseous since the moment Shade told me he couldn't find it. Just knowing it's out there... it gnaws through my soul.
Naturally, I don't say a word.
Instead, as always, I put on my mask.
ARE YOU KIDDING? EASIEST OBJECT FIRST.
SPEE-- ARSENAL, TO THE ARROWCAVE!
Roy loves every minute of it.

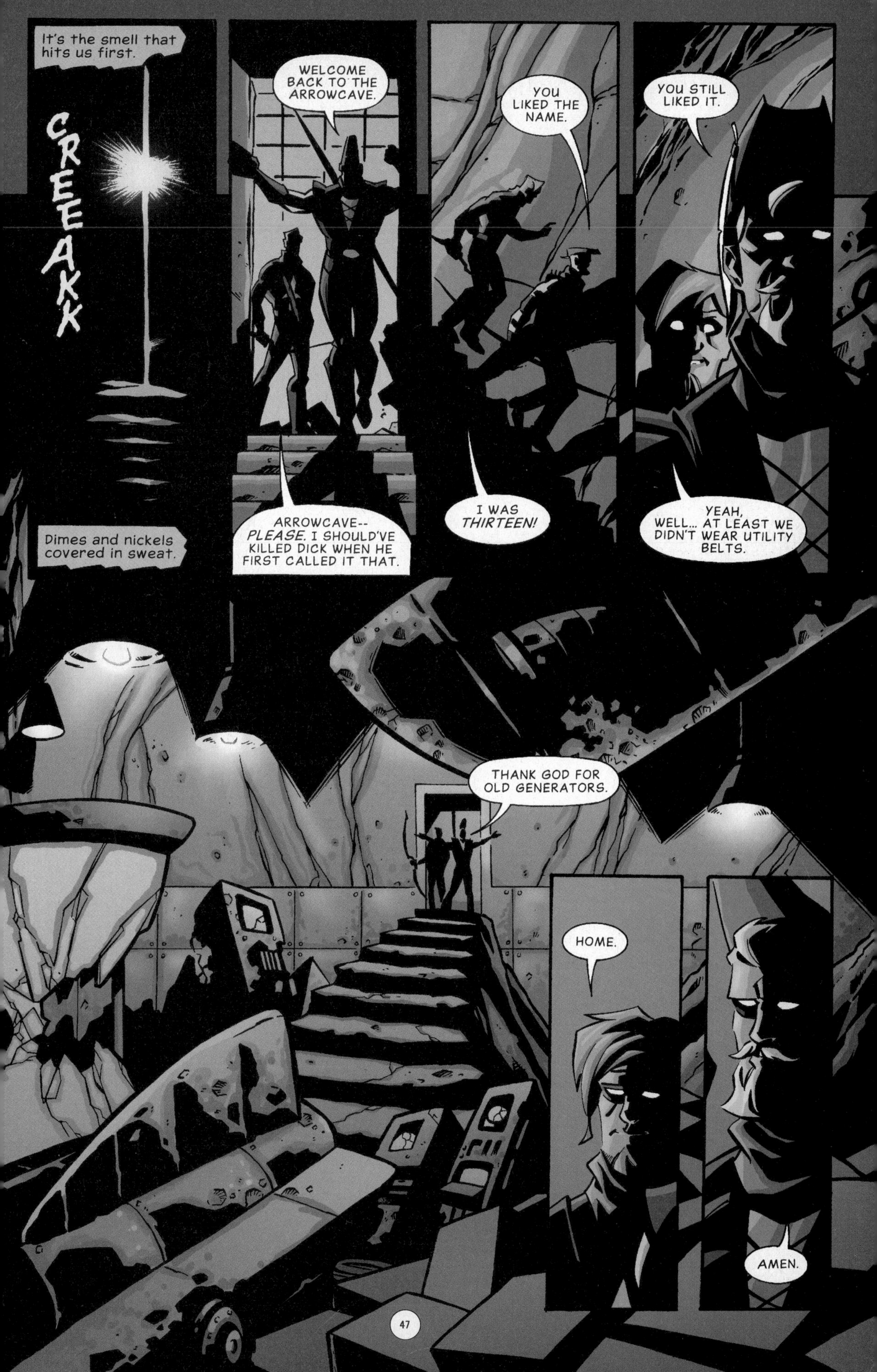
It's the smell that hits us first.
CREEEAKK
WELCOME BACK TO THE ARROWCAVE.
ARROWCAVE-- *PLEASE.* I SHOULD'VE KILLED DICK WHEN HE FIRST CALLED IT THAT.
YOU LIKED THE NAME.
I WAS *THIRTEEN!*
YOU STILL LIKED IT.
YEAH, WELL... AT LEAST WE DIDN'T WEAR UTILITY BELTS.
Dimes and nickels covered in sweat.
THANK GOD FOR OLD GENERATORS.
HOME.
AMEN.

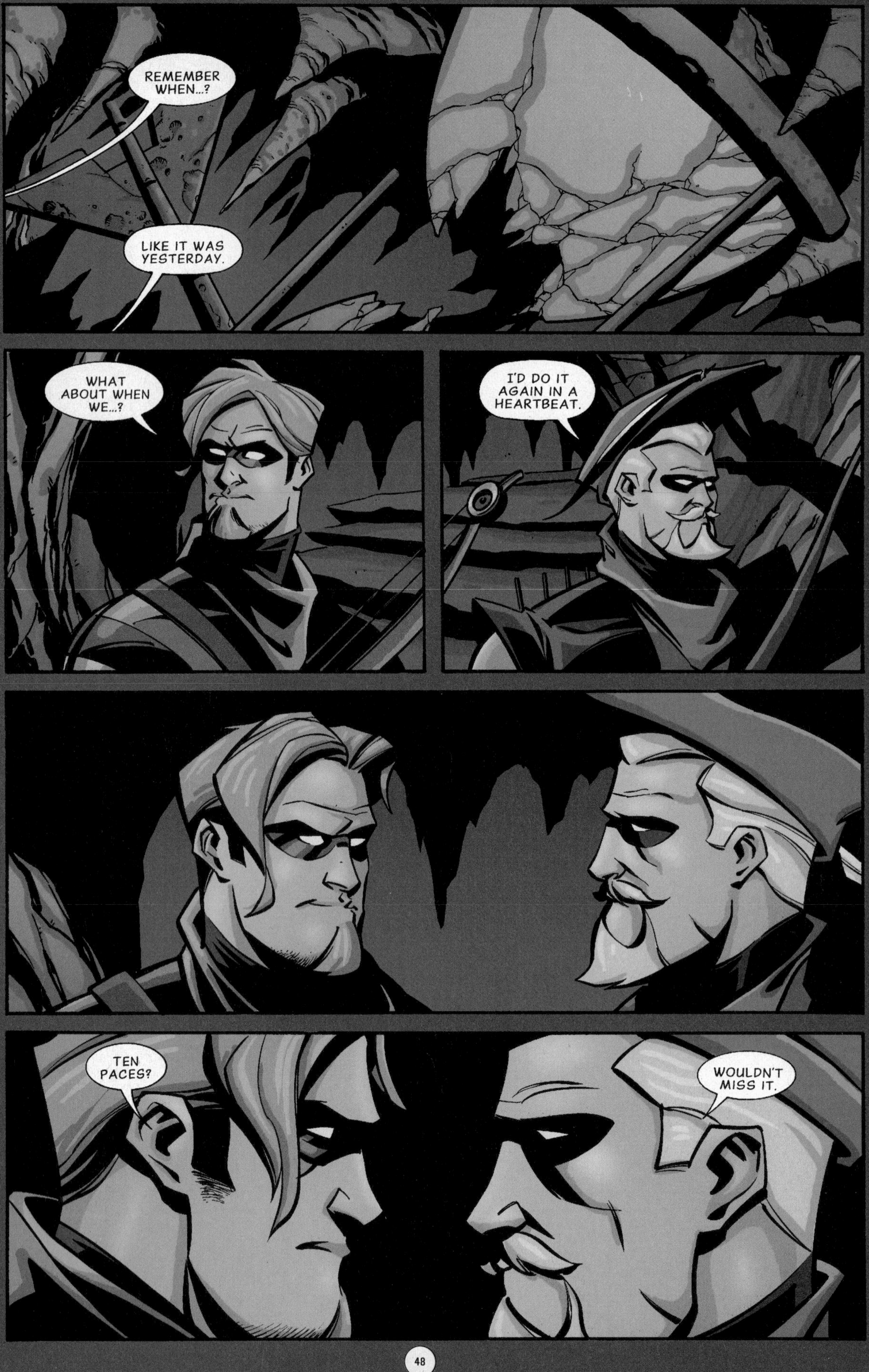
REMEMBER WHEN...?
LIKE IT WAS YESTERDAY.
WHAT ABOUT WHEN WE...?
I'D DO IT AGAIN IN A HEARTBEAT.
TEN PACES?
WOULDN'T MISS IT.

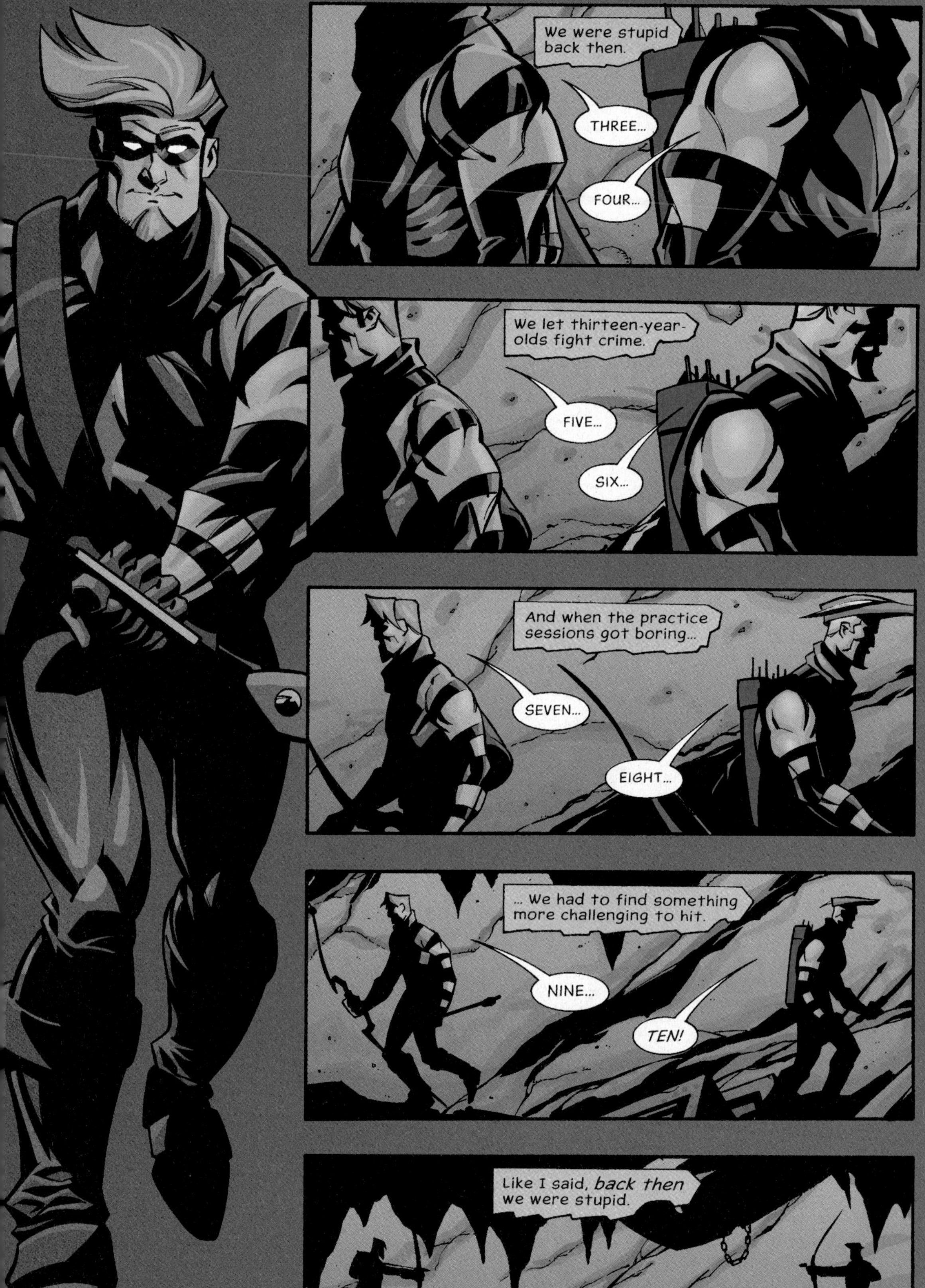
We were stupid back then.
THREE...
FOUR...
We let thirteen-year-olds fight crime.
FIVE...
SIX...
And when the practice sessions got boring...
SEVEN...
EIGHT...
... We had to find something more challenging to hit.
NINE...
TEN!
Like I said, *back then* we were stupid.

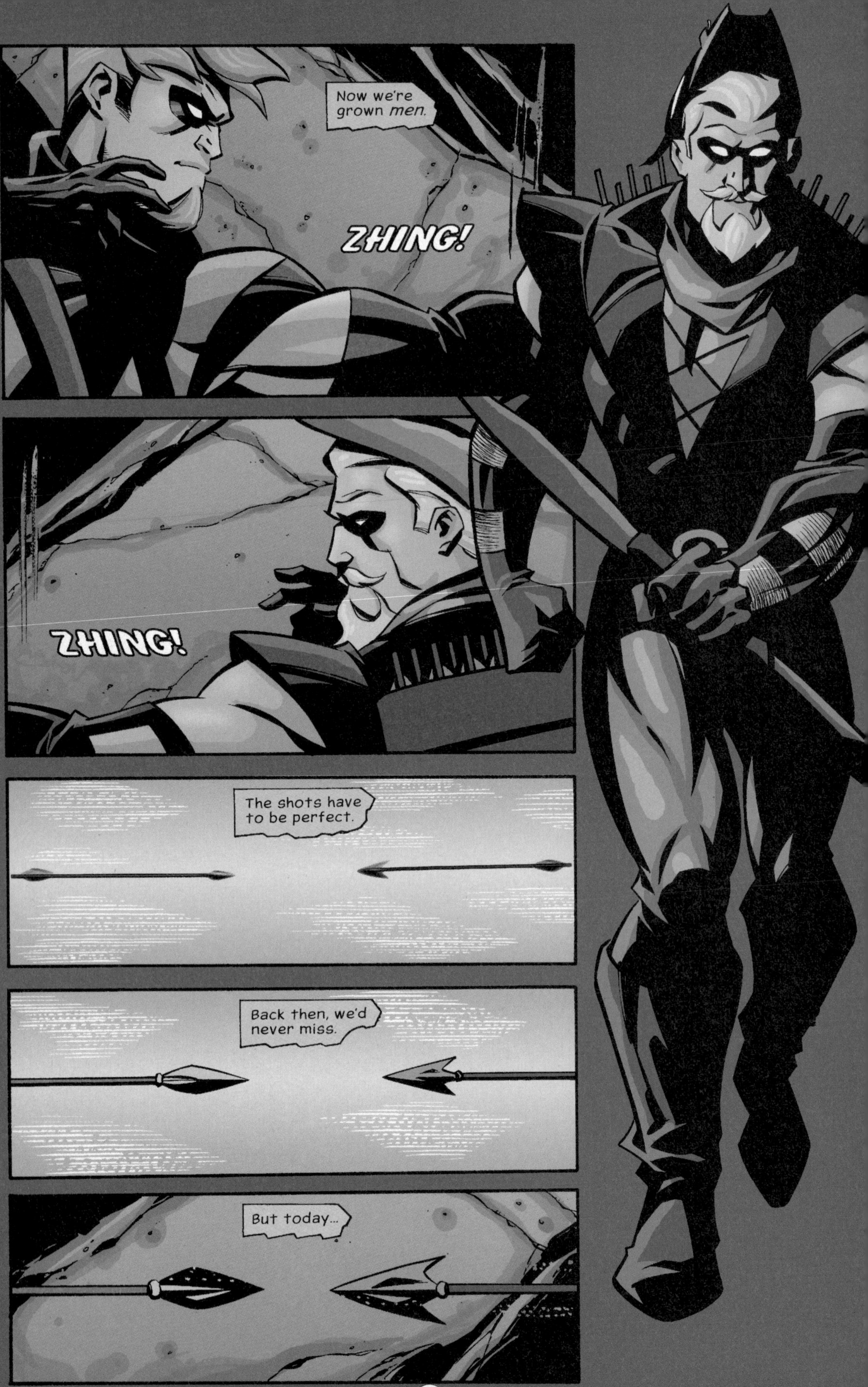

Now we're grown *men.*
ZHING!
ZHING!
The shots have to be perfect.
Back then, we'd never miss.
But today...

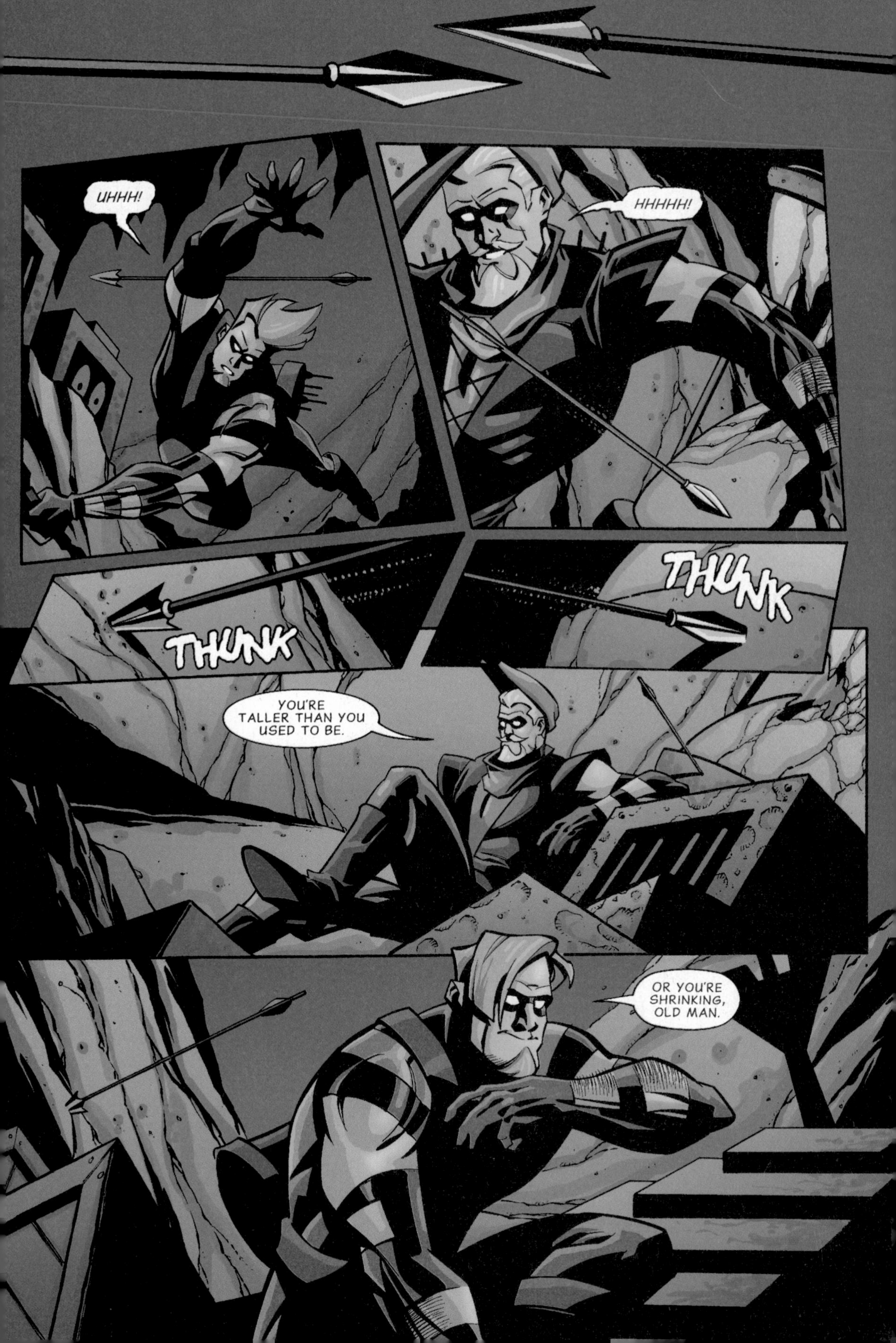
UHHH!
HHHHH!
THUNK
THUNK
YOU'RE TALLER THAN YOU USED TO BE.
OR YOU'RE SHRINKING, OLD MAN.

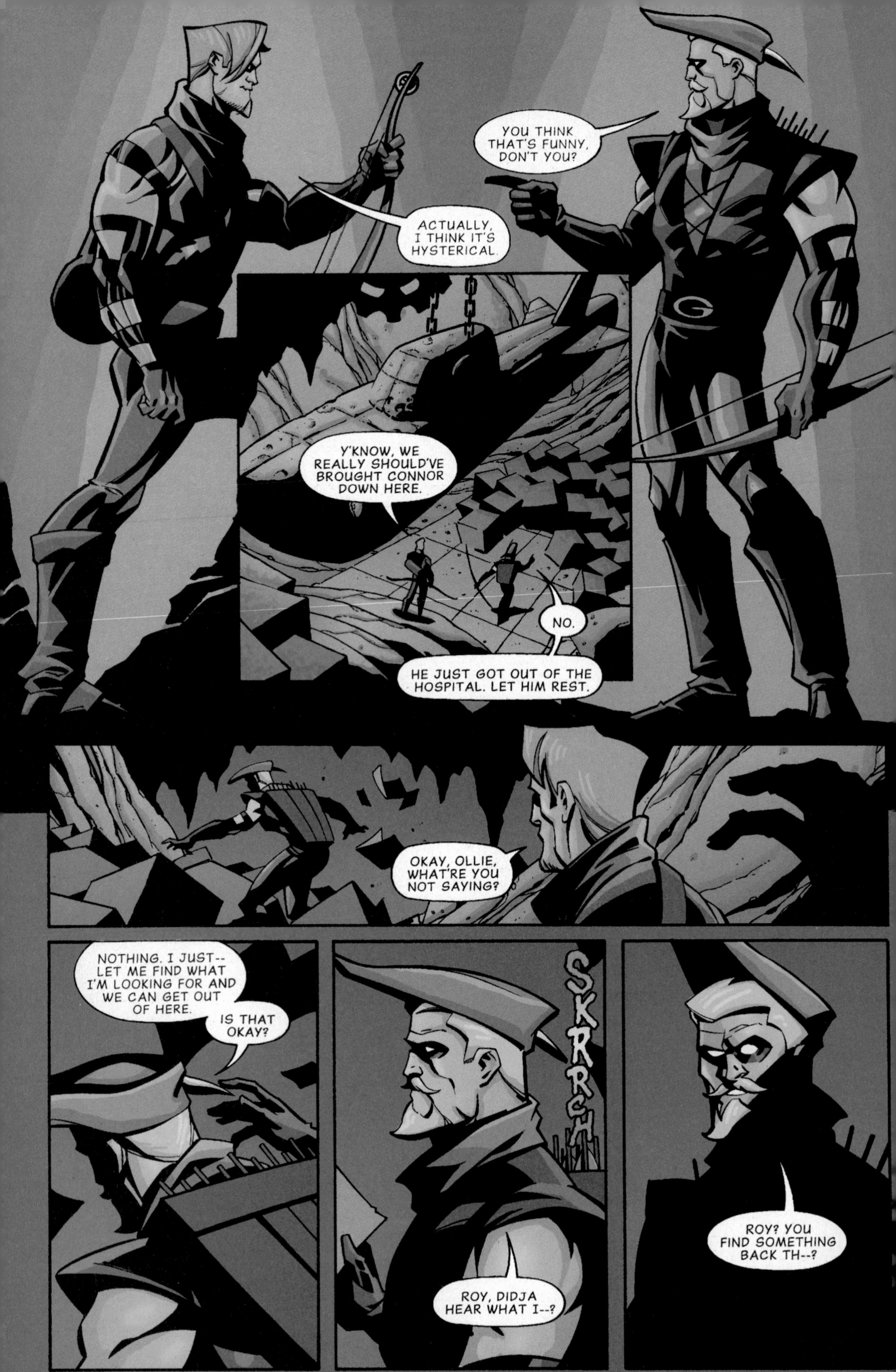
YOU THINK THAT'S FUNNY, DON'T YOU?
ACTUALLY, I THINK IT'S HYSTERICAL.
Y'KNOW, WE REALLY SHOULD'VE BROUGHT CONNOR DOWN HERE.
NO.
HE JUST GOT OUT OF THE HOSPITAL. LET HIM REST.
OKAY, OLLIE, WHAT'RE YOU NOT SAYING?
NOTHING. I JUST-- LET ME FIND WHAT I'M LOOKING FOR AND WE CAN GET OUT OF HERE.
IS THAT OKAY?
SKRRCH
ROY, DIDJA HEAR WHAT I--?
ROY? YOU FIND SOMETHING BACK TH--?

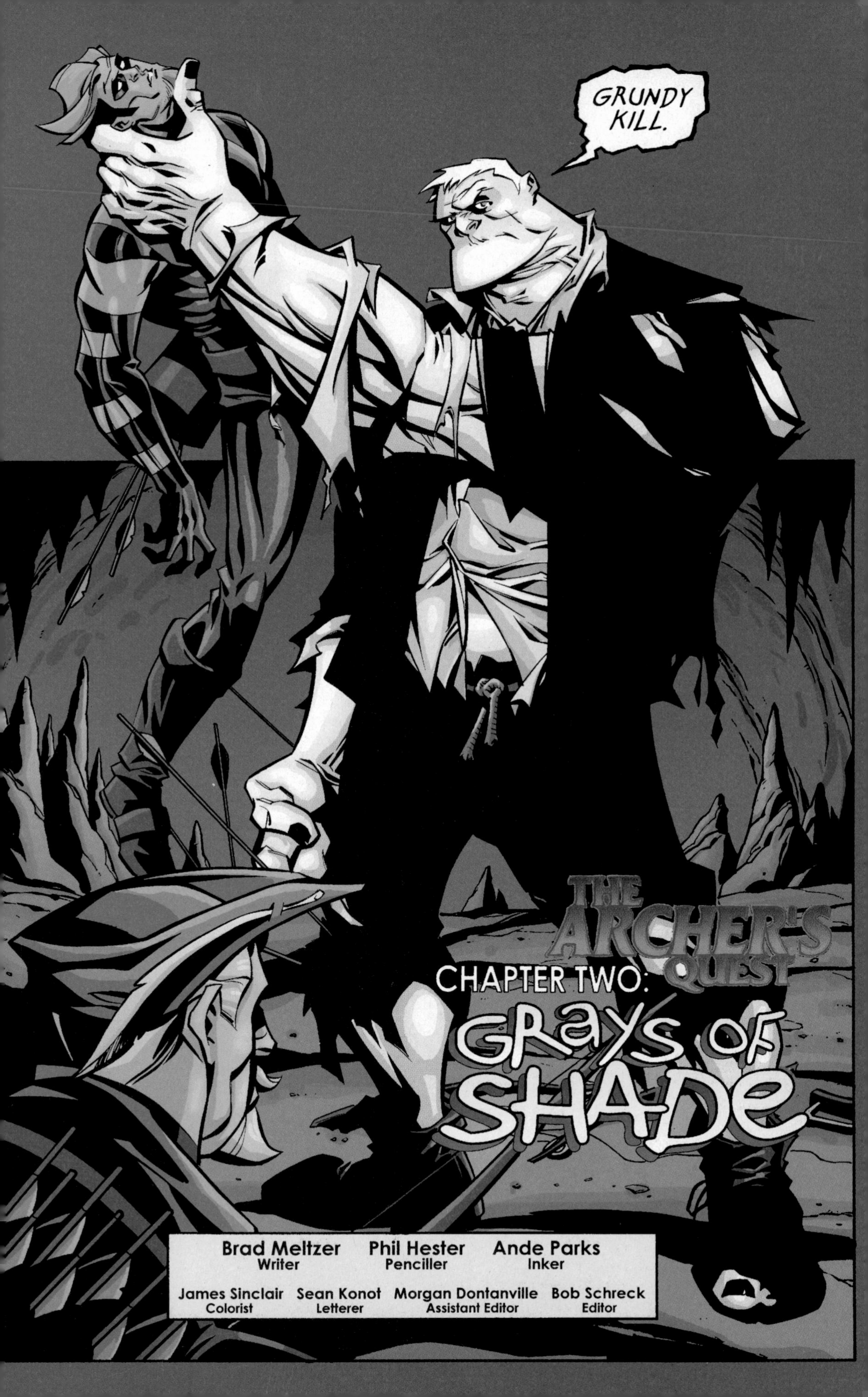
GRUNDY KILL.
THE ARCHER'S QUEST
CHAPTER TWO:
GRAYS OF SHADE
Brad Meltzer Writer
Phil Hester Penciller
Ande Parks Inker
James Sinclair Colorist
Sean Konot Letterer
Morgan Dontanville Assistant Editor
Bob Schreck Editor

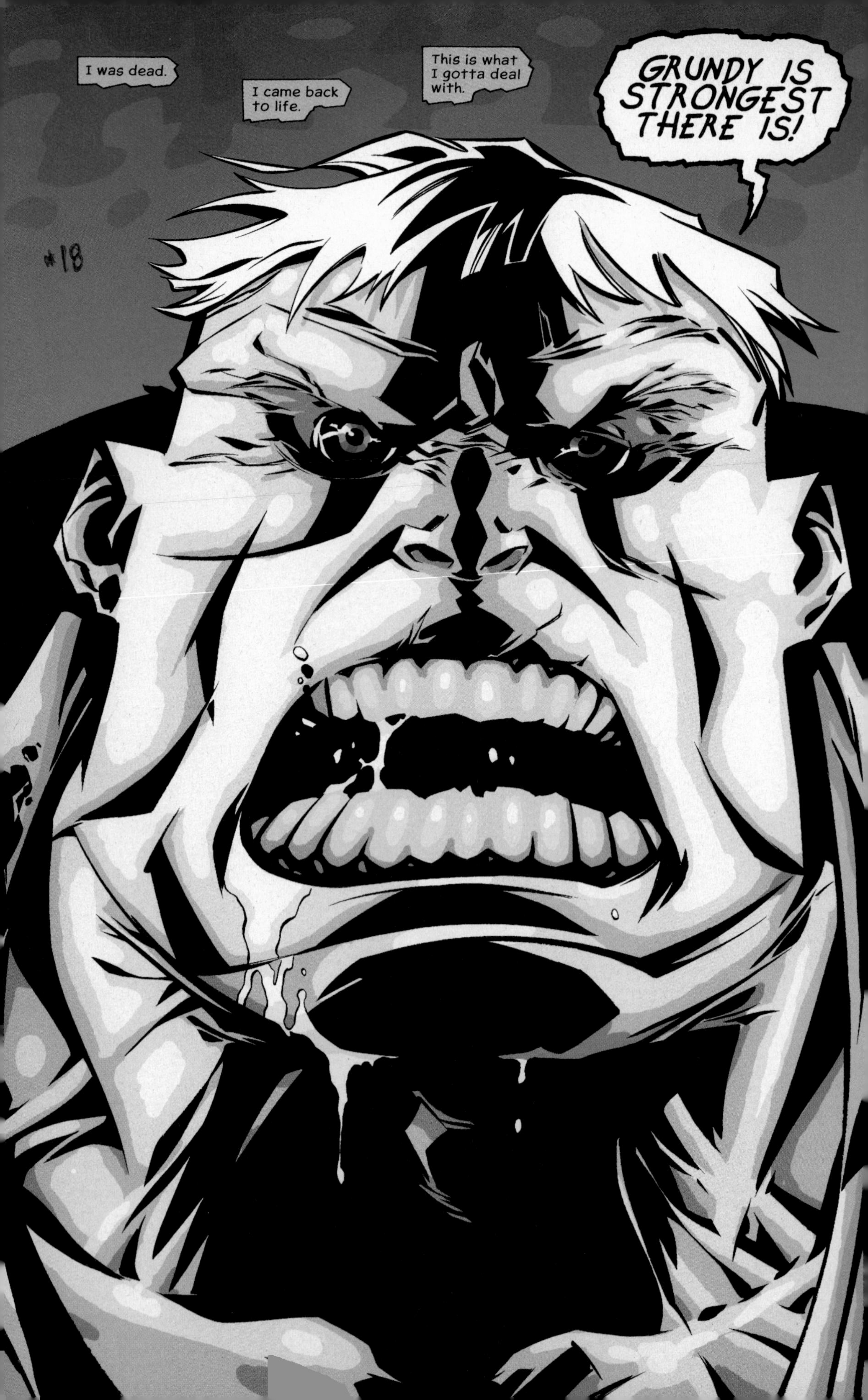
I was dead.
I came back to life.
This is what I gotta deal with.
GRUNDY IS STRONGEST THERE IS!

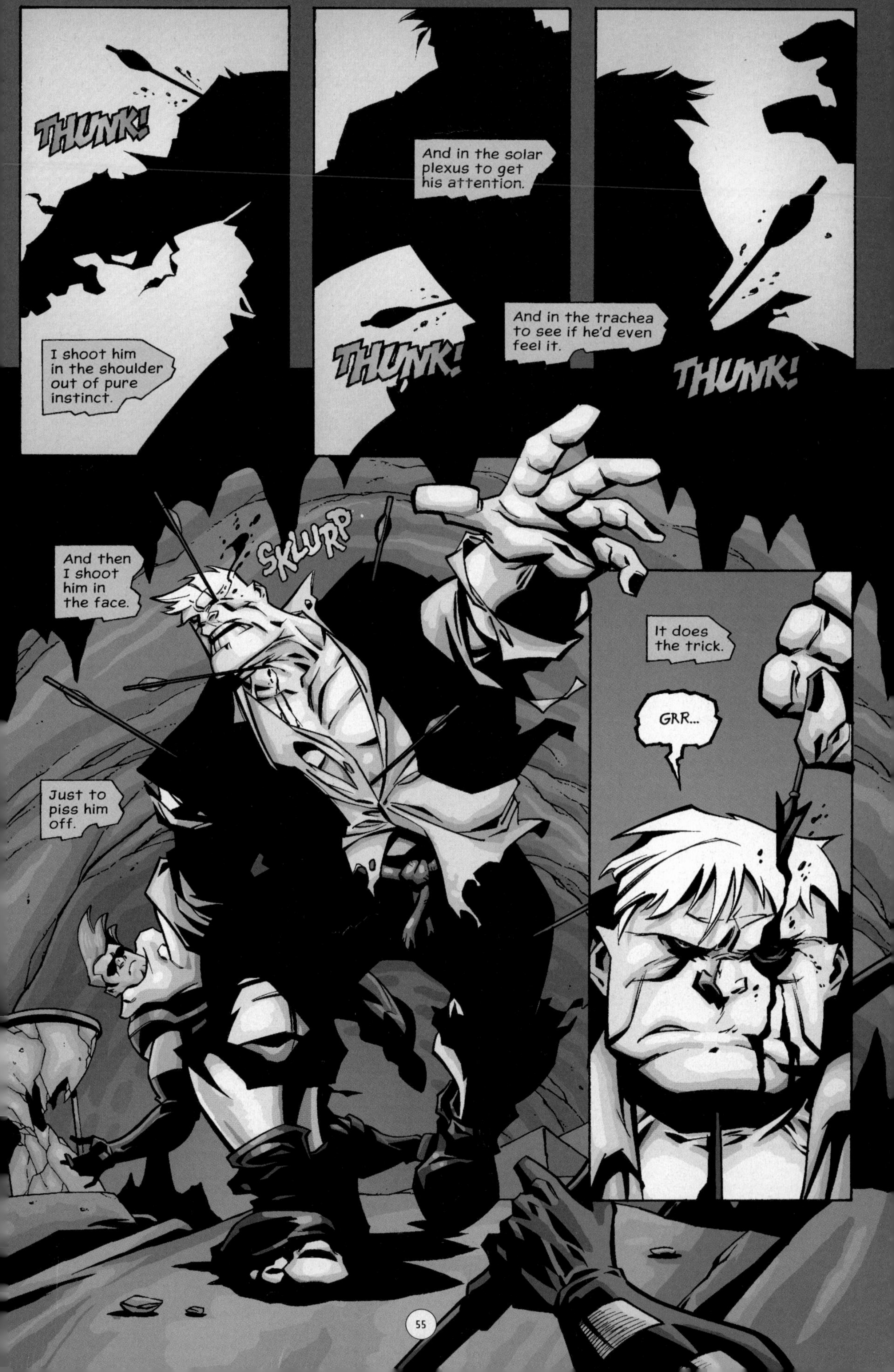
THUNK!
I shoot him in the shoulder out of pure instinct.
And in the solar plexus to get his attention.
THUNK!
And in the trachea to see if he'd even feel it.
THUNK!
And then I shoot him in the face.
SKLURP
Just to piss him off.
It does the trick.
GRR...

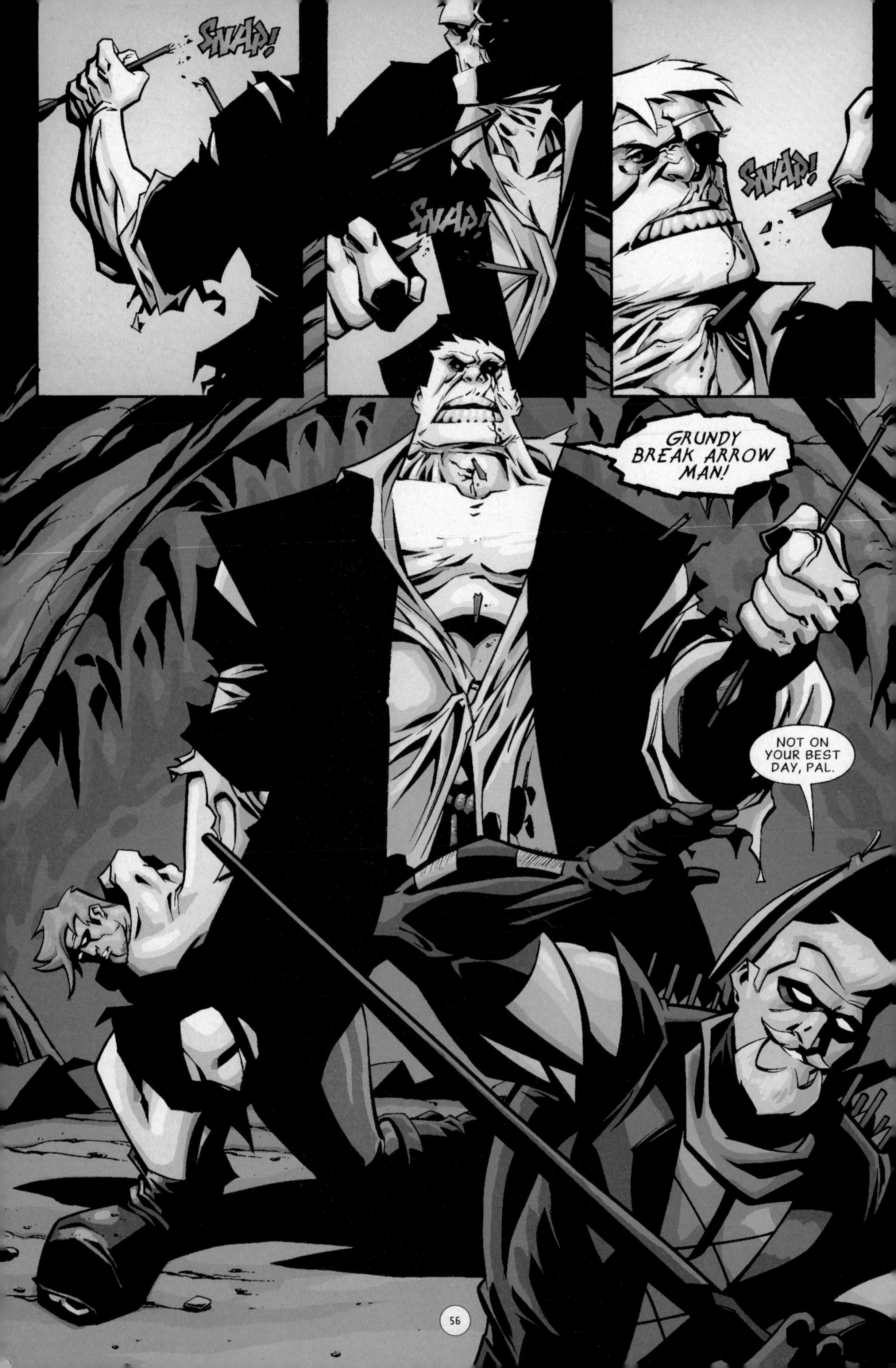
SNAP!
SNAP!
SNAP!
GRUNDY BREAK ARROW MAN!
NOT ON YOUR BEST DAY, PAL.

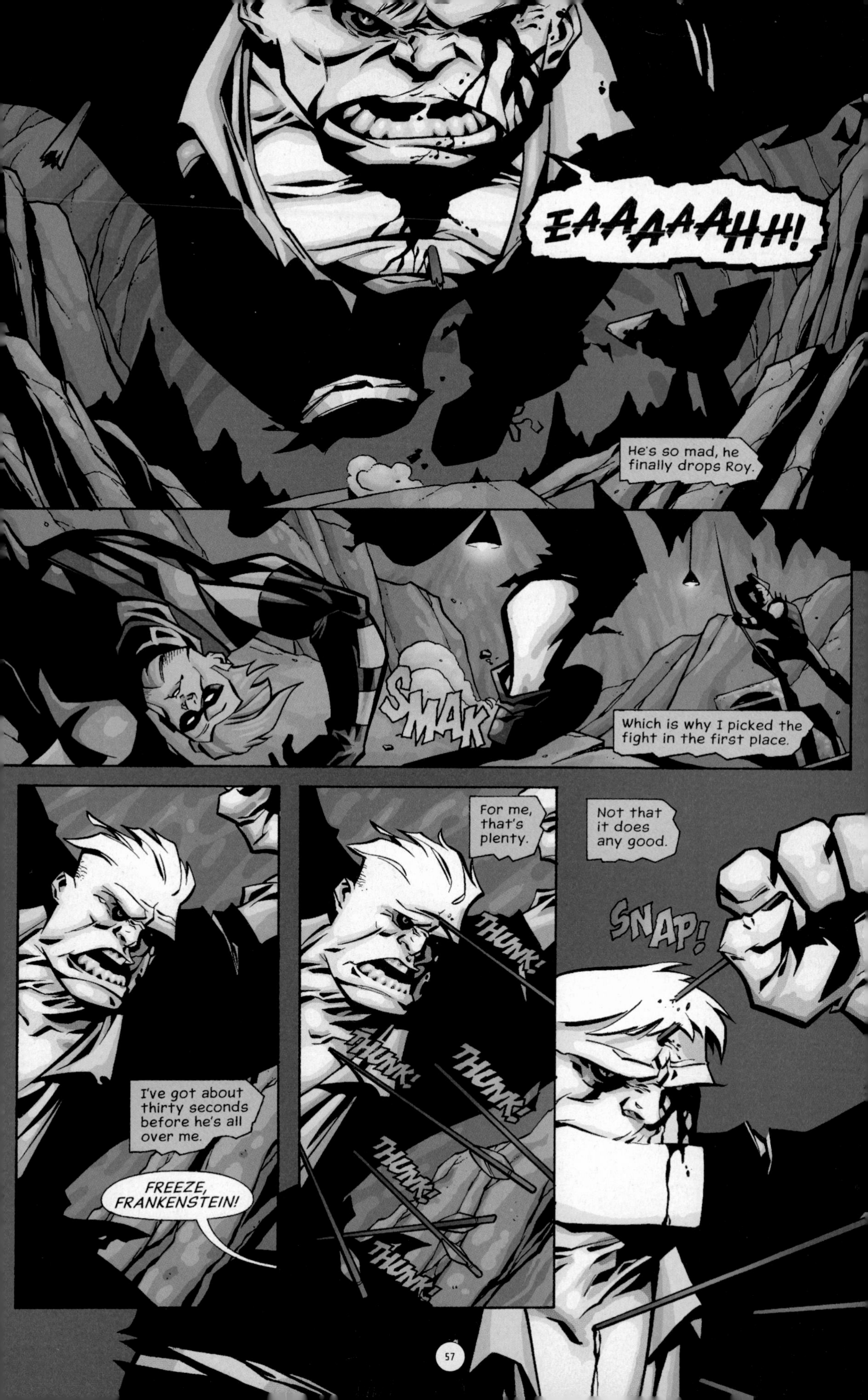

EAAAAAHH!
He's so mad, he finally drops Roy.
SMAK!
Which is why I picked the fight in the first place.
I've got about thirty seconds before he's all over me.
FREEZE, FRANKENSTEIN!
For me, that's plenty.
THUNK!
THUNK!
THUNK!
THUNK!
THUNK!
Not that it does any good.
SNAP!

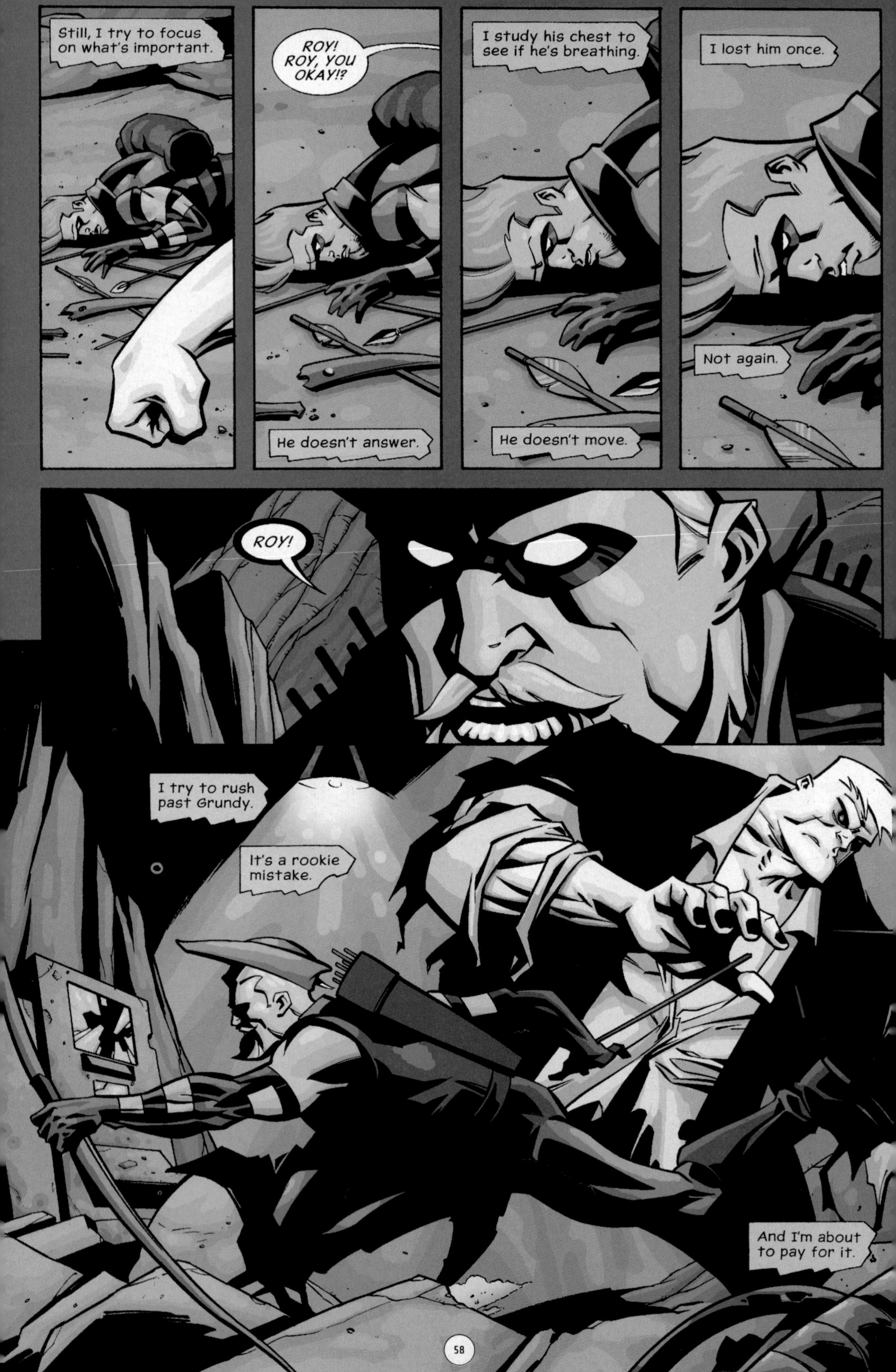
Still, I try to focus on what's important.
ROY! ROY, YOU OKAY!?
He doesn't answer.
I study his chest to see if he's breathing.
He doesn't move.
I lost him once.
Not again.
ROY!
I try to rush past Grundy.
It's a rookie mistake.
And I'm about to pay for it.

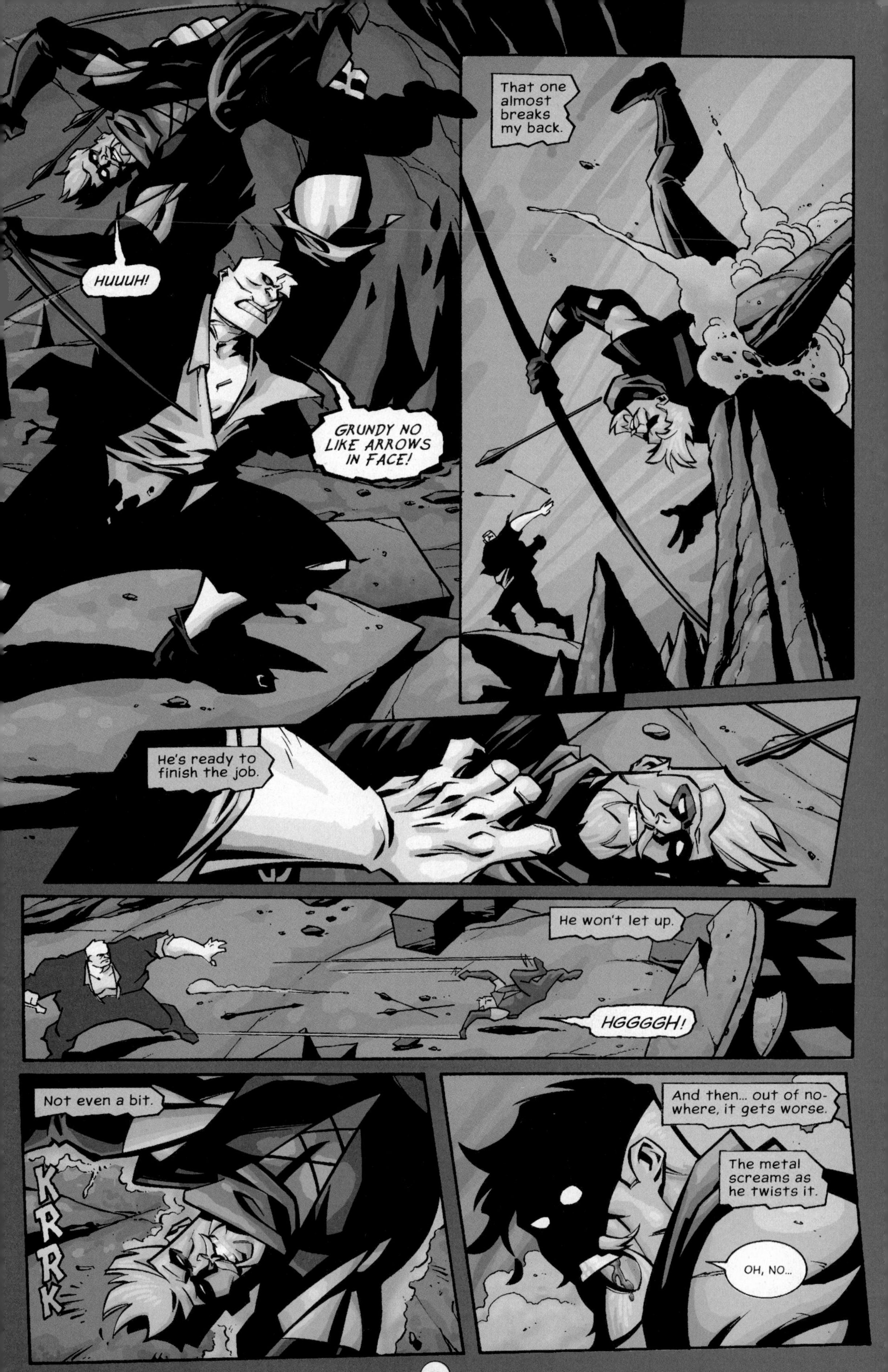
HUUUH!
GRUNDY NO LIKE ARROWS IN FACE!
That one almost breaks my back.
He's ready to finish the job.
He won't let up.
HGGGGH!
Not even a bit.
KRRK
And then... out of no-where, it gets worse.
The metal screams as he twists it.
OH, NO...

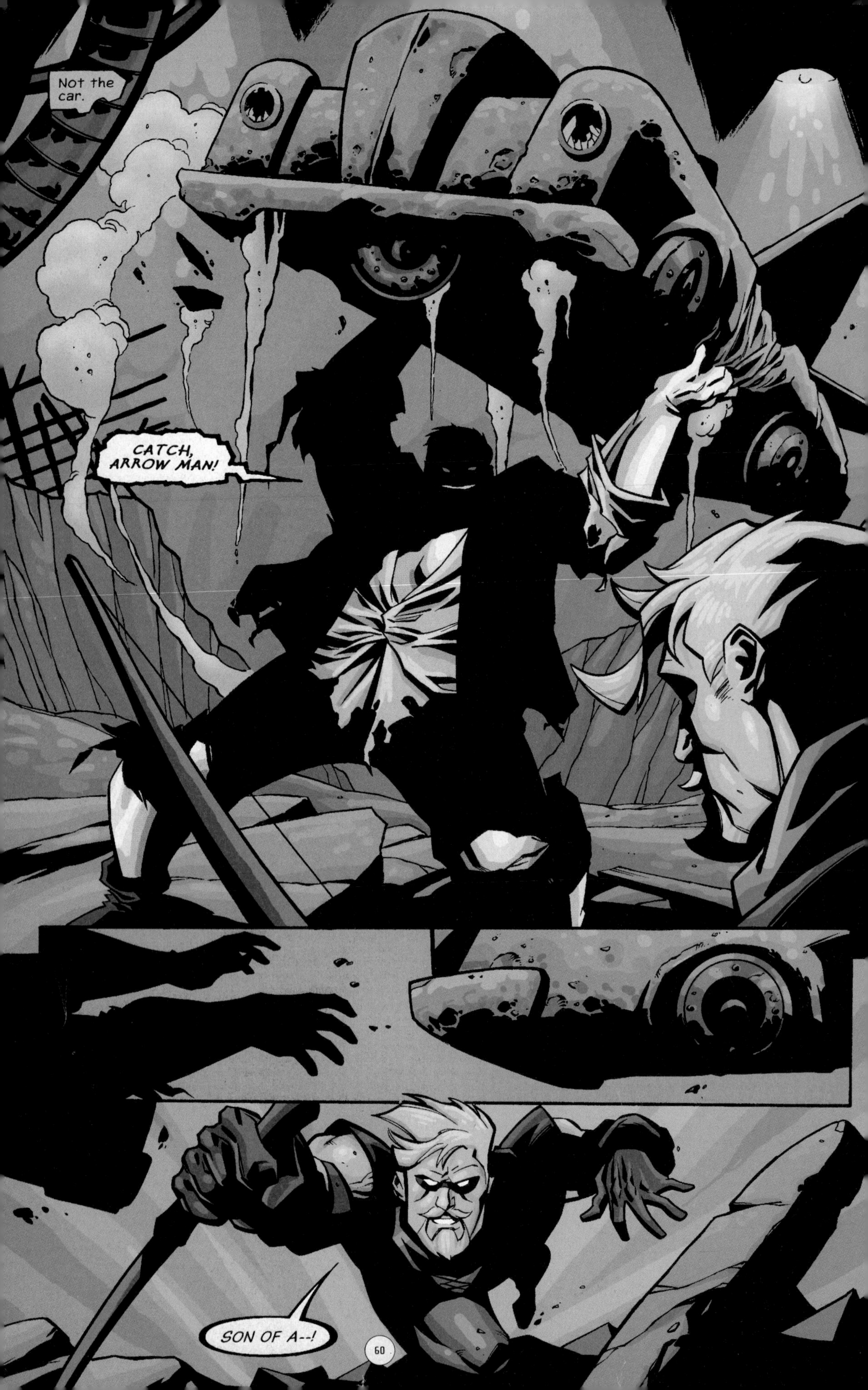
Not the car.
CATCH, ARROW MAN!
SON OF A--!

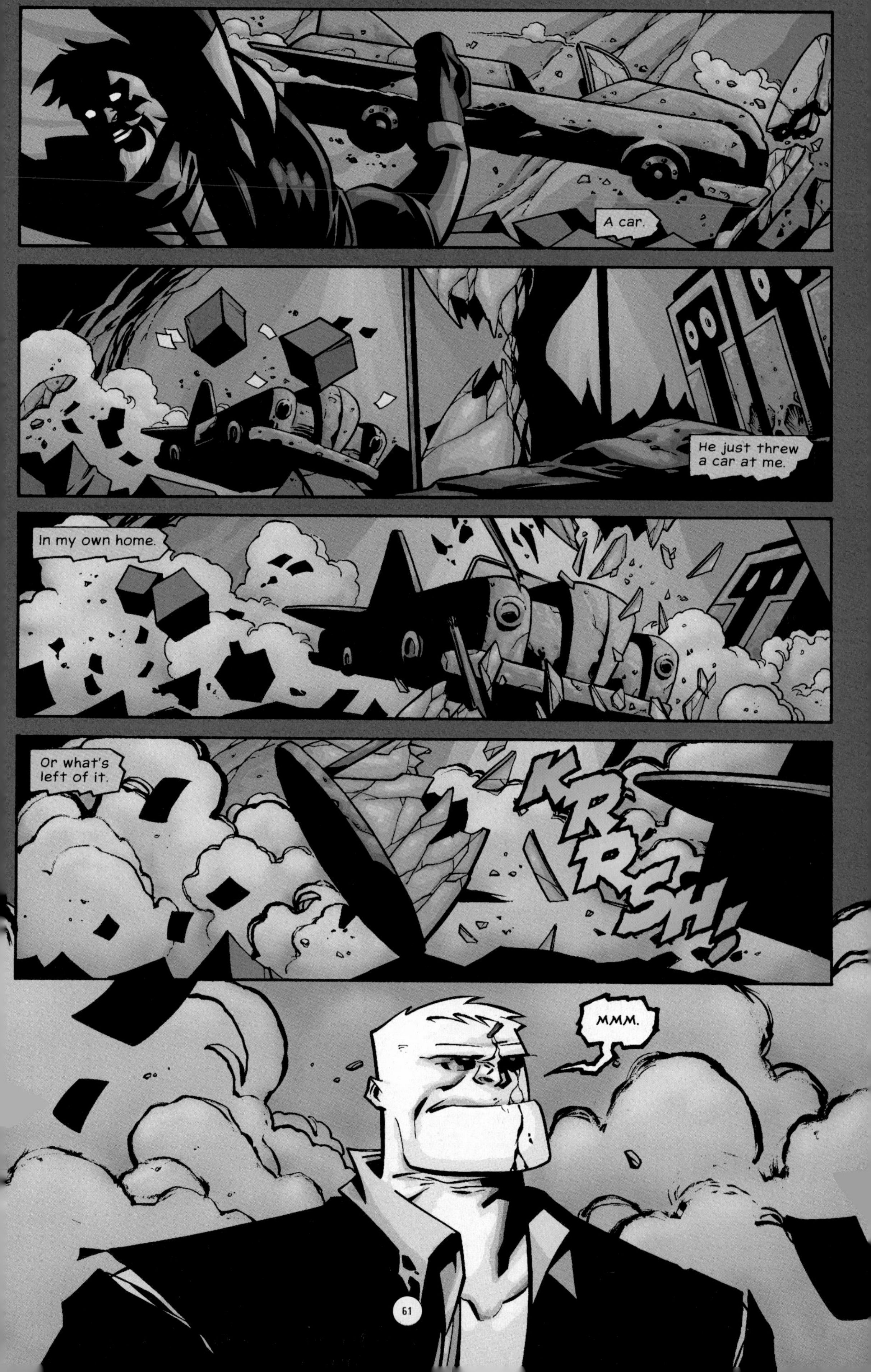
A car.
He just threw a car at me.
In my own home.
Or what's left of it.
KRRSH!
MMM.

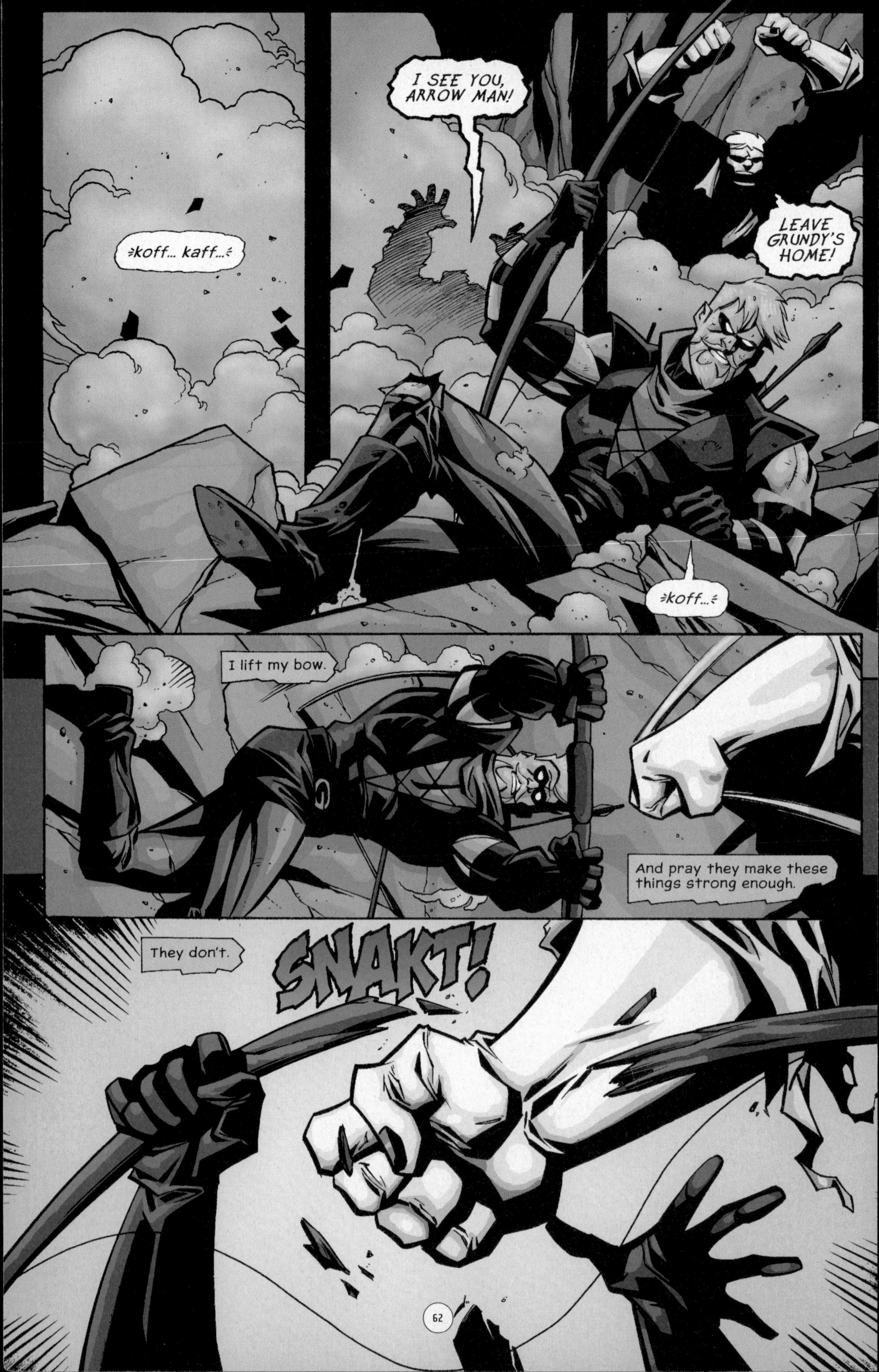

≈koff... kaff...≈
I SEE YOU, ARROW MAN!
LEAVE GRUNDY'S HOME!
≈koff...≈
I lift my bow.
And pray they make these things strong enough.
They don't.
SNAKT!

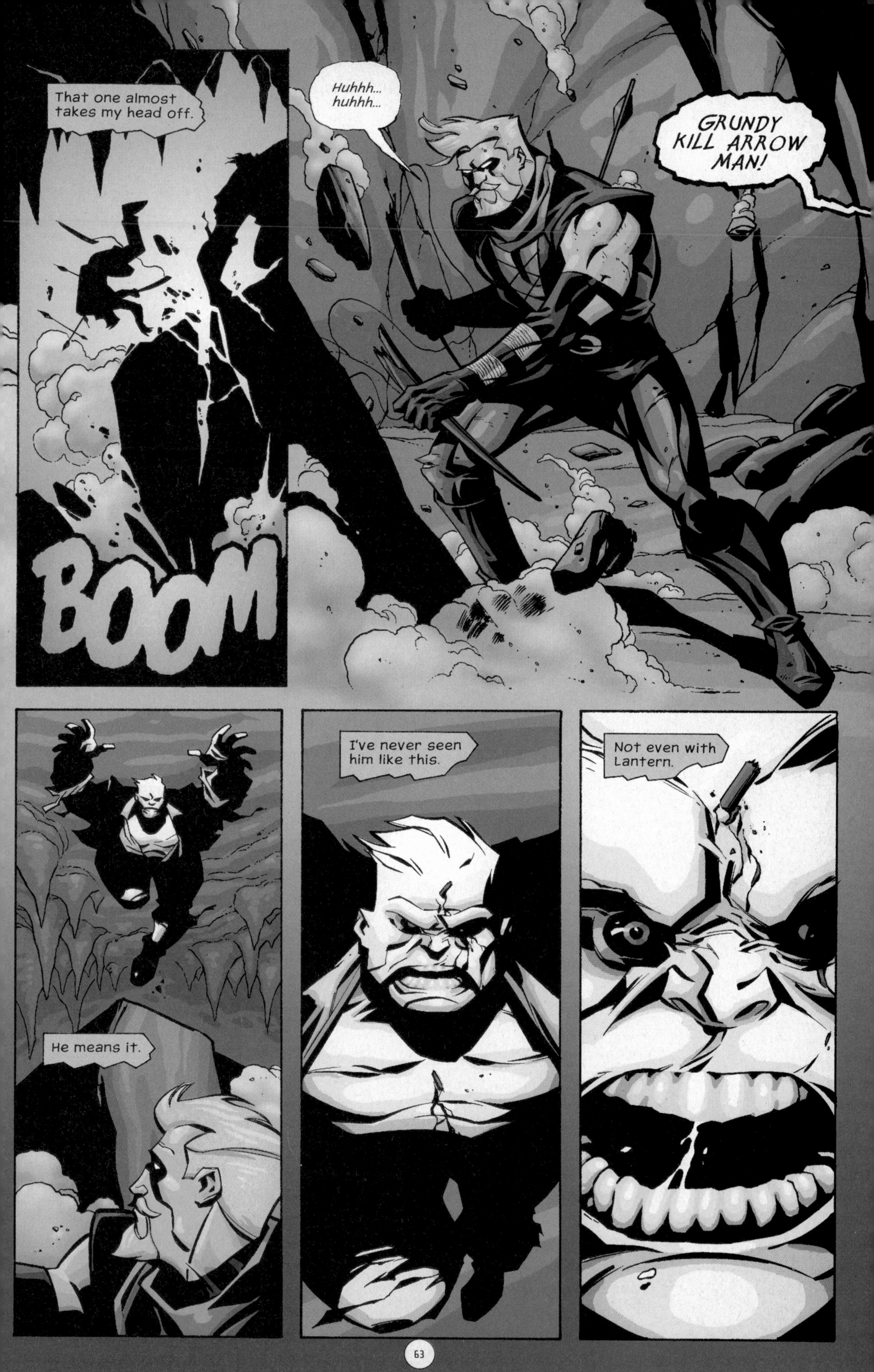
That one almost takes my head off.
Huhhh... huhhh...
GRUNDY KILL ARROW MAN!
BOOM
He means it.
I've never seen him like this.
Not even with Lantern.

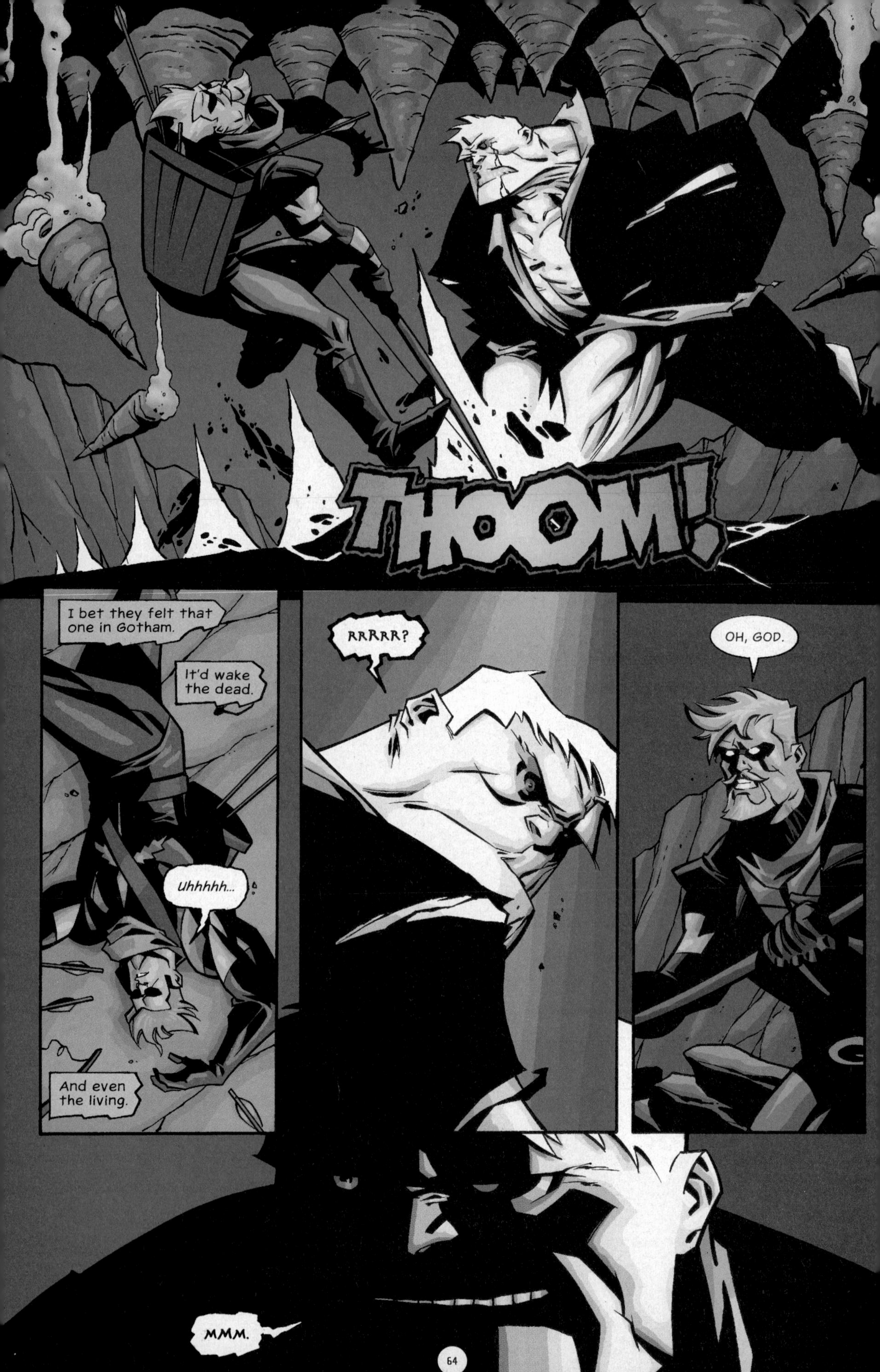
THOOM!
I bet they felt that one in Gotham.
It'd wake the dead.
Uhhhhh...
And even the living.
RRRRR?
OH, GOD.
MMM.

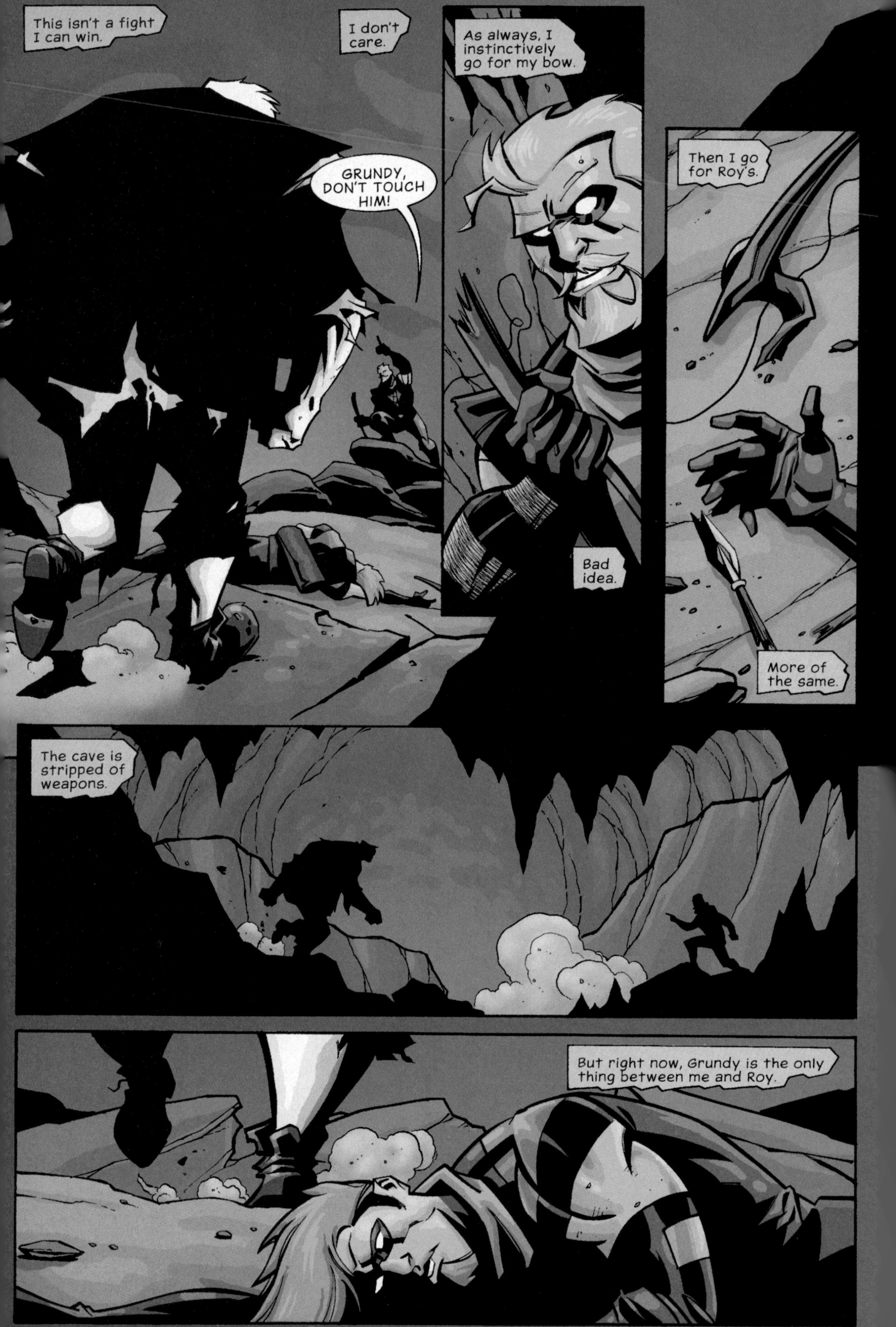

This isn't a fight I can win.
I don't care.
GRUNDY, DON'T TOUCH HIM!
As always, I instinctively go for my bow.
Bad idea.
Then I go for Roy's.
More of the same.
The cave is stripped of weapons.
But right now, Grundy is the only thing between me and Roy.

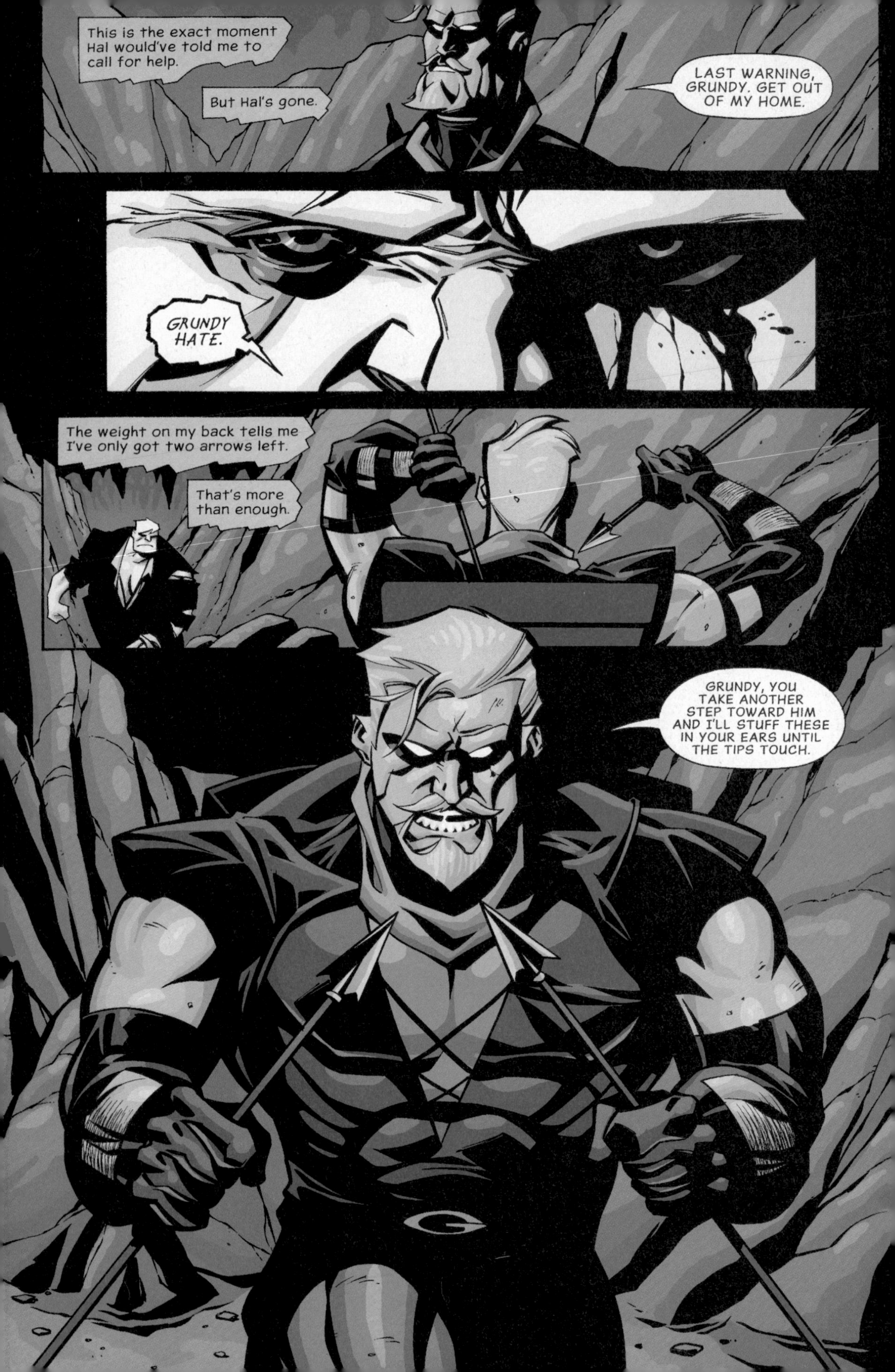
This is the exact moment Hal would've told me to call for help.
But Hal's gone.
LAST WARNING, GRUNDY. GET OUT OF MY HOME.
GRUNDY HATE.
The weight on my back tells me I've only got two arrows left.
That's more than enough.
GRUNDY, YOU TAKE ANOTHER STEP TOWARD HIM AND I'LL STUFF THESE IN YOUR EARS UNTIL THE TIPS TOUCH.

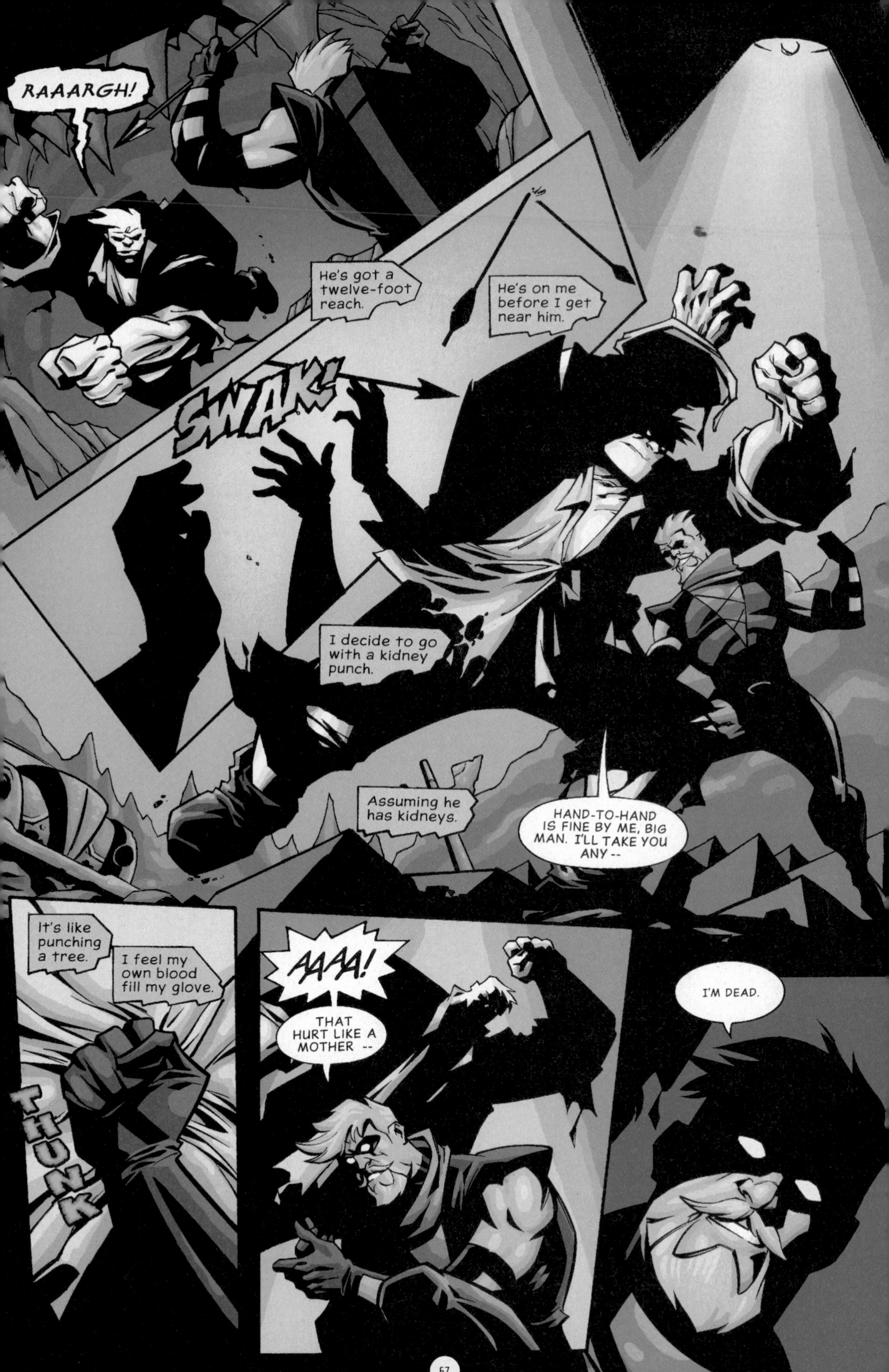
RAAARGH!
He's got a twelve-foot reach.
He's on me before I get near him.
SWAK!
I decide to go with a kidney punch.
Assuming he has kidneys.
HAND-TO-HAND IS FINE BY ME, BIG MAN. I'LL TAKE YOU ANY --
It's like punching a tree.
I feel my own blood fill my glove.
THUNK
AAAA!
THAT HURT LIKE A MOTHER --
I'M DEAD.

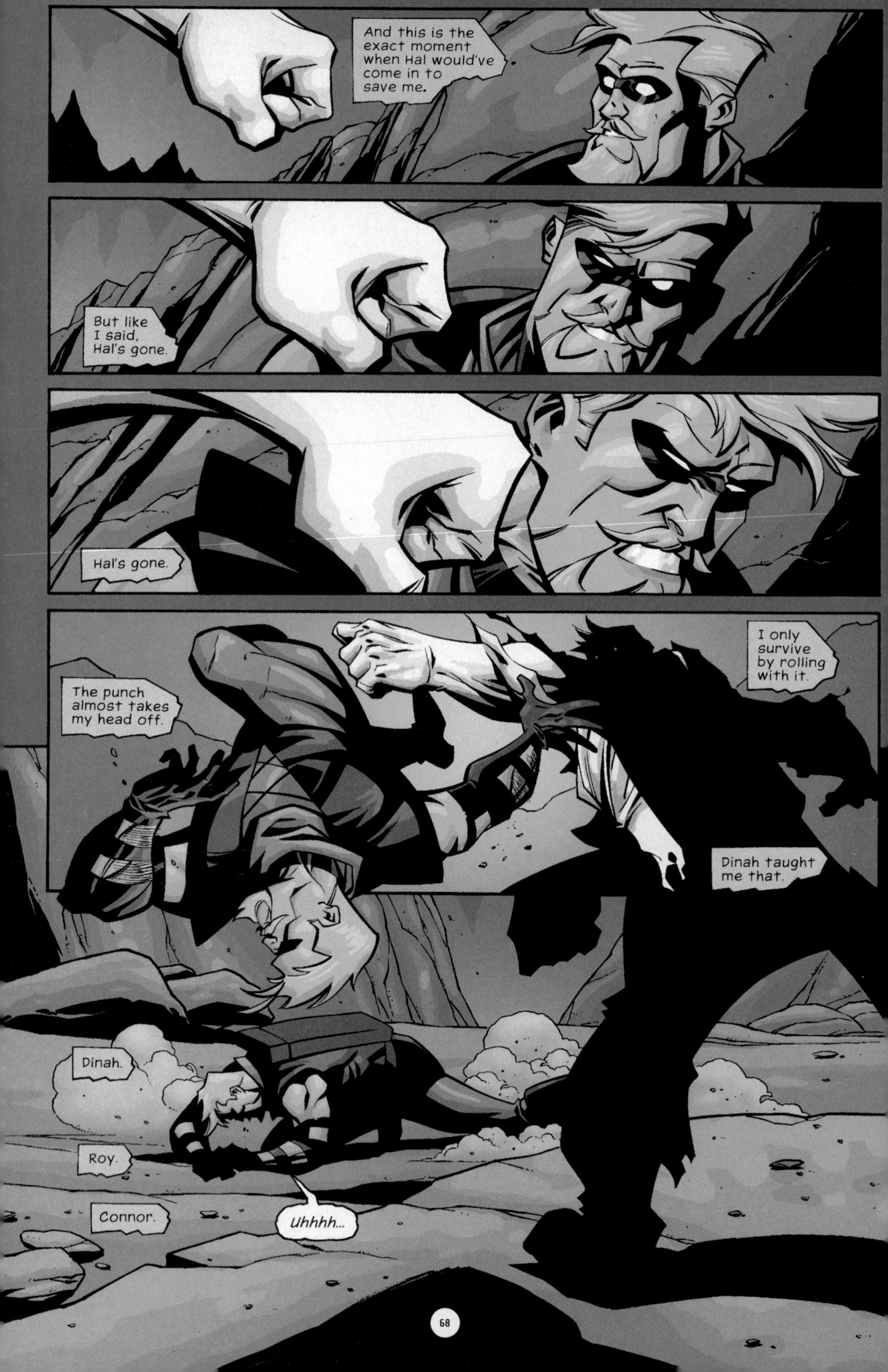
And this is the exact moment when Hal would've come in to save me.
But like I said, Hal's gone.
Hal's gone.
The punch almost takes my head off.
I only survive by rolling with it.
Dinah taught me that.
Dinah.
Roy.
Connor.
Uhhhh...

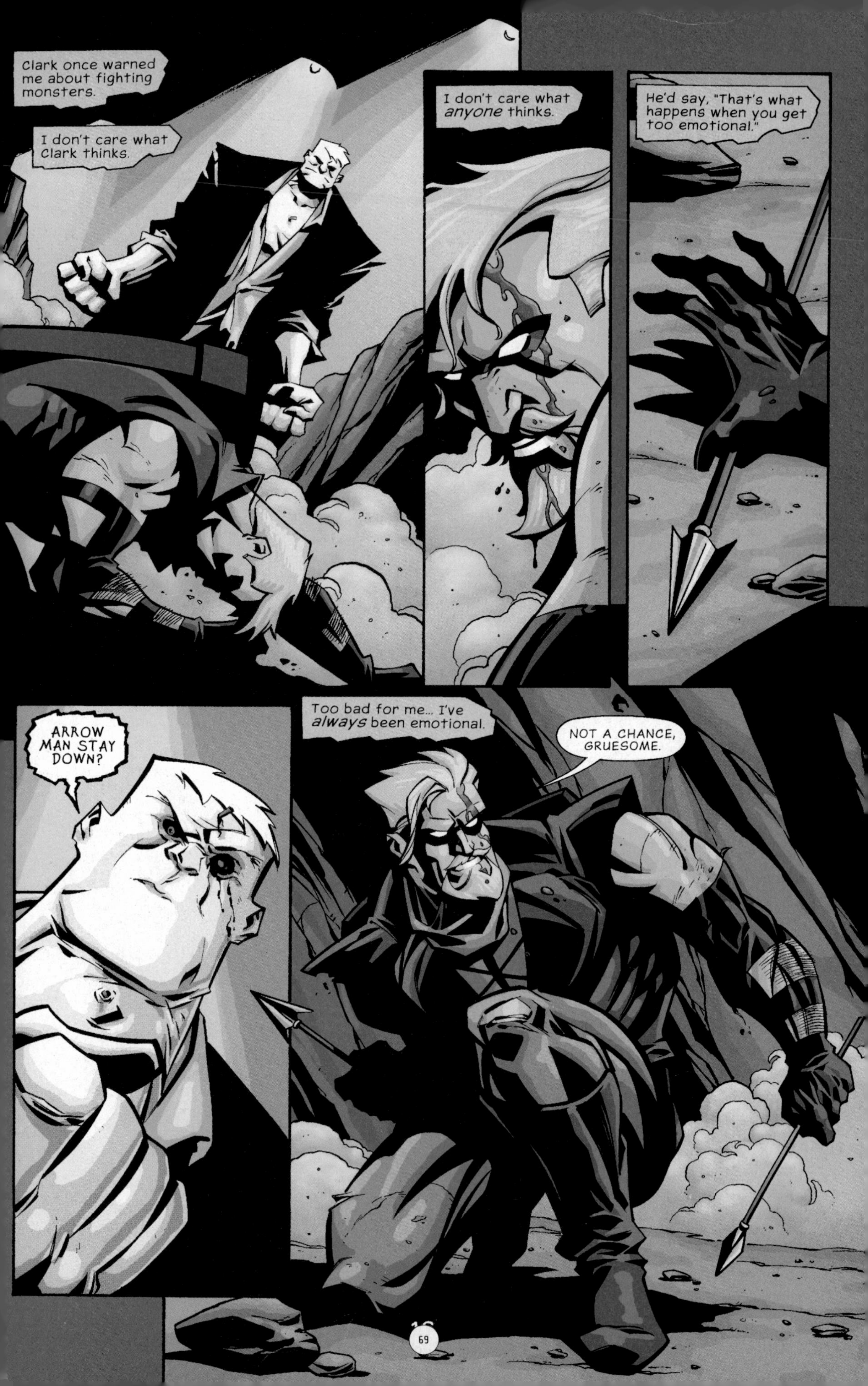
Clark once warned me about fighting monsters.
I don't care what Clark thinks.
I don't care what *anyone* thinks.
He'd say, "That's what happens when you get too emotional."
ARROW MAN STAY DOWN?
Too bad for me... I've *always* been emotional.
NOT A CHANCE, GRUESOME.

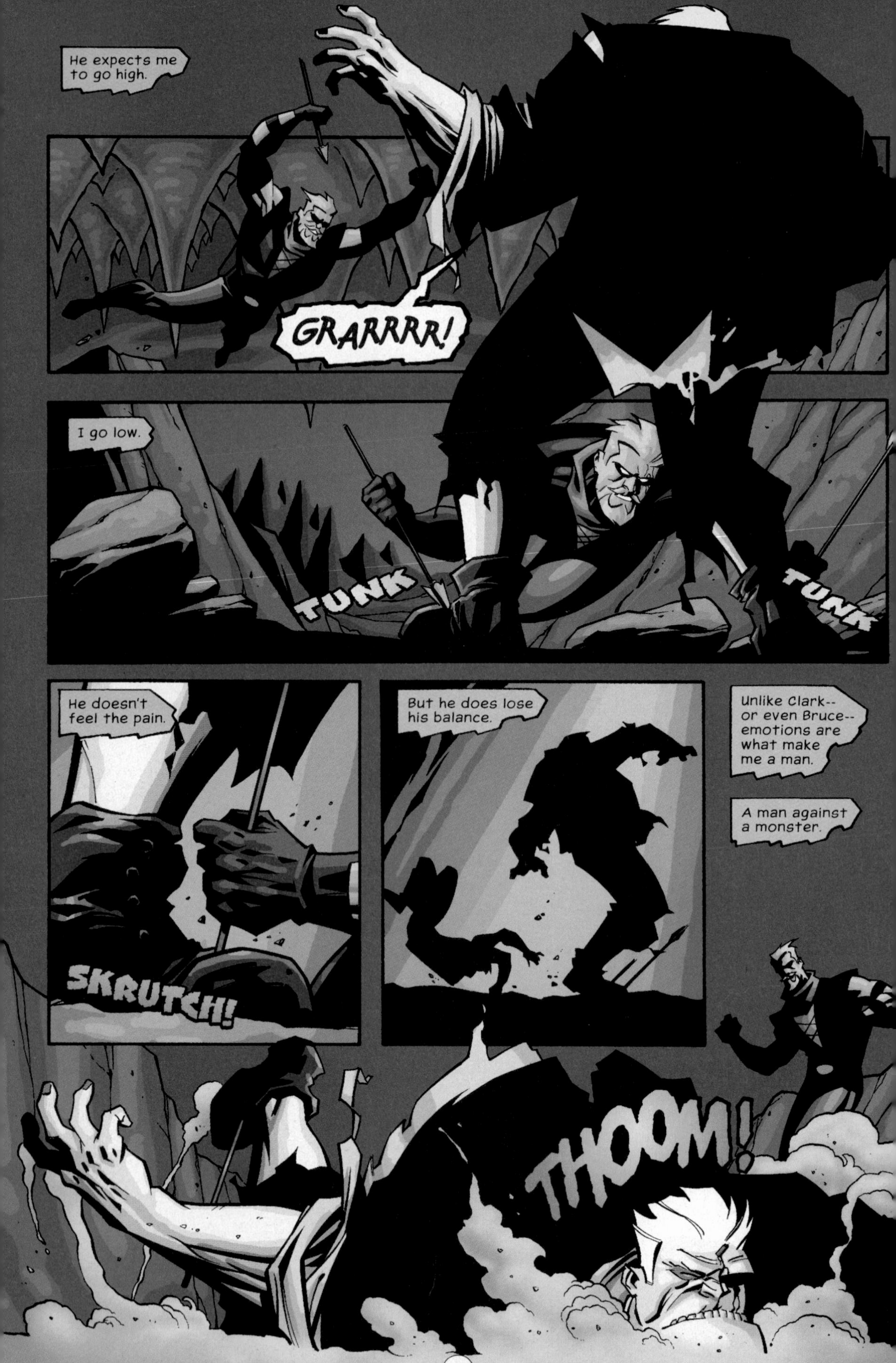

He expects me to go high.
GRARRRR!
I go low.
TUNK
TUNK
He doesn't feel the pain.
SKRUTCH!
But he does lose his balance.
Unlike Clark-- or even Bruce-- emotions are what make me a man.
A man against a monster.
THOOM!

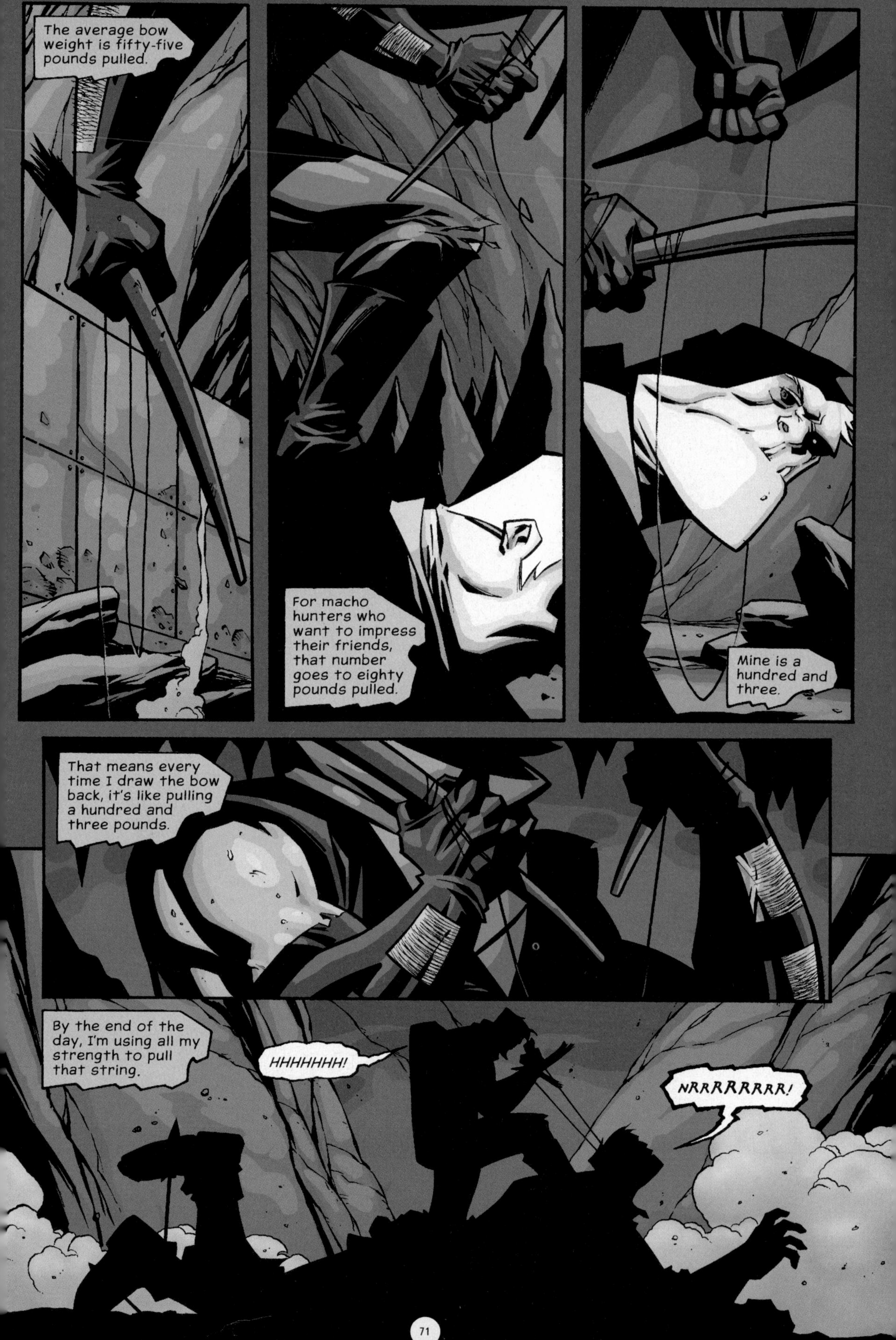

The average bow weight is fifty-five pounds pulled.
For macho hunters who want to impress their friends, that number goes to eighty pounds pulled.
Mine is a hundred and three.
That means every time I draw the bow back, it's like pulling a hundred and three pounds.
By the end of the day, I'm using all my strength to pull that string.
HHHHHHH!
NRRRRRRRR!

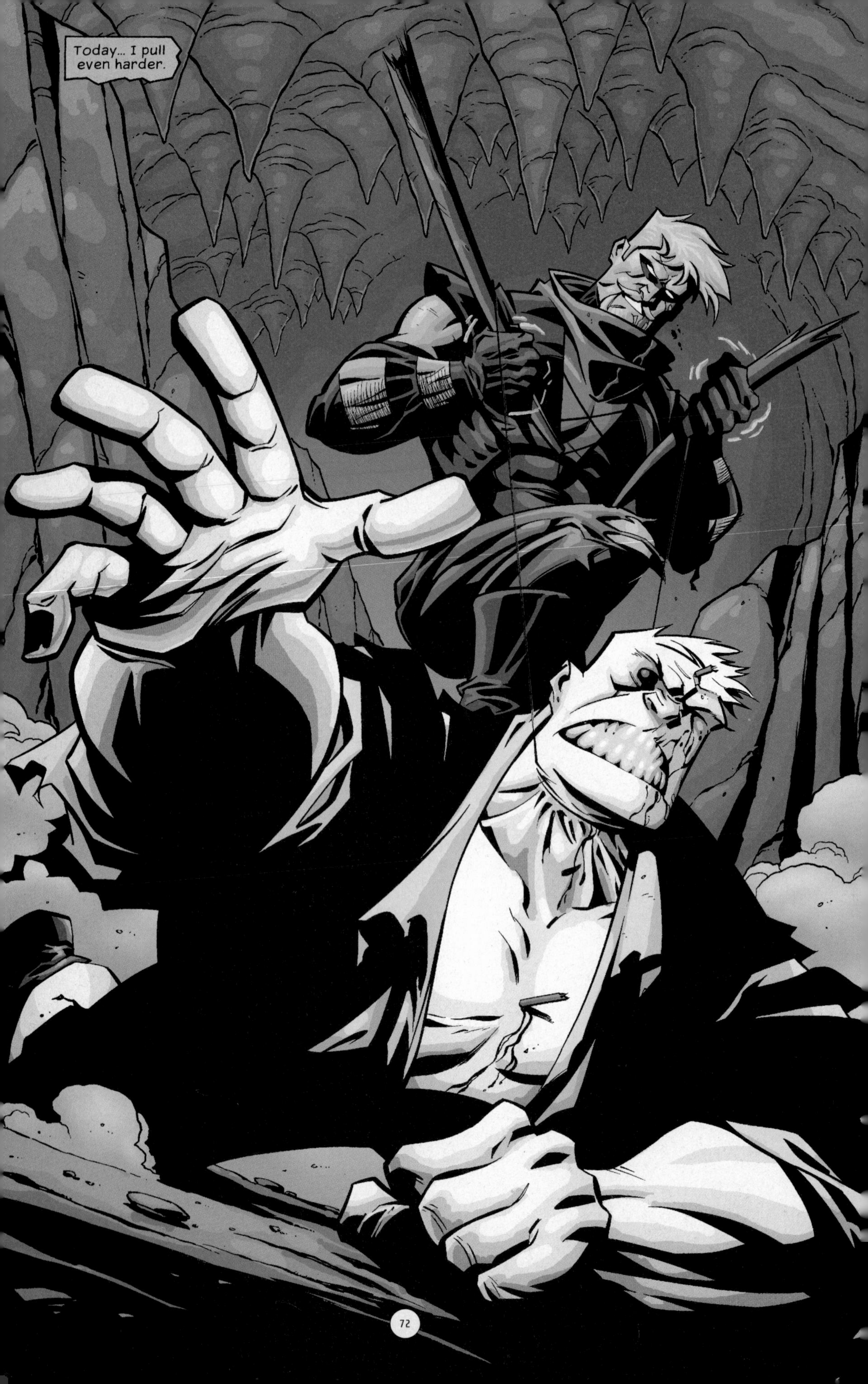
Today... I pull even harder.

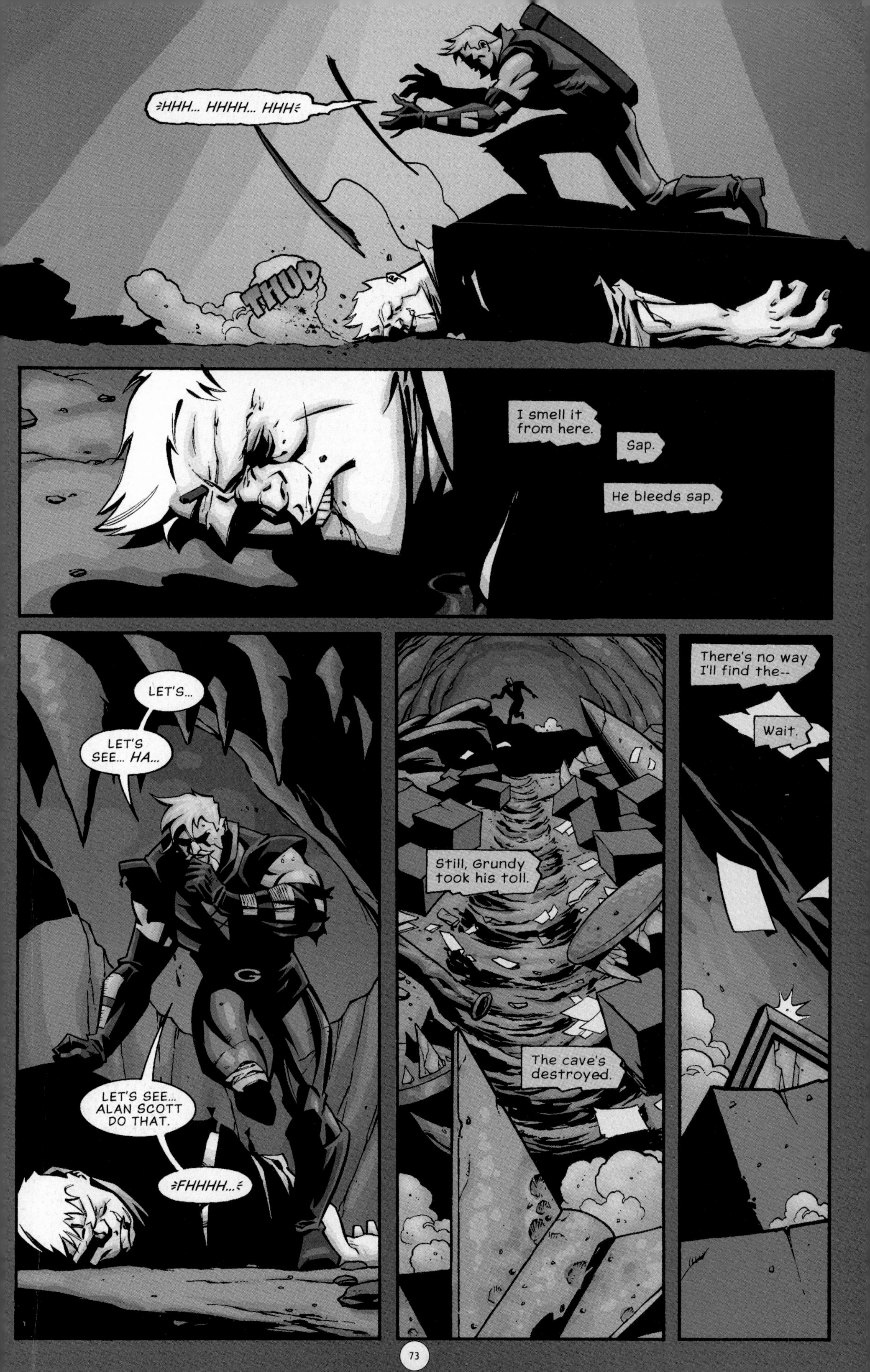
≈HHH... HHHH... HHH≈
THUD
I smell it from here.
Sap.
He bleeds sap.
LET'S...
LET'S SEE... HA...
LET'S SEE... ALAN SCOTT DO THAT.
≈FHHHH...≈
Still, Grundy took his toll.
The cave's destroyed.
There's no way I'll find the--
Wait.

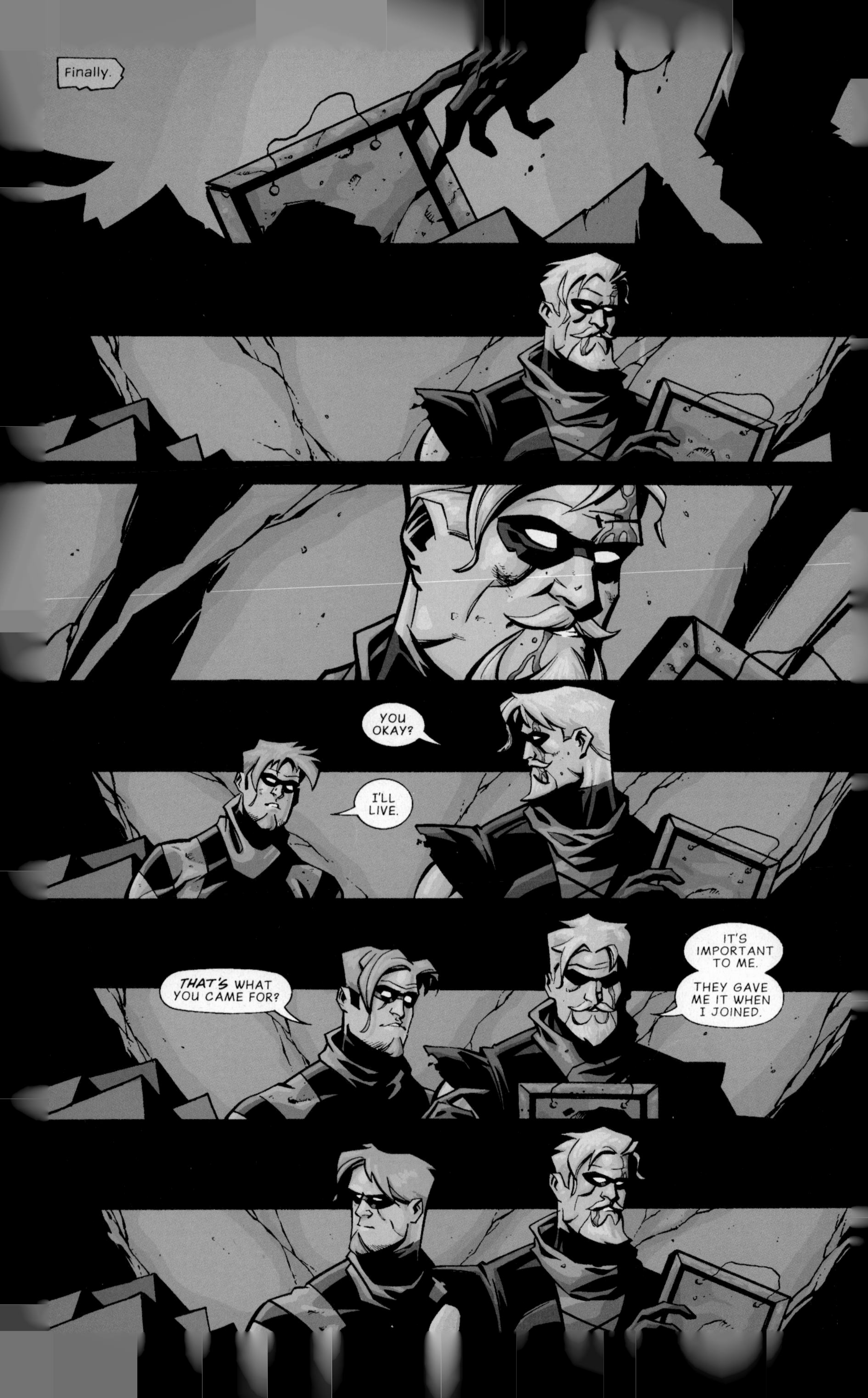
Finally.
YOU OKAY?
I'LL LIVE.
THAT'S WHAT YOU CAME FOR?
IT'S IMPORTANT TO ME.
THEY GAVE ME IT WHEN I JOINED.

YOU REALLY BEAT SOLOMON GRUNDY?

YEP.

hereby elects

GREEN ARR

TO MEMBERSHIP FOR LIFE-- WITH ALL PRIVILEGES AN GRATUITIES INCLUDING THE WEARING OF THE SIGNAL GOLDEN KEY WHICH PERMITS ENTRY INTO THE SEC SOUVENIER ROOMS. IT IS HEREBY FURT

of AMERI

hereby elects

GREEN ARR

TO MEMBERSHIP FOR LIFE-- WITH ALL PRIVILEGES A GRATUITIES INCLUDING THE WEARING OF THE SIGNA GOLDEN KEY WHICH PERMITS ENTRY INTO THE SEC SOUVENIER ROOMS. IT IS HEREBY CUR

"NICE GOING."

"THANKS."

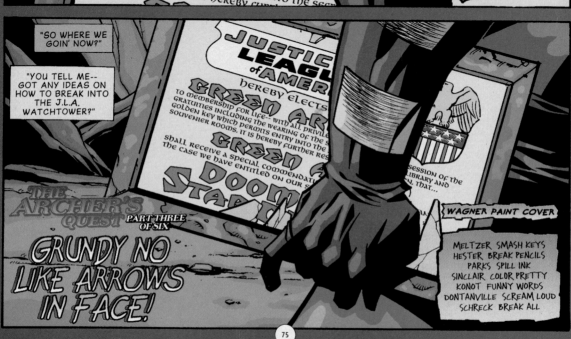

"SO WHERE WE GOIN' NOW?"

"YOU TELL ME-- GOT ANY IDEAS ON HOW TO BREAK INTO THE J.L.A. WATCHTOWER?"

JUSTIC LEAGUE of AMER

hereby elects

GREEN ARR

GREEN

DOOM STAR!

shall receive a special commendat the case we have entitled on our s

ssession of the library and n, that...

THE ARCHER'S QUEST PART THREE OF SIX

GRUNDY NO LIKE ARROWS IN FACE!

WAGNER PAINT COVER

MELTZER SMASH KEYS
HESTER BREAK PENCILS
PARKS SPILL INK
SINCLAIR COLOR PRETTY
KONOT FUNNY WORDS
DONTANVILLE SCREAM LOUD
SCHRECK BREAK ALL

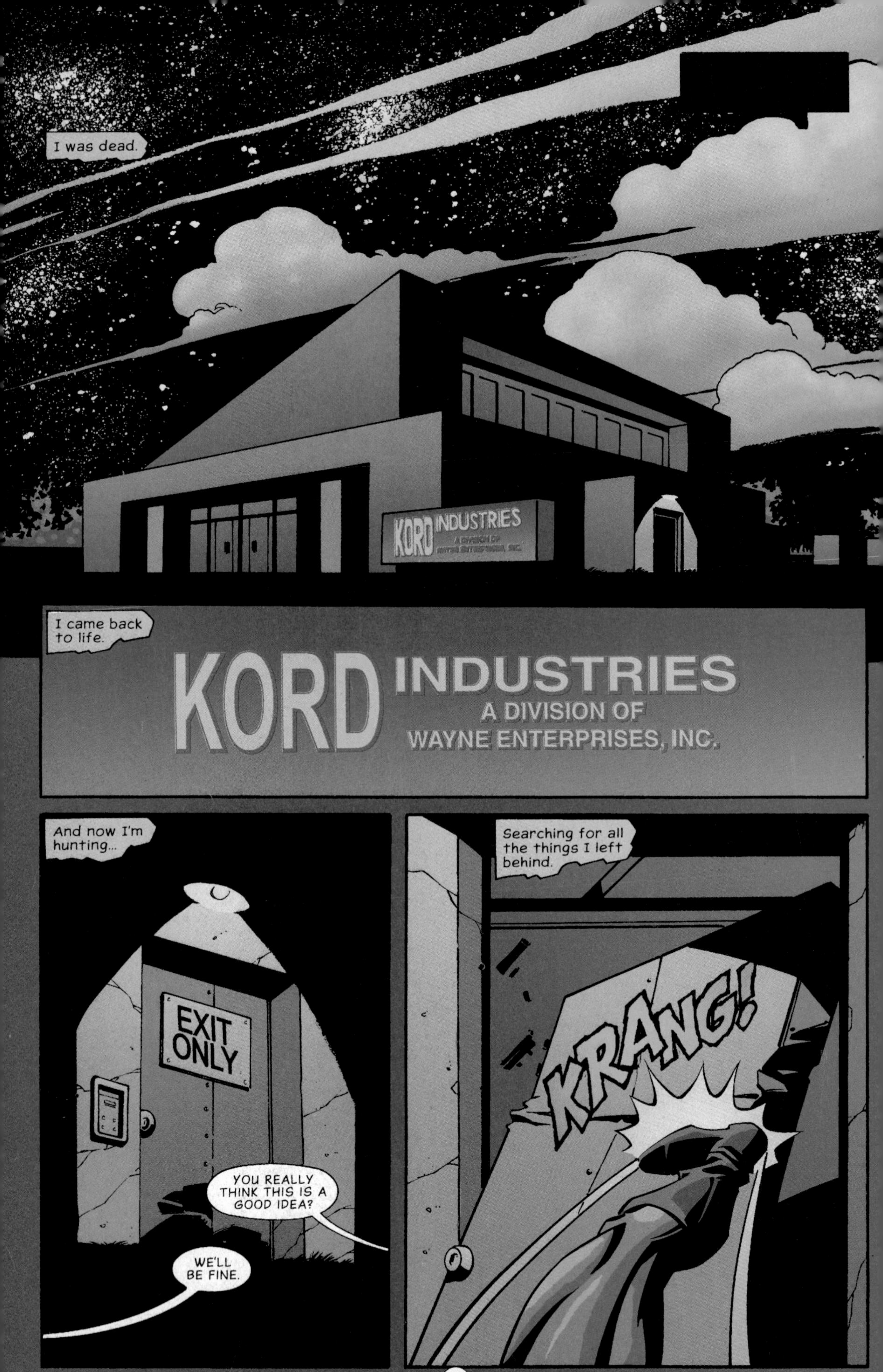
I was dead.
KORD INDUSTRIES
A DIVISION OF WAYNE ENTERPRISES, INC.
I came back to life.
KORD INDUSTRIES
A DIVISION OF
WAYNE ENTERPRISES, INC.
And now I'm hunting...
EXIT ONLY
YOU REALLY THINK THIS IS A GOOD IDEA?
WE'LL BE FINE.
Searching for all the things I left behind.
KRANG!

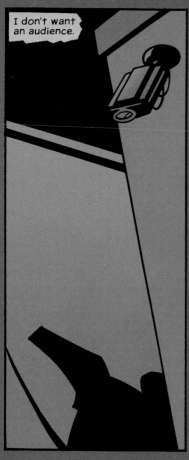

I don't want an audience.

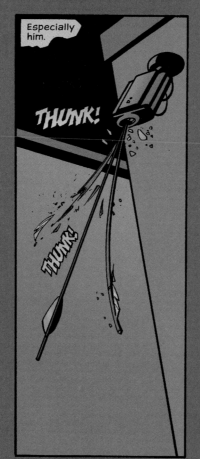

Especially him.

THUNK!

THUNK!

Most of my belongings were gathered by The Shade and destroyed.

He did it as a favor to me.

PING!

But there were a few items he missed.

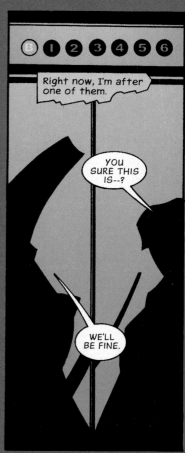

Right now, I'm after one of them.

YOU SURE THIS IS--?

WE'LL BE FINE.

And that's what brings me here.

BUT IF THEY--

ROY, THEY KNEW WE WERE HERE THE MOMENT I KICKED IN THE DOOR.

YOU THINK?

I *KNOW.* IF THEY DON'T, THEY SHOULDN'T BE IN THIS BUSINESS.

HAZARDOUS MATERIALS

KEEP OUT

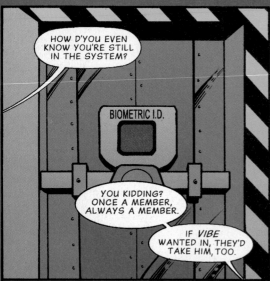

HOW D'YOU EVEN KNOW YOU'RE STILL IN THE SYSTEM?

BIOMETRIC I.D.

YOU KIDDING? ONCE A MEMBER, ALWAYS A MEMBER.

IF *VIBE* WANTED IN, THEY'D TAKE HIM, TOO.

IDENTITY: OLIVER QUEEN
STATUS: DECEASED
ACCESS: APPROVED

VIBE'S DEAD.

APPARENTLY, THAT WOULDN'T STOP HIM. BRUCE IS GETTING LAZY IN HIS OLD AGE.

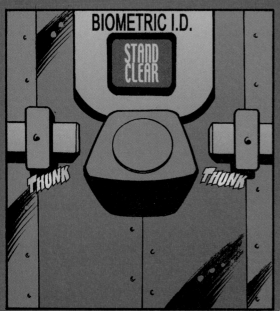

BIOMETRIC I.D.
STAND CLEAR

THUNK   *THUNK*

YOU PROMISE WE WON'T--

ROY, LISTEN TO ME-- WE USED THE SAME ONE ON THE SATELLITE...

78

YOU ARE IN STAR CITY TRANSPORTER 1527
IF YOU WANNA GO UP, YOU GOTTA START SOMEWHERE.
YOU SURE YOU DON'T WANT ME TO COME?
I WAS UP THERE LAST MONTH, ROY. I KNOW THESE PEOPLE.
FZZZZZ

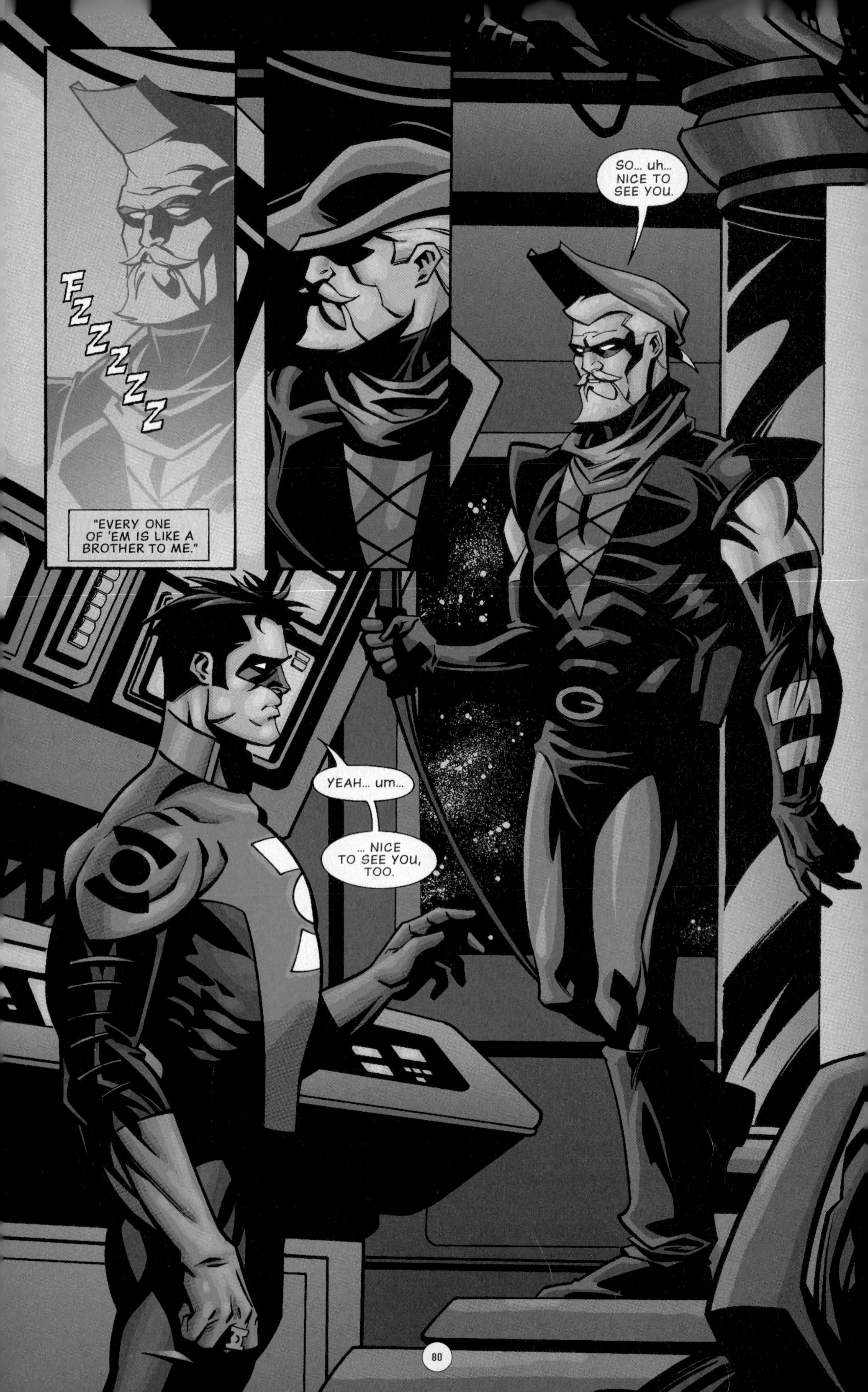
FZZZZZZ
"EVERY ONE OF 'EM IS LIKE A BROTHER TO ME."
SO... uh... NICE TO SEE YOU.
YEAH... um...
... NICE TO SEE YOU, TOO.

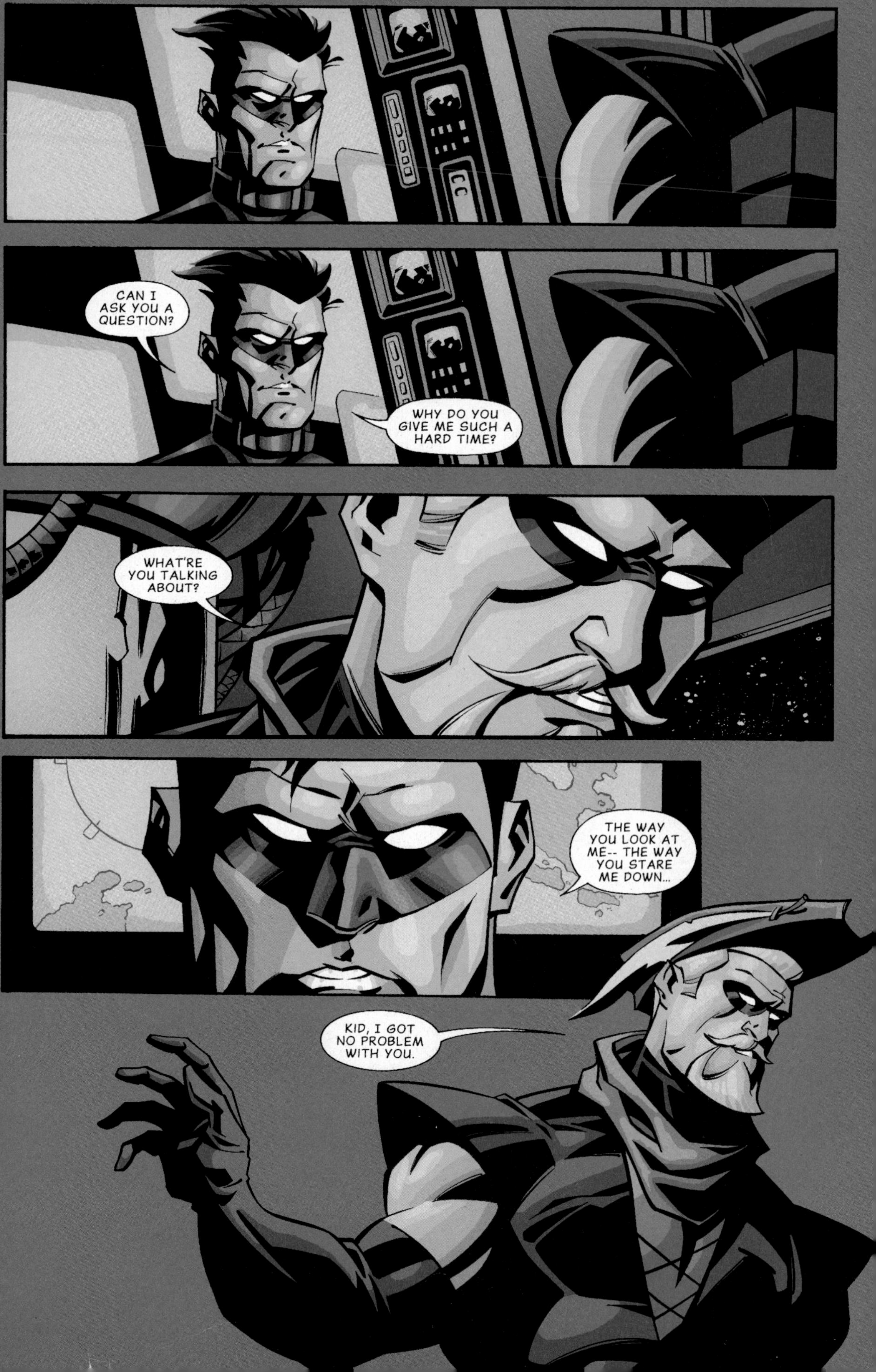
CAN I ASK YOU A QUESTION?
WHY DO YOU GIVE ME SUCH A HARD TIME?
WHAT'RE YOU TALKING ABOUT?
THE WAY YOU LOOK AT ME-- THE WAY YOU STARE ME DOWN...
KID, I GOT NO PROBLEM WITH YOU.

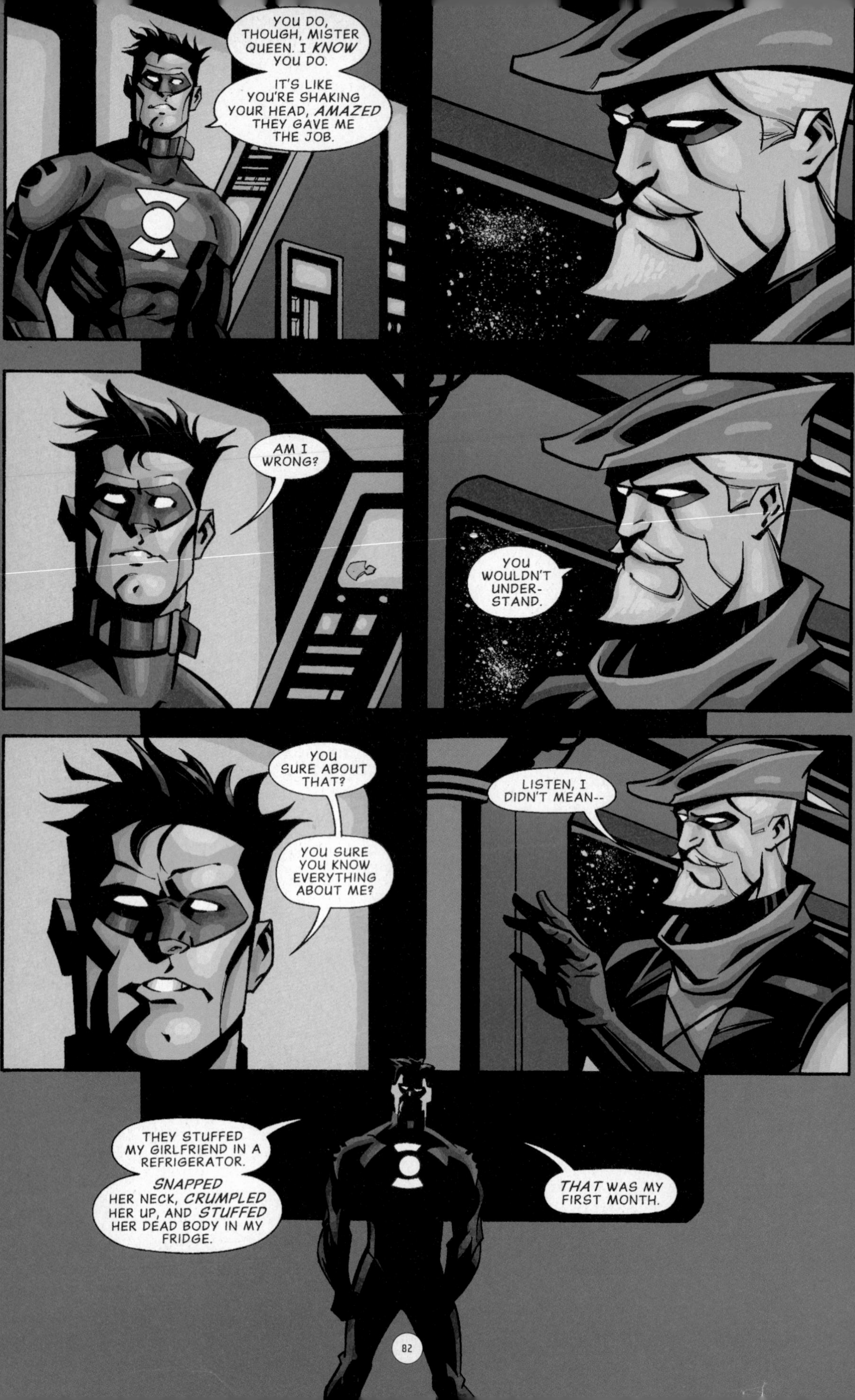
YOU DO, THOUGH, MISTER QUEEN. I KNOW YOU DO.
IT'S LIKE YOU'RE SHAKING YOUR HEAD, AMAZED THEY GAVE ME THE JOB.
AM I WRONG?
YOU WOULDN'T UNDER-STAND.
YOU SURE ABOUT THAT?
YOU SURE YOU KNOW EVERYTHING ABOUT ME?
LISTEN, I DIDN'T MEAN--
THEY STUFFED MY GIRLFRIEND IN A REFRIGERATOR.
SNAPPED HER NECK, CRUMPLED HER UP, AND STUFFED HER DEAD BODY IN MY FRIDGE.
THAT WAS MY FIRST MONTH.

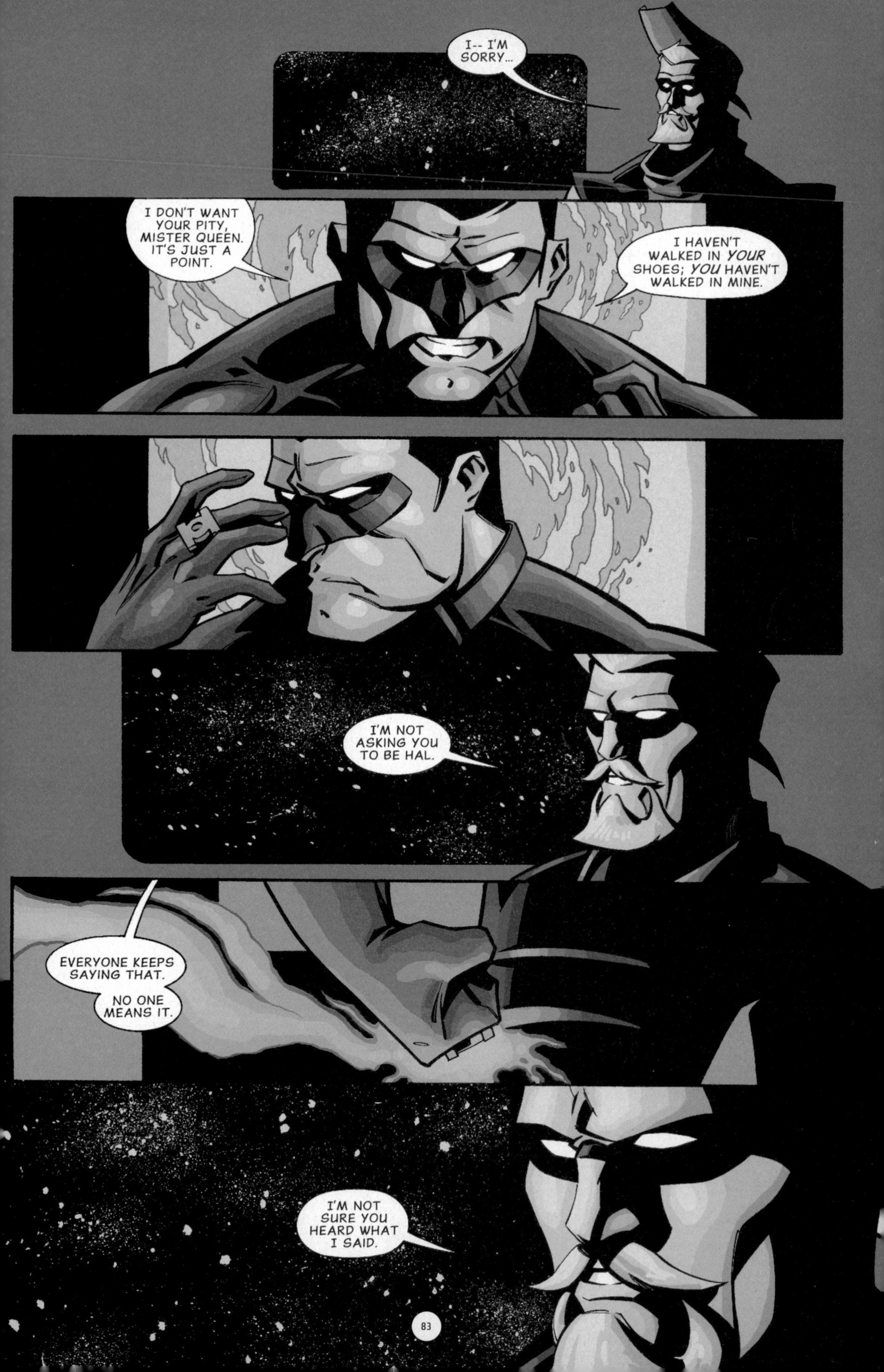
I-- I'M SORRY...
I DON'T WANT YOUR PITY, MISTER QUEEN. IT'S JUST A POINT.
I HAVEN'T WALKED IN YOUR SHOES; YOU HAVEN'T WALKED IN MINE.
I'M NOT ASKING YOU TO BE HAL.
EVERYONE KEEPS SAYING THAT.
NO ONE MEANS IT.
I'M NOT SURE YOU HEARD WHAT I SAID.

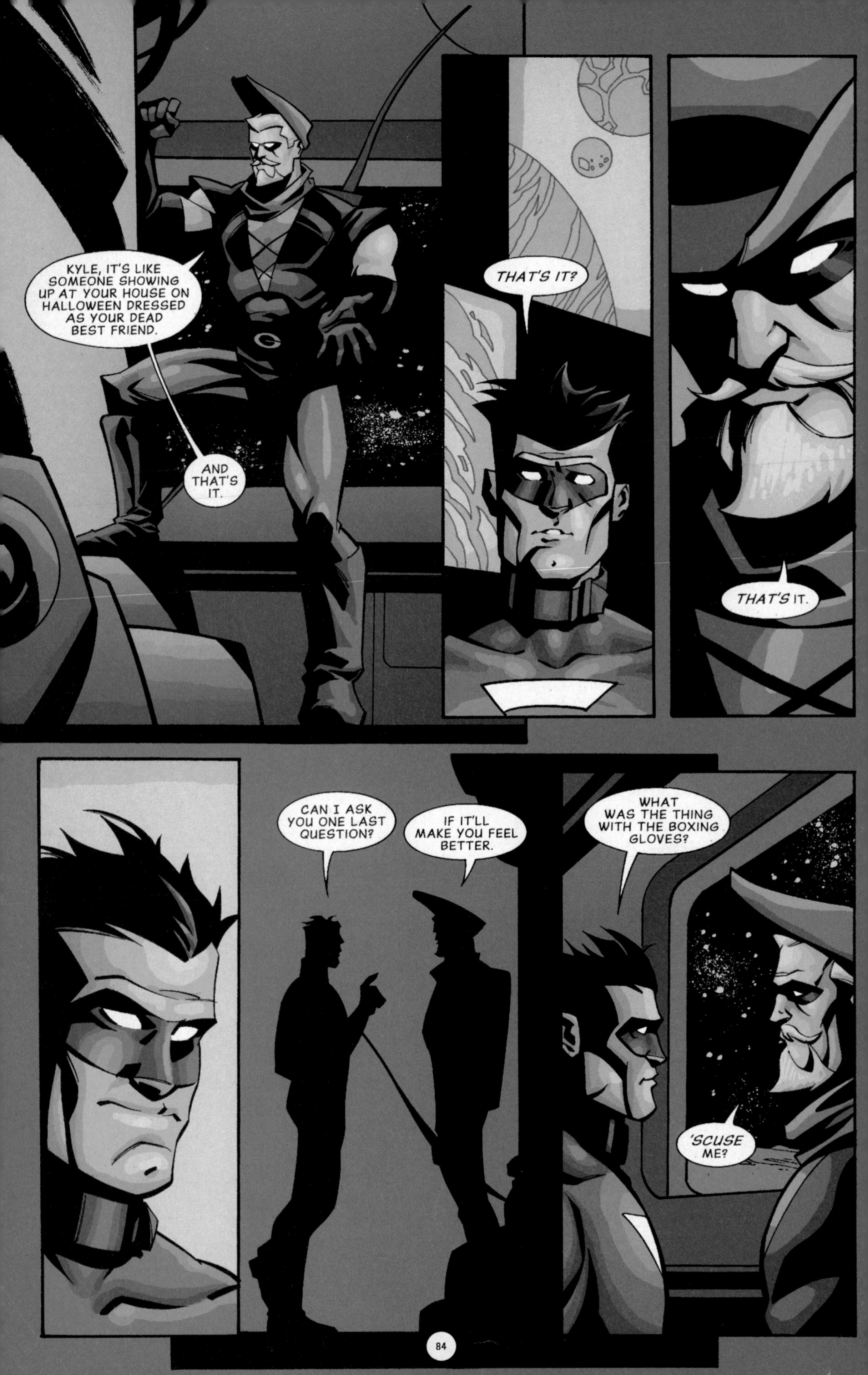
KYLE, IT'S LIKE SOMEONE SHOWING UP AT YOUR HOUSE ON HALLOWEEN DRESSED AS YOUR DEAD BEST FRIEND.
AND THAT'S IT.
THAT'S IT?
THAT'S IT.
CAN I ASK YOU ONE LAST QUESTION?
IF IT'LL MAKE YOU FEEL BETTER.
WHAT WAS THE THING WITH THE BOXING GLOVES?
'SCUSE ME?

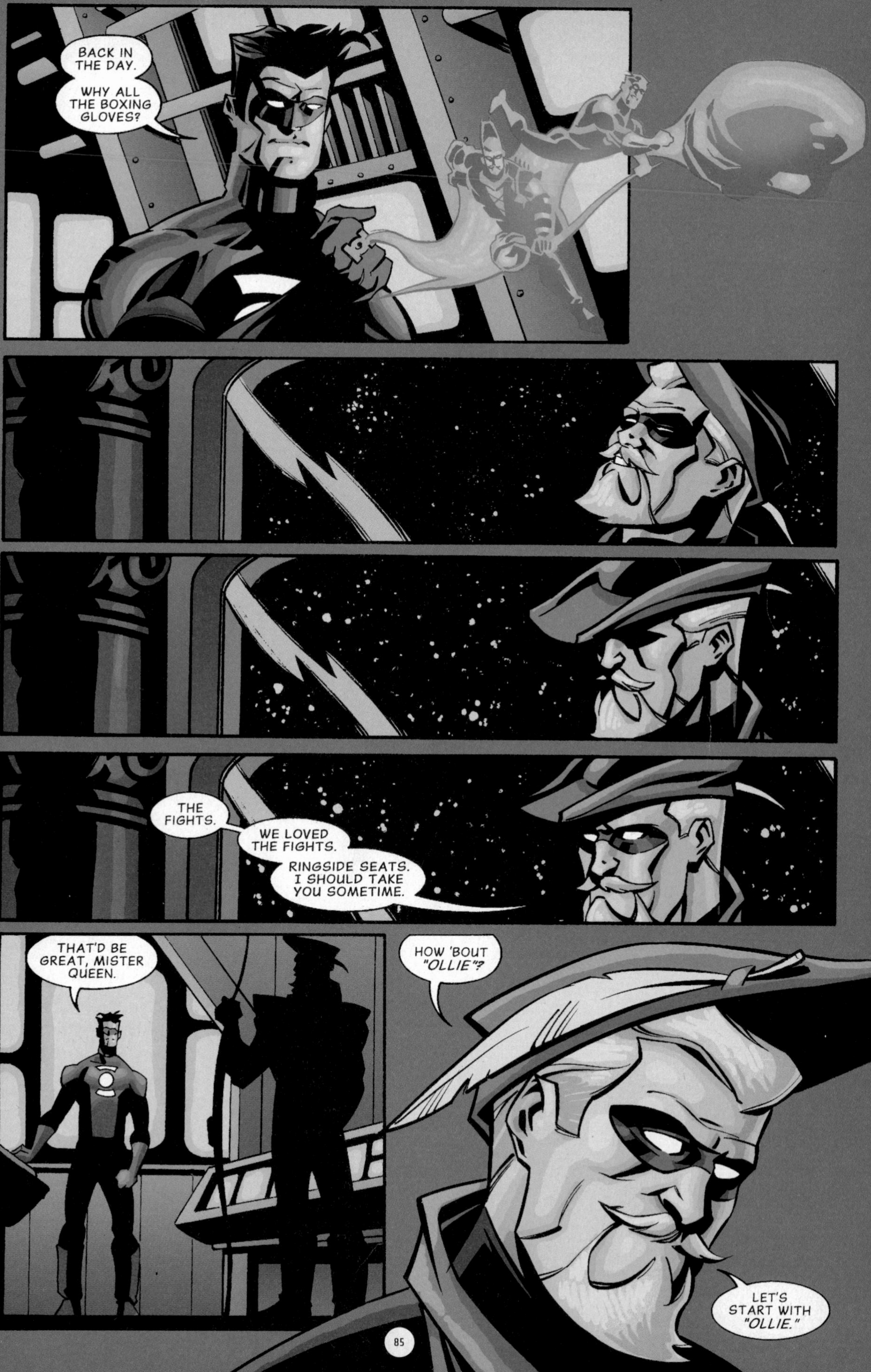
BACK IN THE DAY.
WHY ALL THE BOXING GLOVES?
THE FIGHTS.
WE LOVED THE FIGHTS.
RINGSIDE SEATS. I SHOULD TAKE YOU SOMETIME.
THAT'D BE GREAT, MISTER QUEEN.
HOW 'BOUT "OLLIE"?
LET'S START WITH "OLLIE."

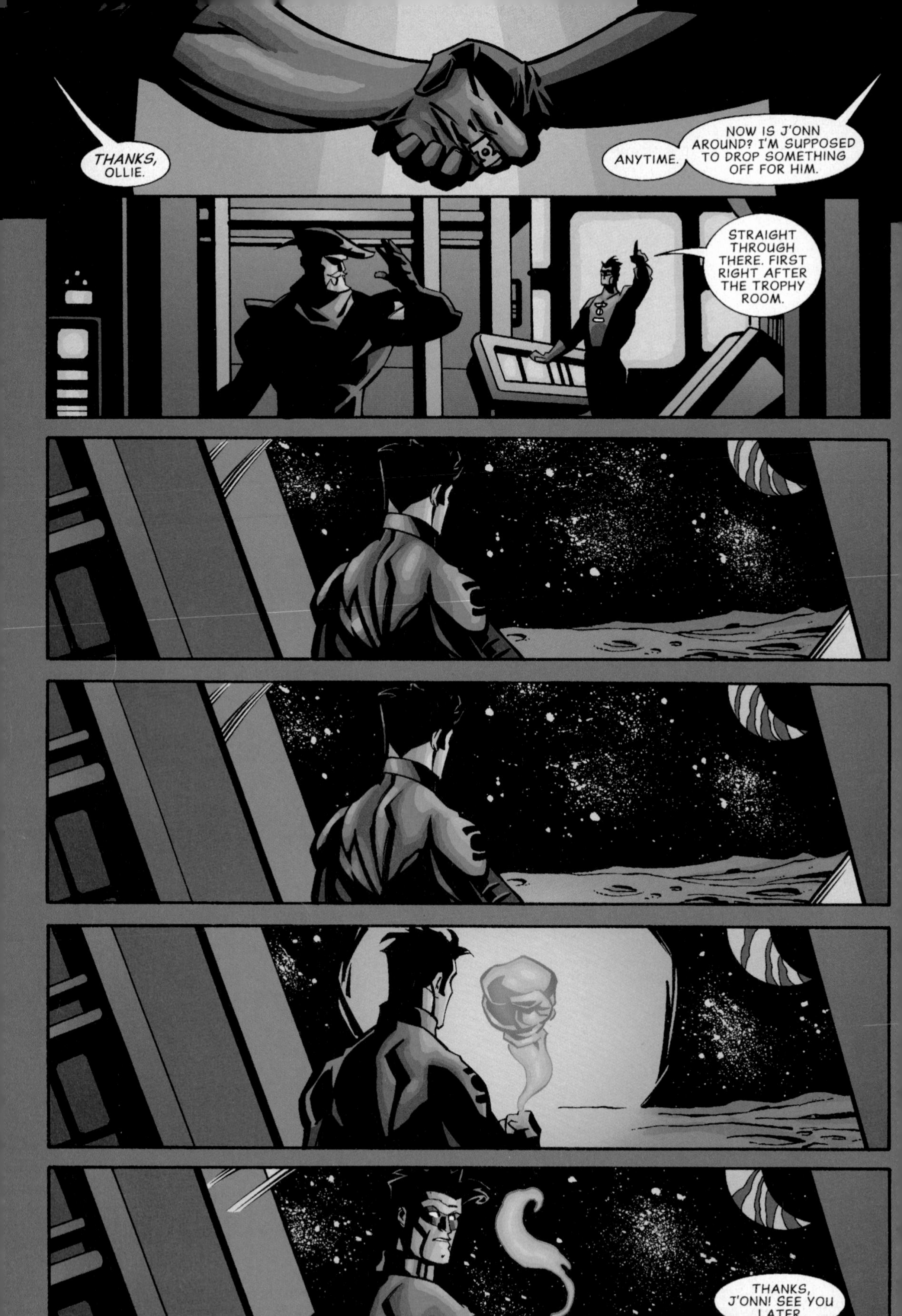

THANKS, OLLIE.
ANYTIME.
NOW IS J'ONN AROUND? I'M SUPPOSED TO DROP SOMETHING OFF FOR HIM.
STRAIGHT THROUGH THERE. FIRST RIGHT AFTER THE TROPHY ROOM.
THANKS, J'ONN! SEE YOU LATER.

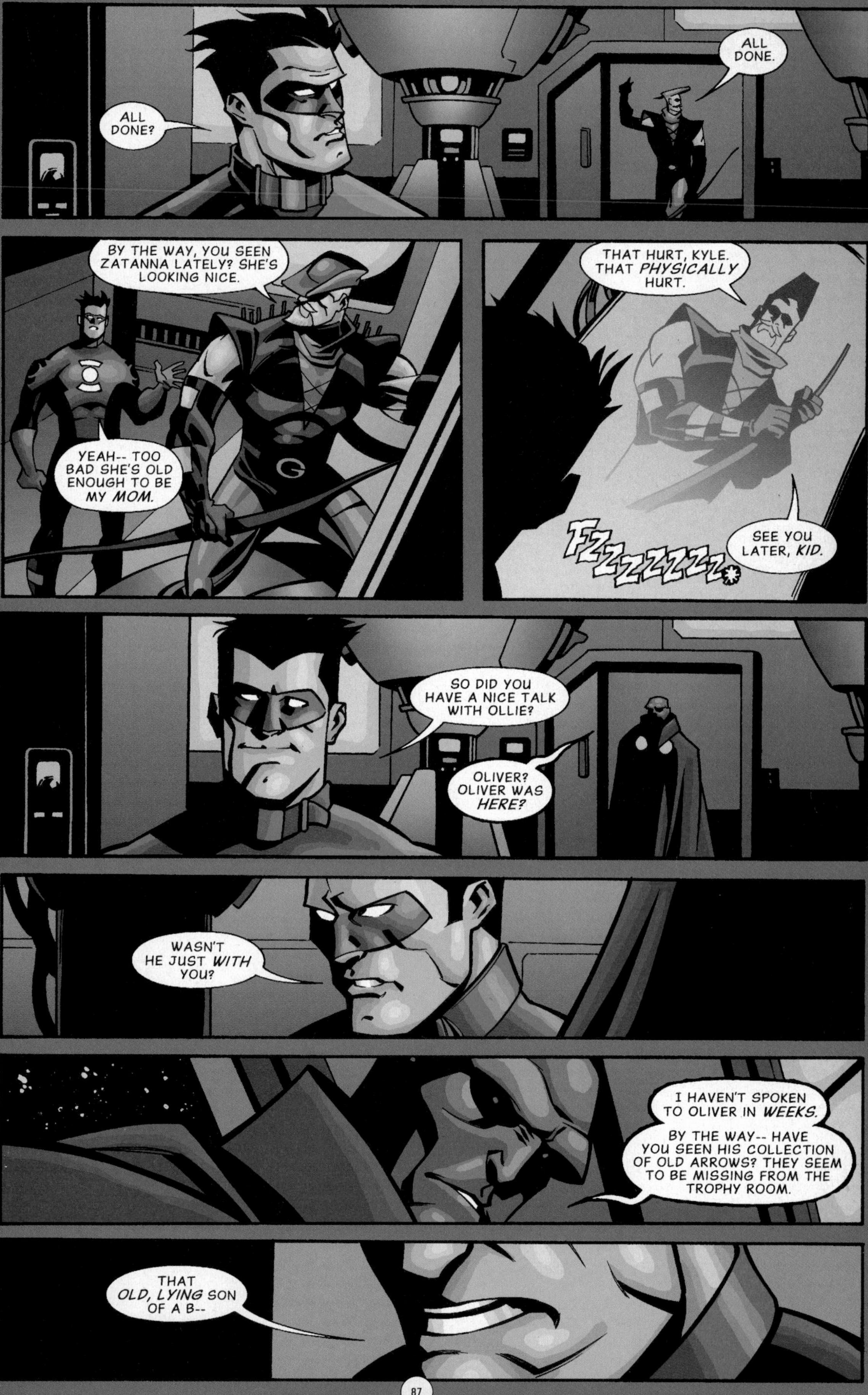
ALL DONE?
ALL DONE.
BY THE WAY, YOU SEEN ZATANNA LATELY? SHE'S LOOKING NICE.
YEAH-- TOO BAD SHE'S OLD ENOUGH TO BE MY MOM.
THAT HURT, KYLE. THAT PHYSICALLY HURT.
FZZZZZZZZ
SEE YOU LATER, KID.
SO DID YOU HAVE A NICE TALK WITH OLLIE?
OLIVER? OLIVER WAS HERE?
WASN'T HE JUST WITH YOU?
I HAVEN'T SPOKEN TO OLIVER IN WEEKS.
BY THE WAY-- HAVE YOU SEEN HIS COLLECTION OF OLD ARROWS? THEY SEEM TO BE MISSING FROM THE TROPHY ROOM.
THAT OLD, LYING SON OF A B--

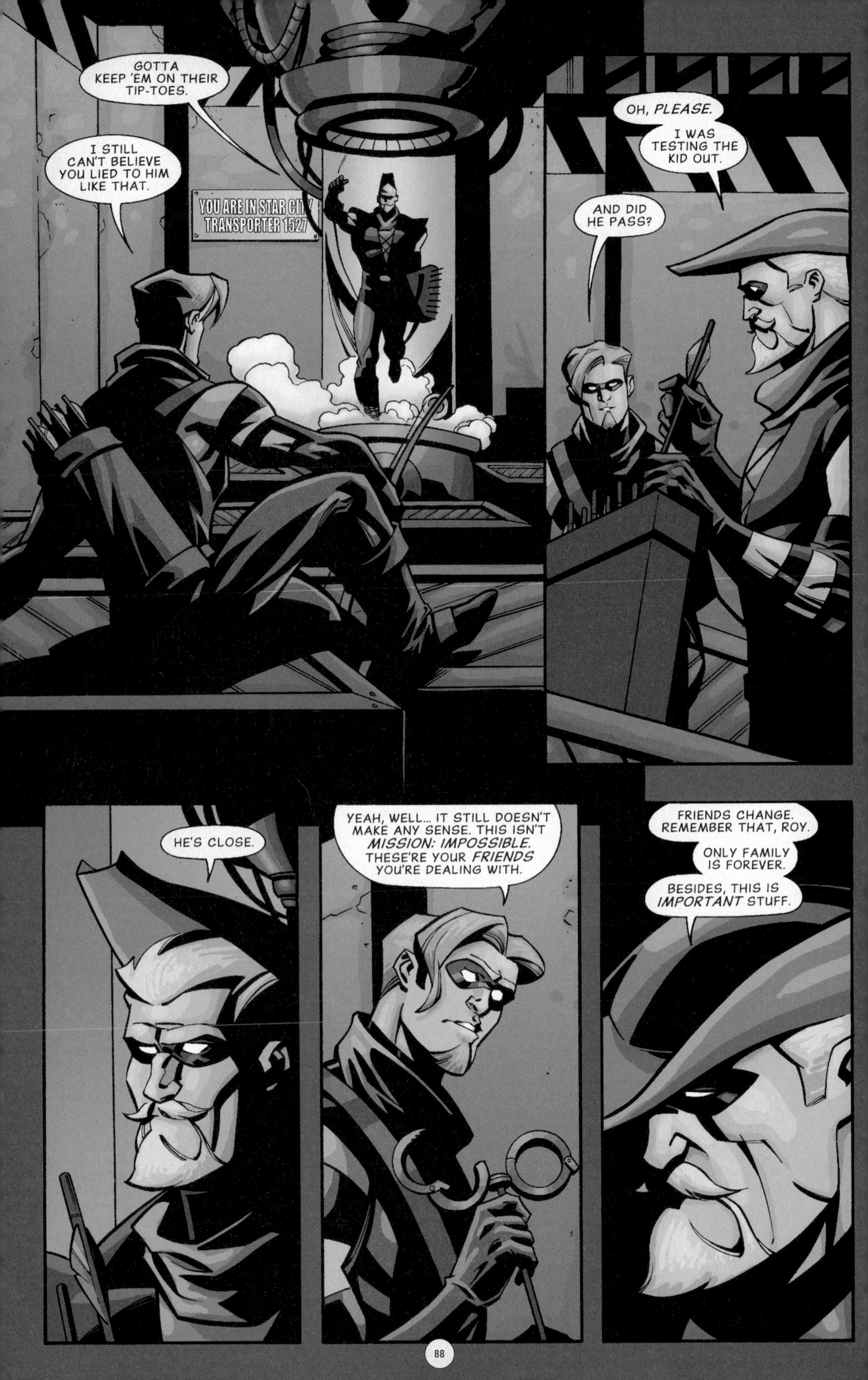
GOTTA KEEP 'EM ON THEIR TIP-TOES.
I STILL CAN'T BELIEVE YOU LIED TO HIM LIKE THAT.
YOU ARE IN STAR CITY TRANSPORTER 1527
OH, *PLEASE.*
I WAS TESTING THE KID OUT.
AND DID HE PASS?
HE'S CLOSE.
YEAH, WELL... IT STILL DOESN'T MAKE ANY SENSE. THIS ISN'T *MISSION: IMPOSSIBLE.* THESE'RE YOUR *FRIENDS* YOU'RE DEALING WITH.
FRIENDS CHANGE. REMEMBER THAT, ROY.
ONLY FAMILY IS FOREVER.
BESIDES, THIS IS *IMPORTANT* STUFF.

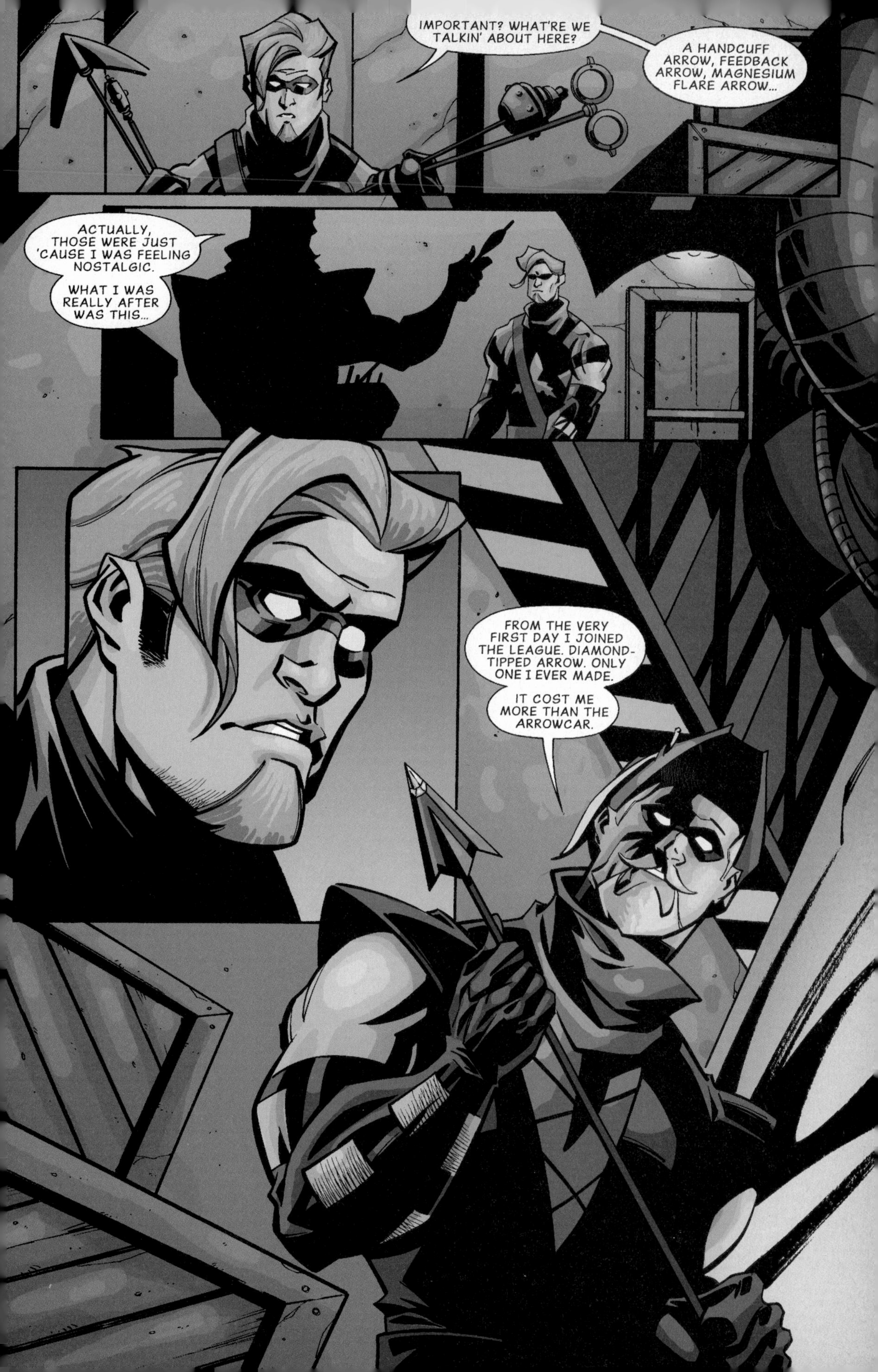

IMPORTANT? WHAT'RE WE TALKIN' ABOUT HERE?
A HANDCUFF ARROW, FEEDBACK ARROW, MAGNESIUM FLARE ARROW...
ACTUALLY, THOSE WERE JUST 'CAUSE I WAS FEELING NOSTALGIC.
WHAT I WAS REALLY AFTER WAS THIS...
FROM THE VERY FIRST DAY I JOINED THE LEAGUE. DIAMOND-TIPPED ARROW. ONLY ONE I EVER MADE.
IT COST ME MORE THAN THE ARROWCAR.

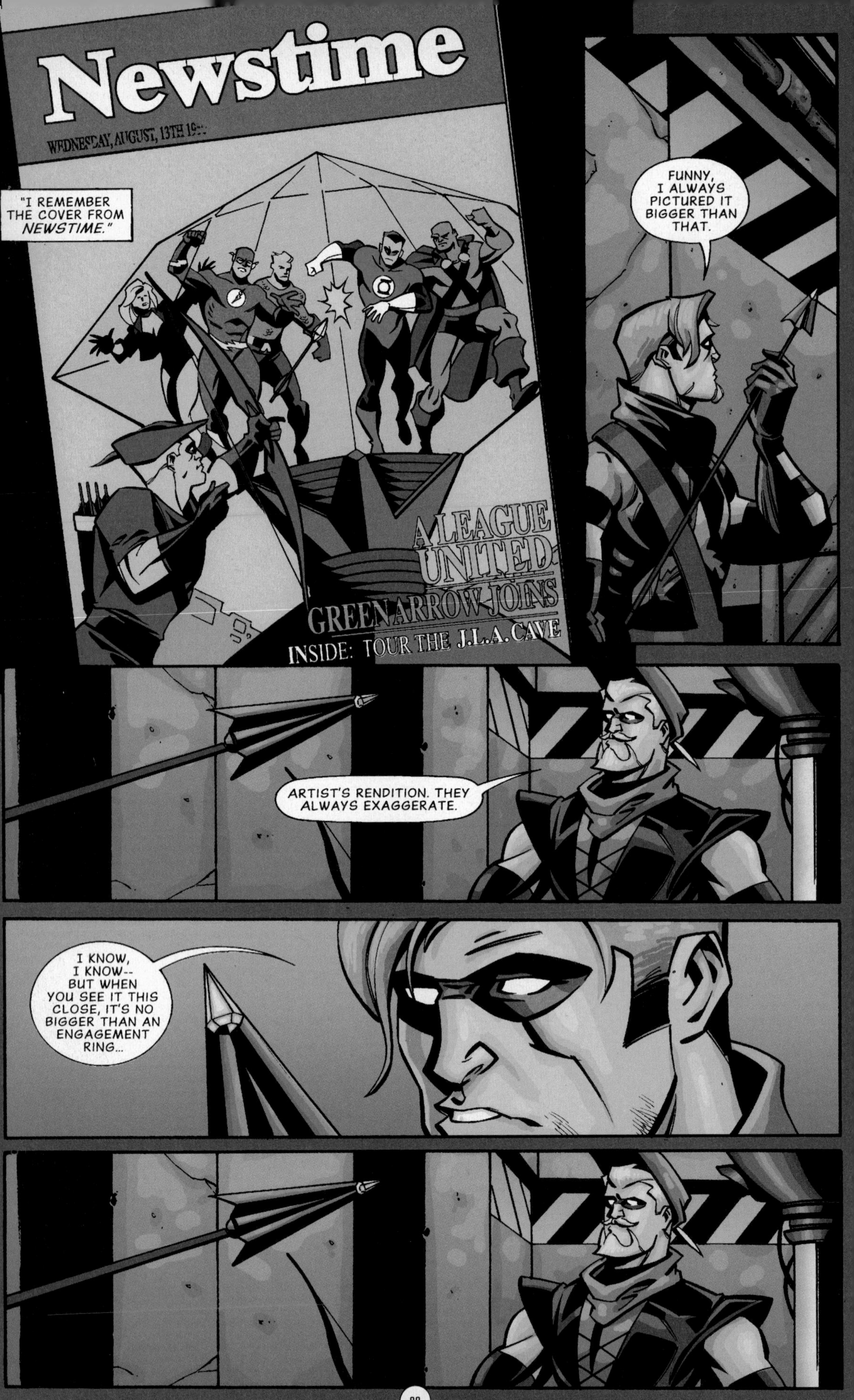
Newstime
WEDNESDAY, AUGUST, 13TH 19
"I REMEMBER THE COVER FROM *NEWSTIME.*"
A LEAGUE UNITED
GREEN ARROW JOINS
INSIDE: TOUR THE J.L.A. CAVE
FUNNY, I ALWAYS PICTURED IT BIGGER THAN THAT.
ARTIST'S RENDITION. THEY ALWAYS EXAGGERATE.
I KNOW, I KNOW-- BUT WHEN YOU SEE IT THIS CLOSE, IT'S NO BIGGER THAN AN ENGAGEMENT RING...

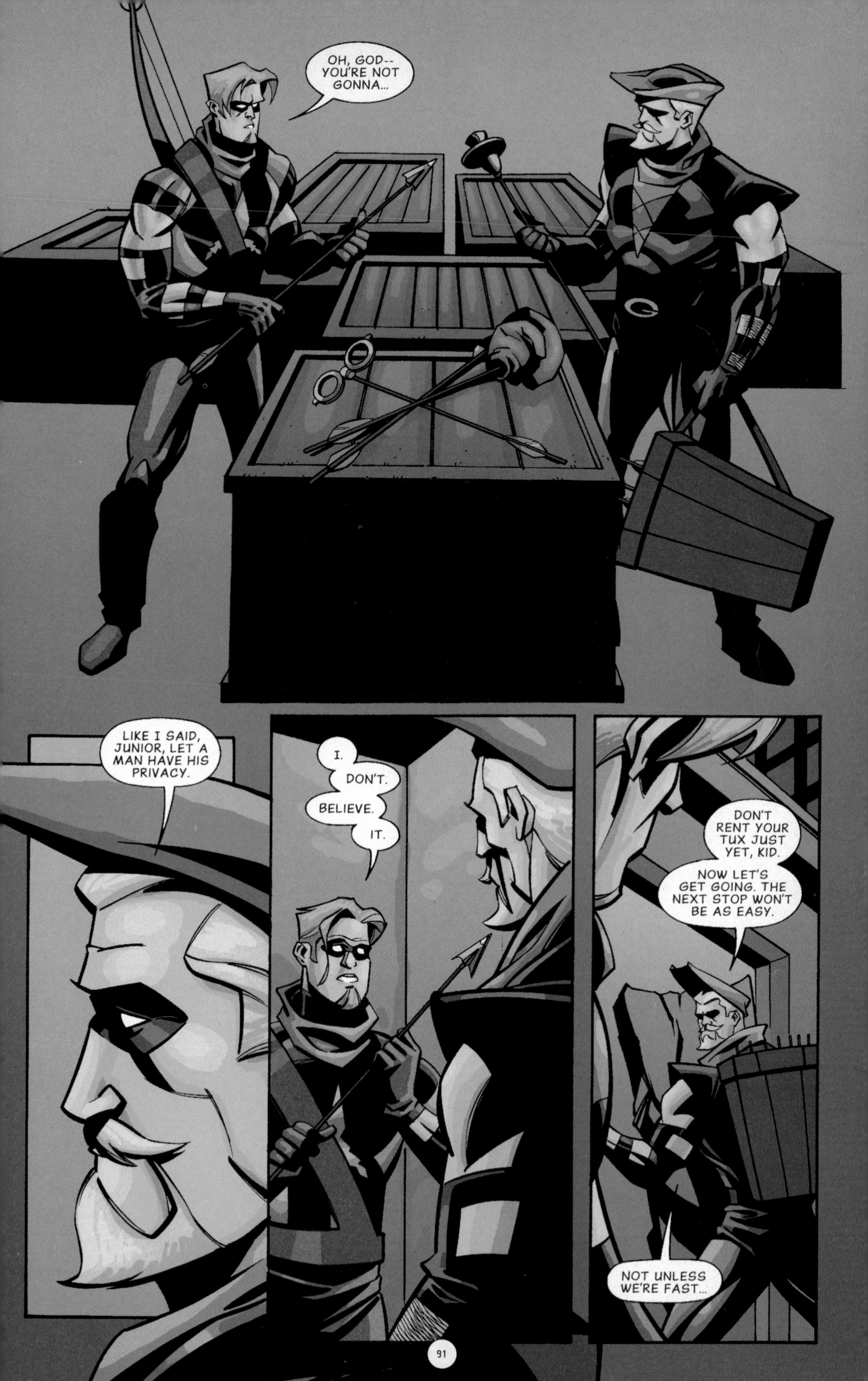
OH, GOD-- YOU'RE NOT GONNA...
LIKE I SAID, JUNIOR, LET A MAN HAVE HIS PRIVACY.
I.
DON'T.
BELIEVE.
IT.
DON'T RENT YOUR TUX JUST YET, KID.
NOW LET'S GET GOING. THE NEXT STOP WON'T BE AS EASY.
NOT UNLESS WE'RE FAST...

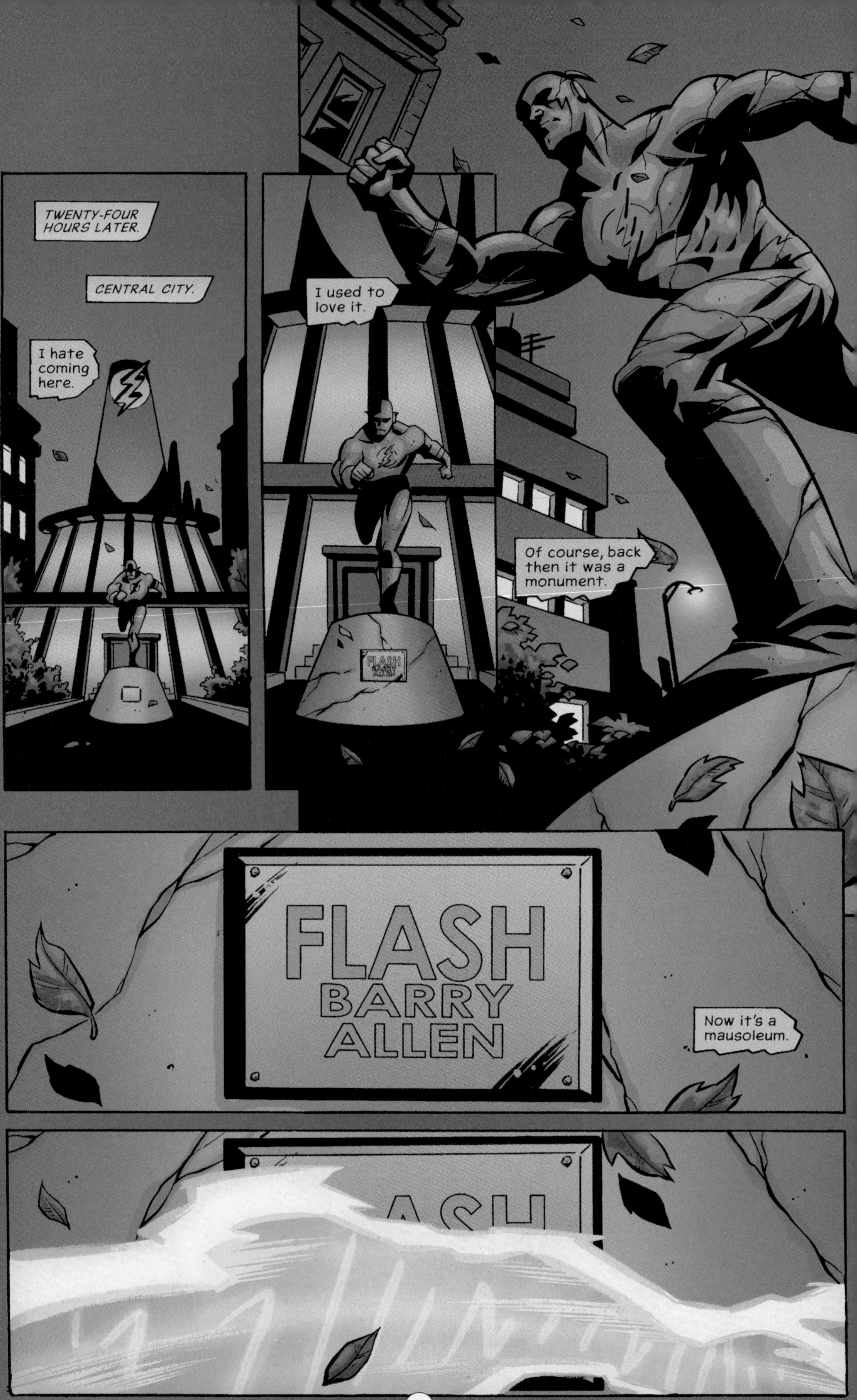
TWENTY-FOUR HOURS LATER.
CENTRAL CITY.
I hate coming here.
I used to love it.
Of course, back then it was a monument.
FLASH BARRY ALLEN
Now it's a mausoleum.

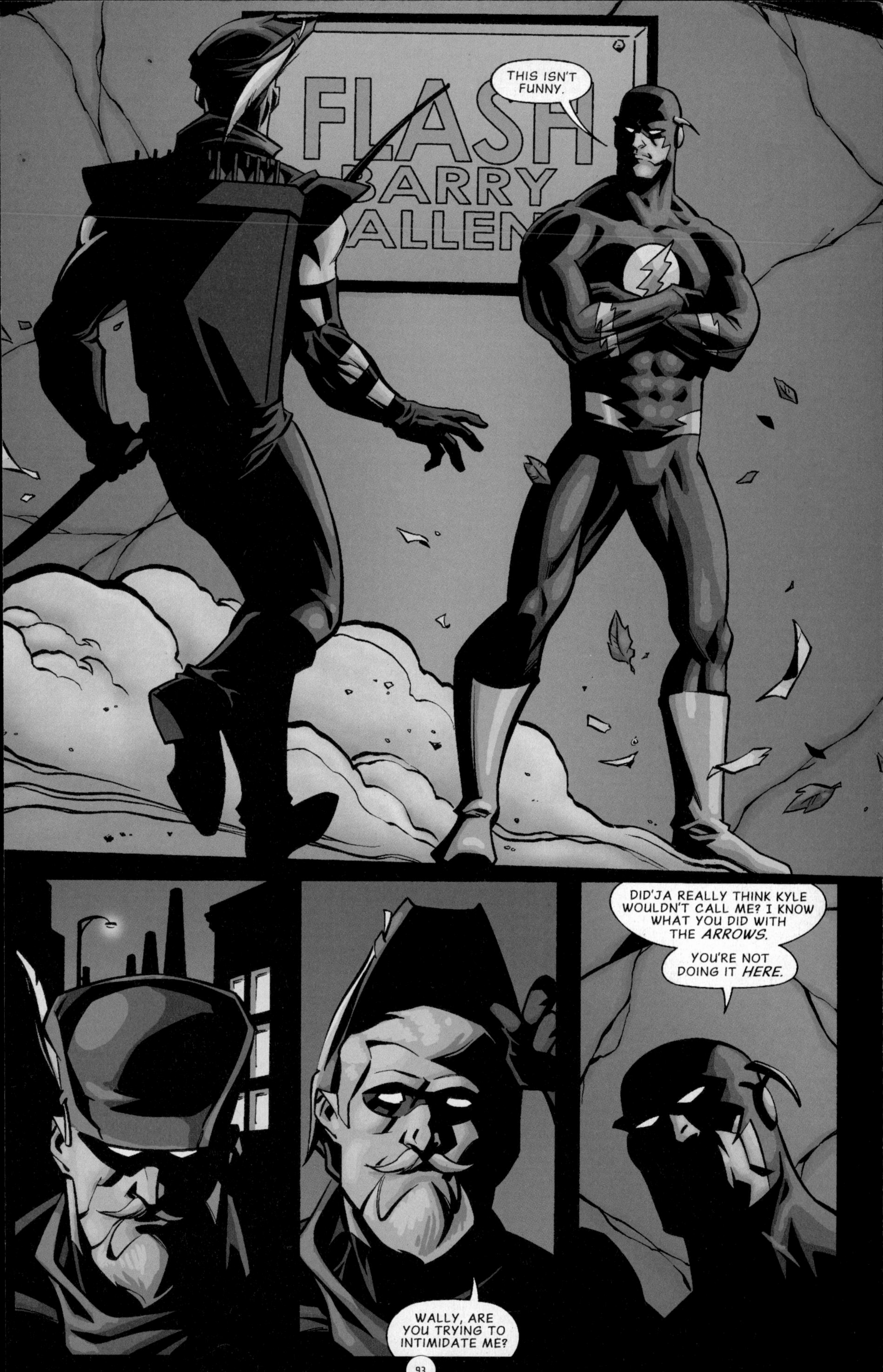
FLASH
BARRY
ALLEN
THIS ISN'T FUNNY.
DID'JA REALLY THINK KYLE WOULDN'T CALL ME? I KNOW WHAT YOU DID WITH THE *ARROWS*.
YOU'RE NOT DOING IT *HERE*.
WALLY, ARE YOU TRYING TO INTIMIDATE ME?

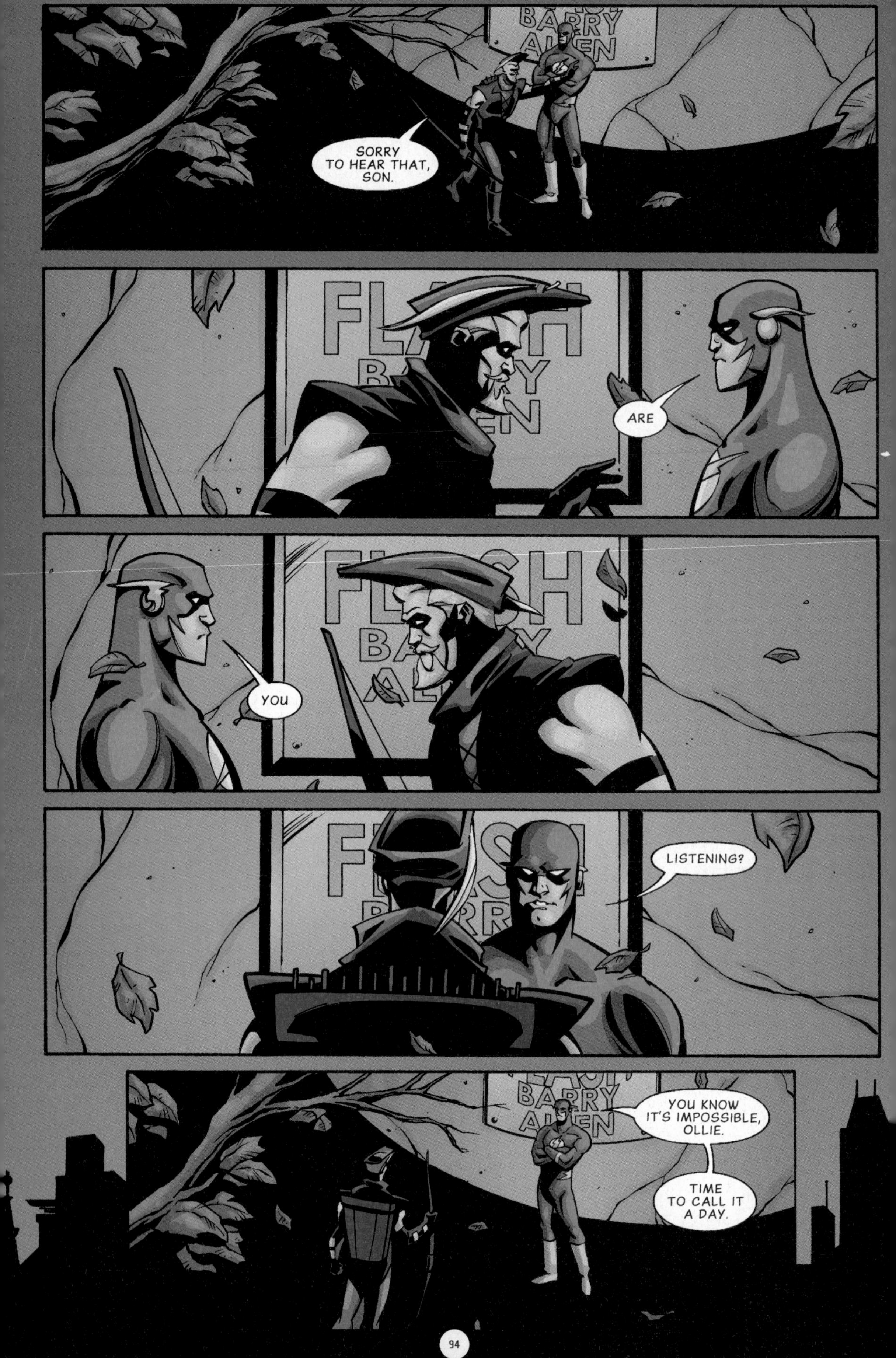
SORRY TO HEAR THAT, SON.
ARE
YOU
LISTENING?
YOU KNOW IT'S IMPOSSIBLE, OLLIE.
TIME TO CALL IT A DAY.

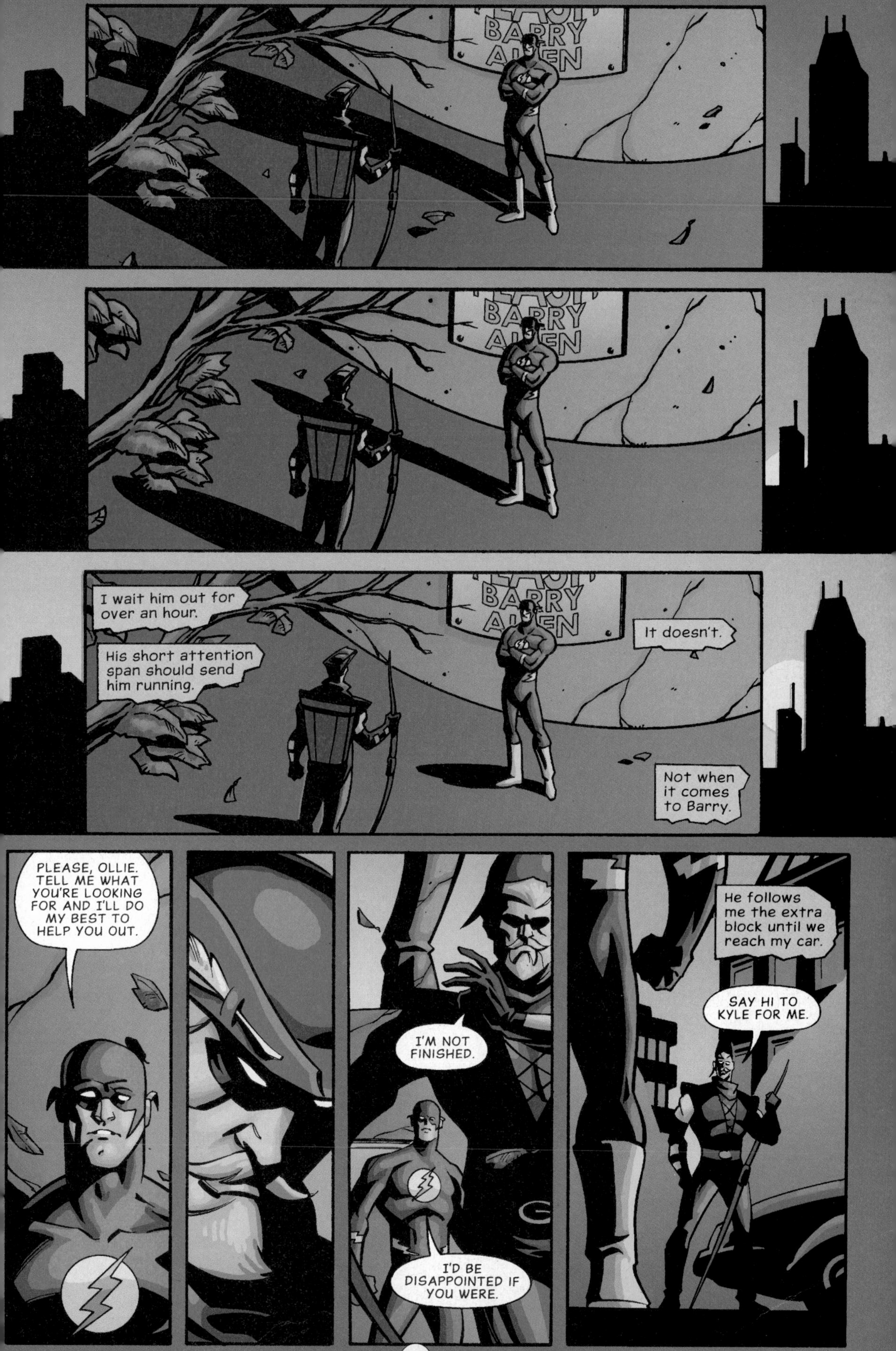

FLASH BARRY ALLEN
I wait him out for over an hour.
His short attention span should send him running.
It doesn't.
Not when it comes to Barry.
PLEASE, OLLIE. TELL ME WHAT YOU'RE LOOKING FOR AND I'LL DO MY BEST TO HELP YOU OUT.
I'M NOT FINISHED.
I'D BE DISAPPOINTED IF YOU WERE.
He follows me the extra block until we reach my car.
SAY HI TO KYLE FOR ME.

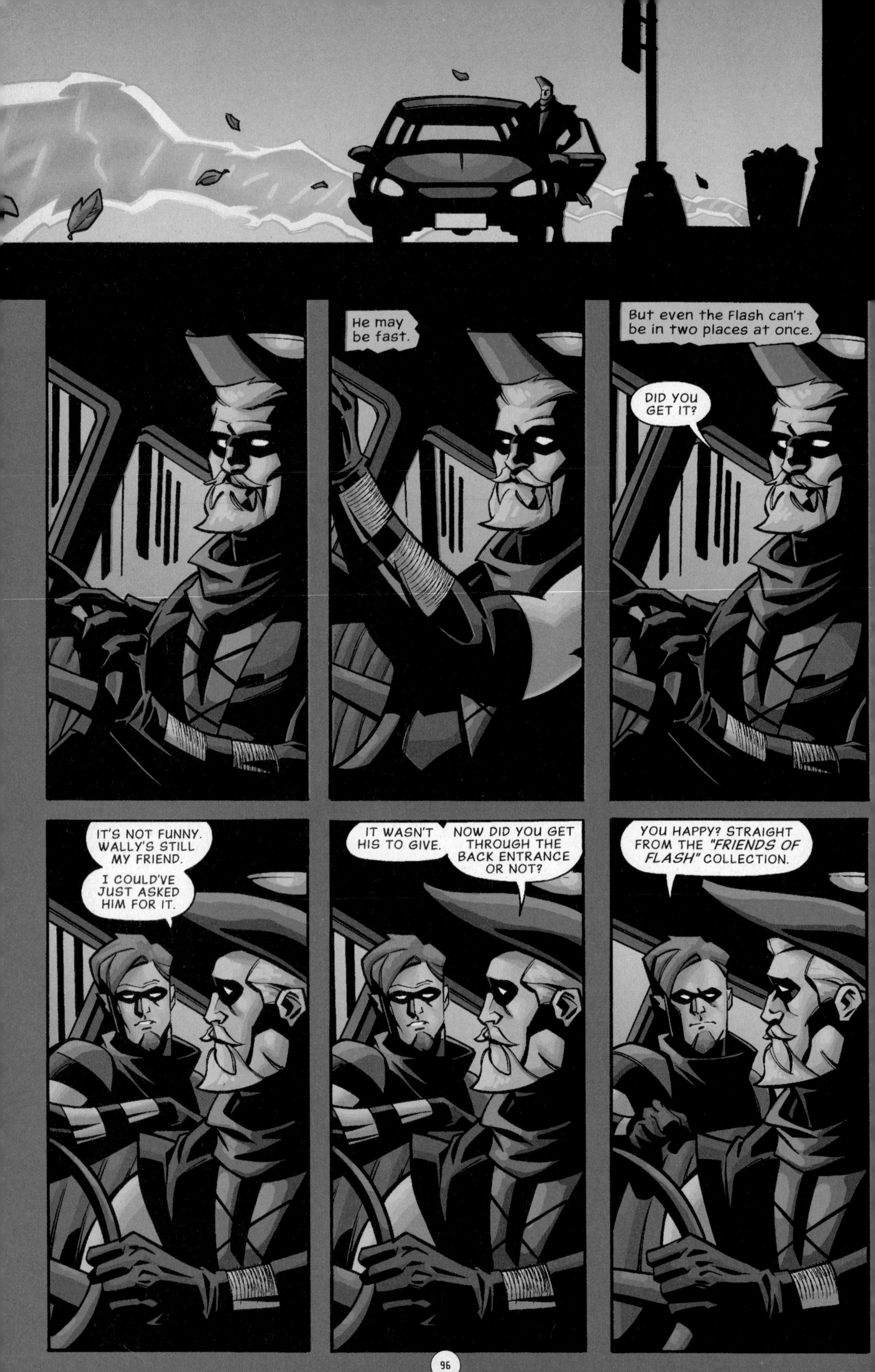
He may be fast.
But even the Flash can't be in two places at once.
DID YOU GET IT?
IT'S NOT FUNNY. WALLY'S STILL MY FRIEND.
I COULD'VE JUST ASKED HIM FOR IT.
IT WASN'T HIS TO GIVE.
NOW DID YOU GET THROUGH THE BACK ENTRANCE OR NOT?
YOU HAPPY? STRAIGHT FROM THE "FRIENDS OF FLASH" COLLECTION.

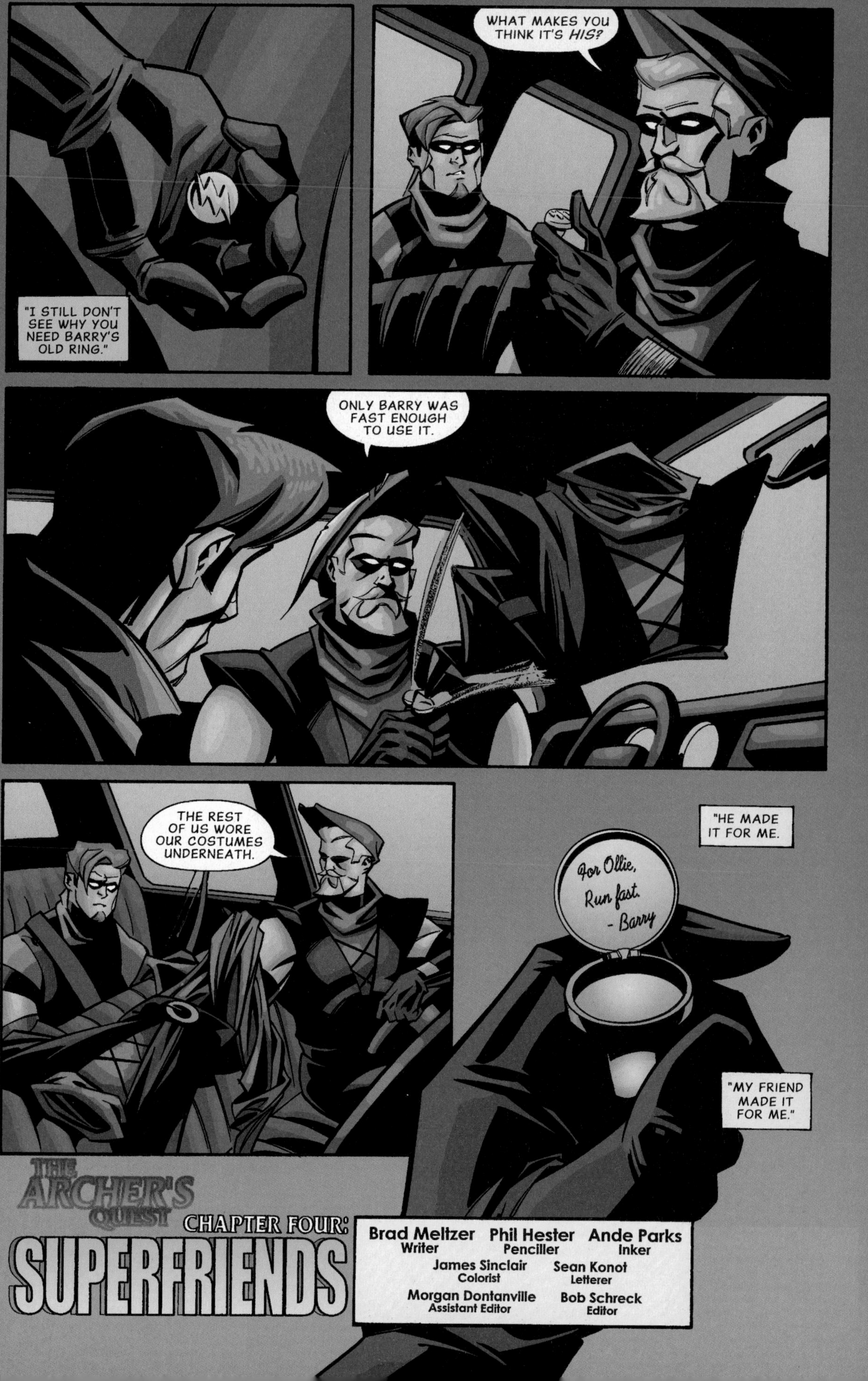
"I STILL DON'T SEE WHY YOU NEED BARRY'S OLD RING."
WHAT MAKES YOU THINK IT'S *HIS?*
ONLY BARRY WAS FAST ENOUGH TO USE IT.
THE REST OF US WORE OUR COSTUMES UNDERNEATH.
"HE MADE IT FOR ME.
For Ollie, Run fast. - Barry
"MY FRIEND MADE IT FOR ME."
THE ARCHER'S QUEST
CHAPTER FOUR:
SUPERFRIENDS
Brad Meltzer Writer
Phil Hester Penciller
Ande Parks Inker
James Sinclair Colorist
Sean Konot Letterer
Morgan Dontanville Assistant Editor
Bob Schreck Editor

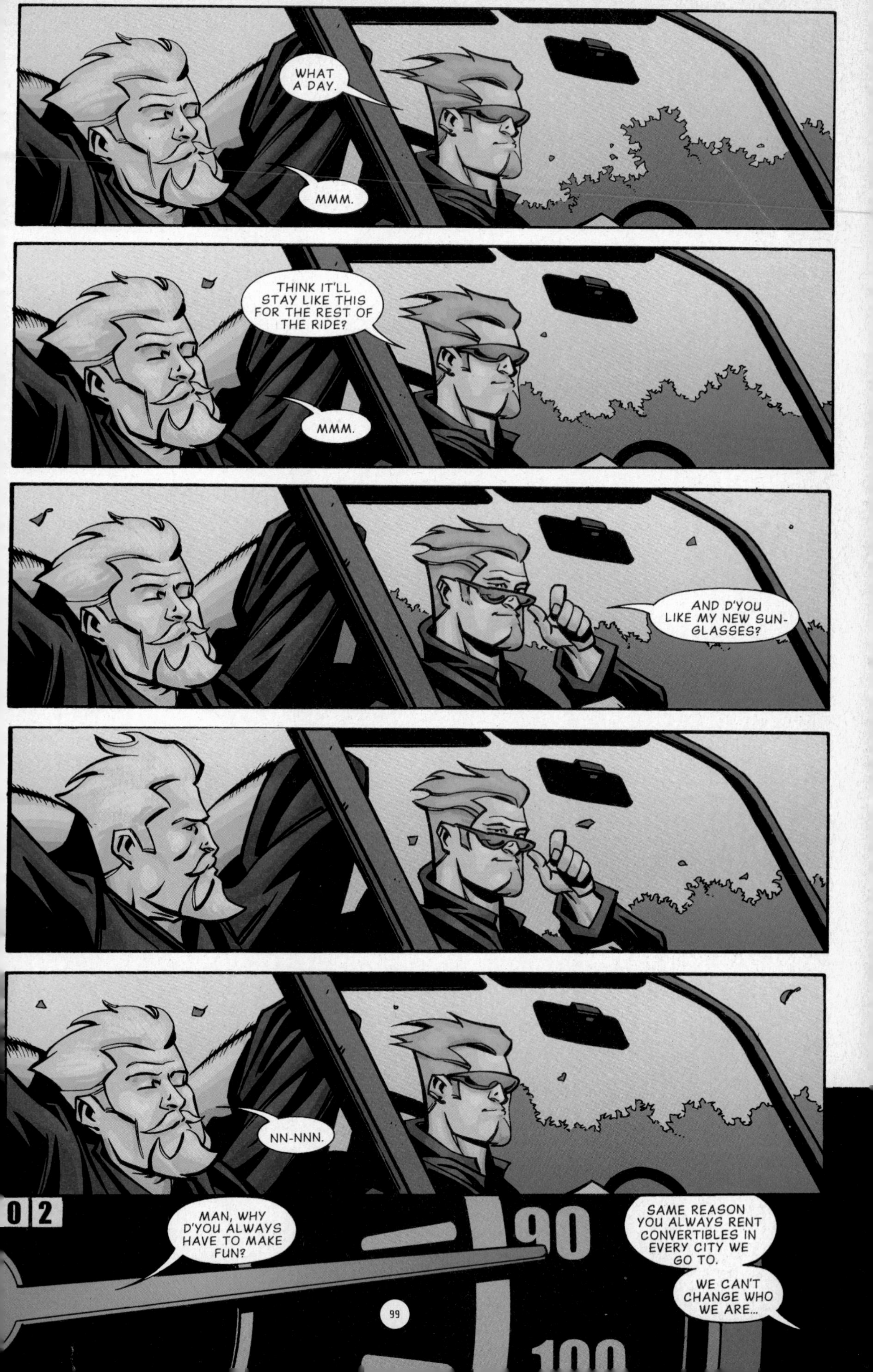
WHAT A DAY.
MMM.
THINK IT'LL STAY LIKE THIS FOR THE REST OF THE RIDE?
MMM.
AND D'YOU LIKE MY NEW SUN-GLASSES?
NN-NNN.
MAN, WHY D'YOU ALWAYS HAVE TO MAKE FUN?
SAME REASON YOU ALWAYS RENT CONVERTIBLES IN EVERY CITY WE GO TO.
WE CAN'T CHANGE WHO WE ARE...
90
100

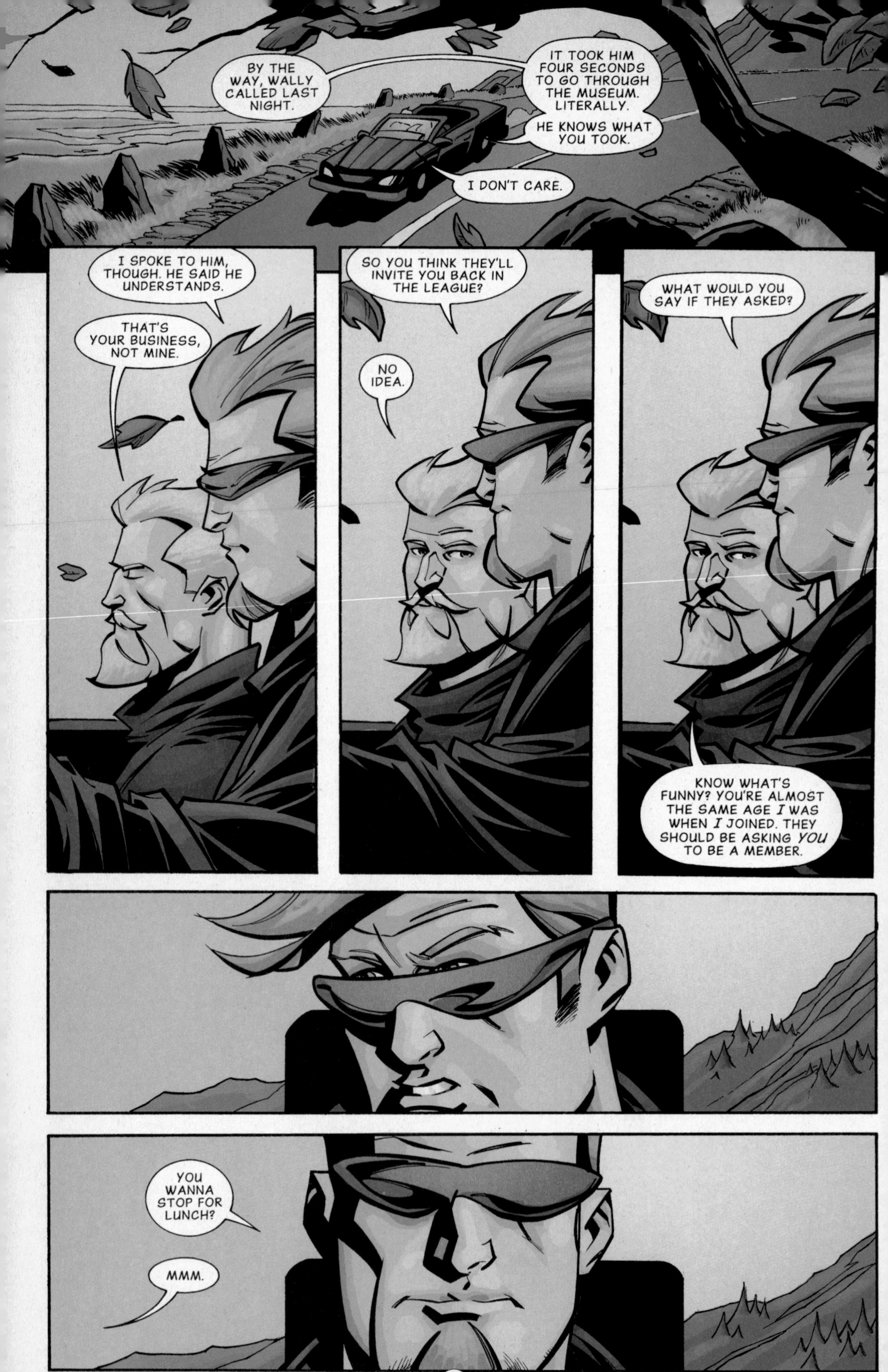
BY THE WAY, WALLY CALLED LAST NIGHT.
IT TOOK HIM FOUR SECONDS TO GO THROUGH THE MUSEUM. LITERALLY.
HE KNOWS WHAT YOU TOOK.
I DON'T CARE.
I SPOKE TO HIM, THOUGH. HE SAID HE UNDERSTANDS.
THAT'S YOUR BUSINESS, NOT MINE.
SO YOU THINK THEY'LL INVITE YOU BACK IN THE LEAGUE?
NO IDEA.
WHAT WOULD YOU SAY IF THEY ASKED?
KNOW WHAT'S FUNNY? YOU'RE ALMOST THE SAME AGE *I* WAS WHEN *I* JOINED. THEY SHOULD BE ASKING *YOU* TO BE A MEMBER.
YOU WANNA STOP FOR LUNCH?
MMM.

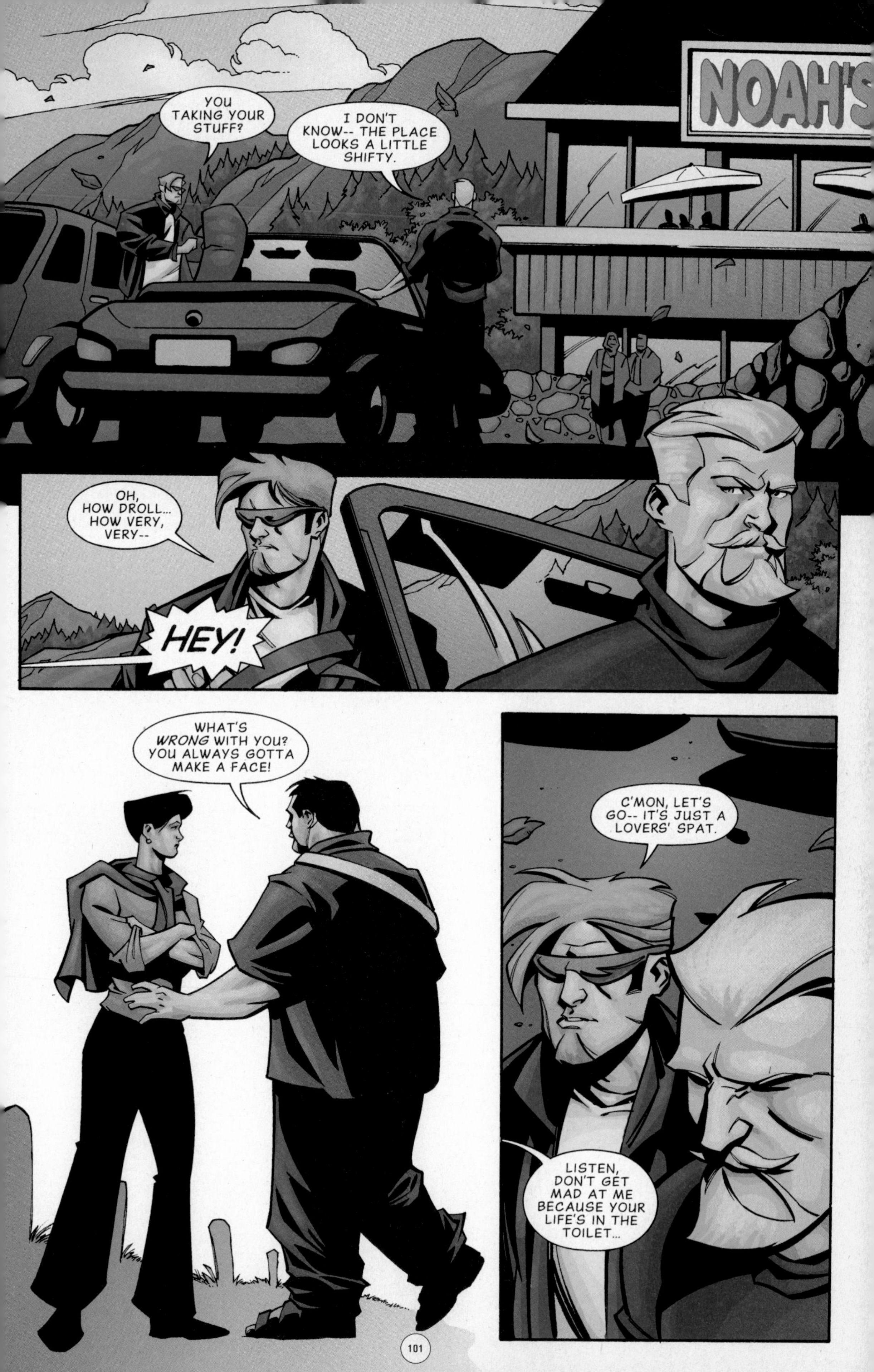
YOU TAKING YOUR STUFF?
I DON'T KNOW-- THE PLACE LOOKS A LITTLE SHIFTY.
NOAH'S
OH, HOW DROLL... HOW VERY, VERY--
HEY!
WHAT'S *WRONG* WITH YOU? YOU ALWAYS GOTTA MAKE A FACE!
C'MON, LET'S GO-- IT'S JUST A LOVERS' SPAT.
LISTEN, DON'T GET MAD AT ME BECAUSE YOUR LIFE'S IN THE TOILET...

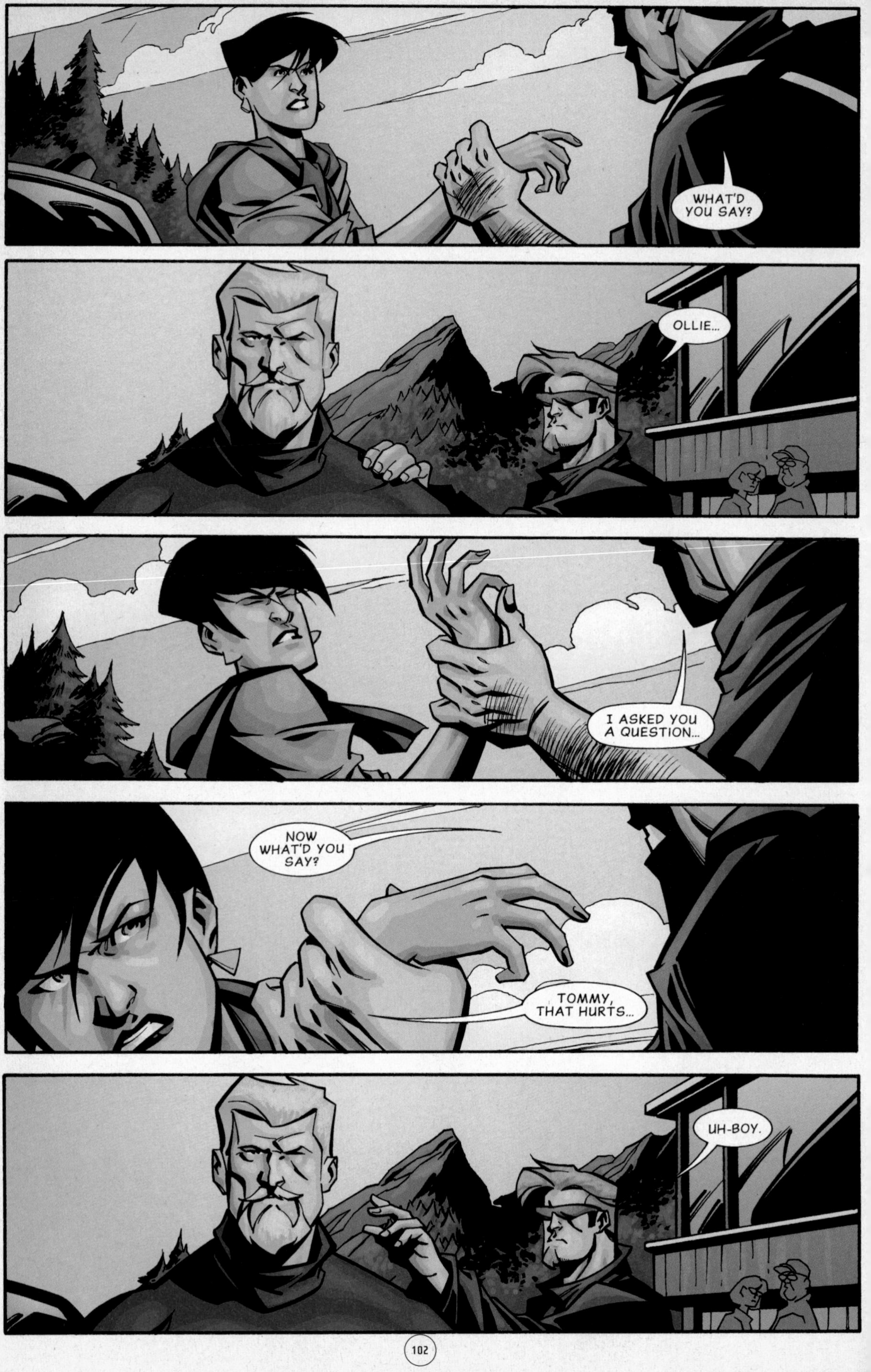
WHAT'D YOU SAY?
OLLIE...
I ASKED YOU A QUESTION...
NOW WHAT'D YOU SAY?
TOMMY, THAT HURTS...
UH-BOY.

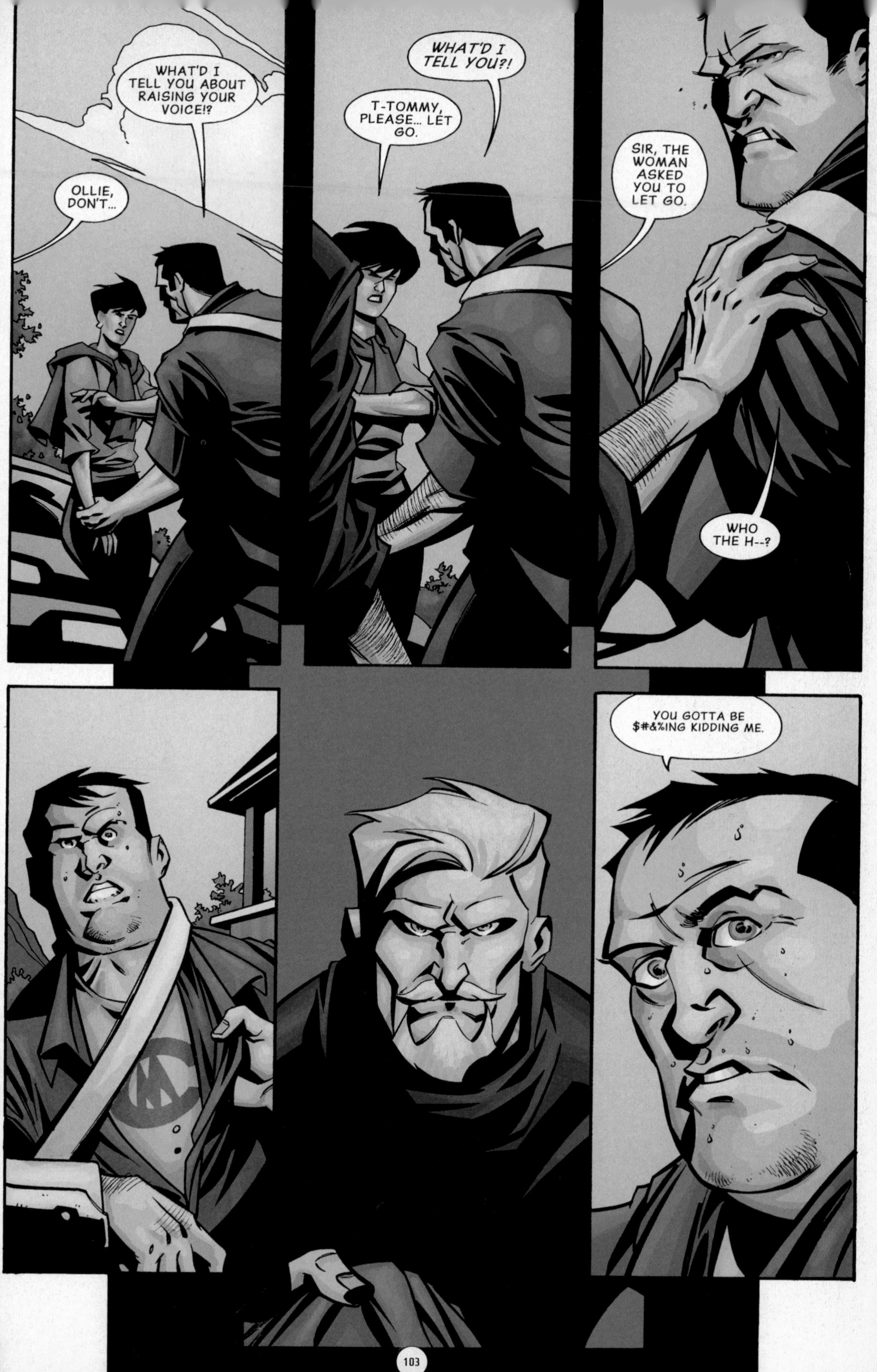
WHAT'D I TELL YOU ABOUT RAISING YOUR VOICE!?
OLLIE, DON'T...
T-TOMMY, PLEASE... LET GO.
WHAT'D I TELL YOU?!
SIR, THE WOMAN ASKED YOU TO LET GO.
WHO THE H--?
YOU GOTTA BE $#&%ING KIDDING ME.

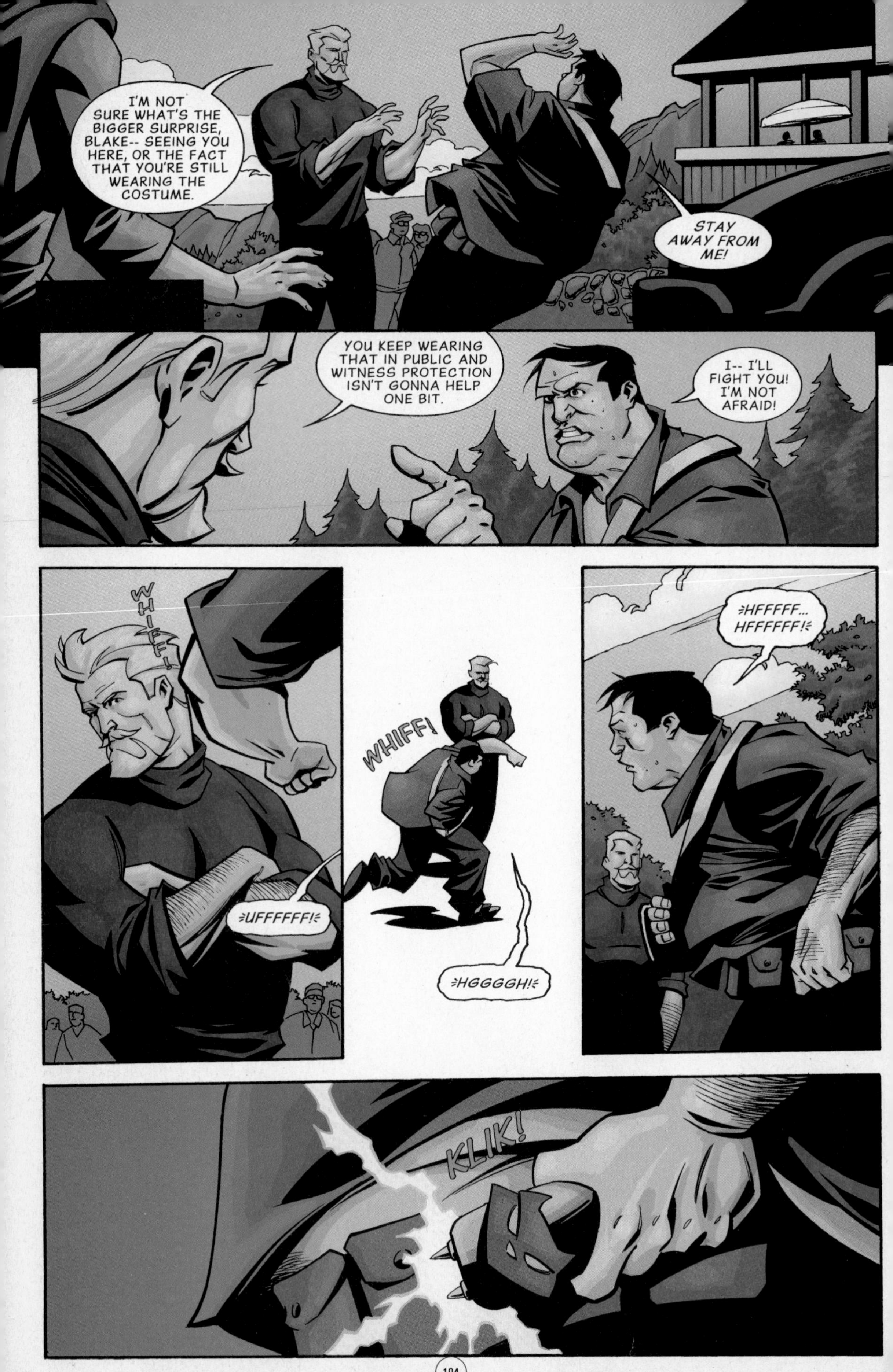

I'M NOT SURE WHAT'S THE BIGGER SURPRISE, BLAKE-- SEEING YOU HERE, OR THE FACT THAT YOU'RE STILL WEARING THE COSTUME.
STAY AWAY FROM ME!
YOU KEEP WEARING THAT IN PUBLIC AND WITNESS PROTECTION ISN'T GONNA HELP ONE BIT.
I-- I'LL FIGHT YOU! I'M NOT AFRAID!
WHIFF!
UFFFFFF!
WHIFF!
HGGGGH!
HFFFFF... HFFFFFF!
KLIK!

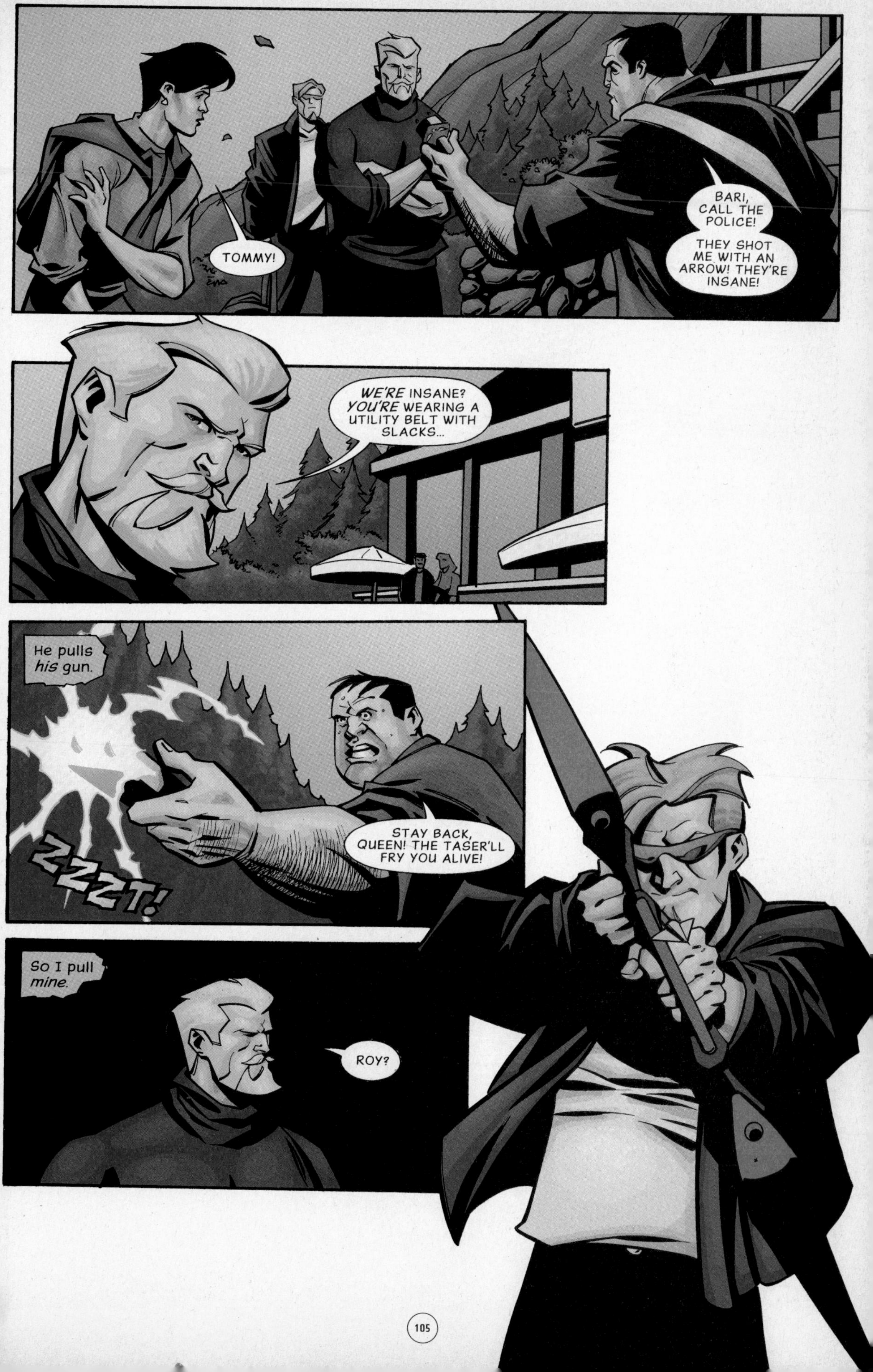
TOMMY!
BARI, CALL THE POLICE!
THEY SHOT ME WITH AN ARROW! THEY'RE INSANE!
WE'RE INSANE? YOU'RE WEARING A UTILITY BELT WITH SLACKS...
He pulls his gun.
ZZZT!
STAY BACK, QUEEN! THE TASER'LL FRY YOU ALIVE!
So I pull mine.
ROY?

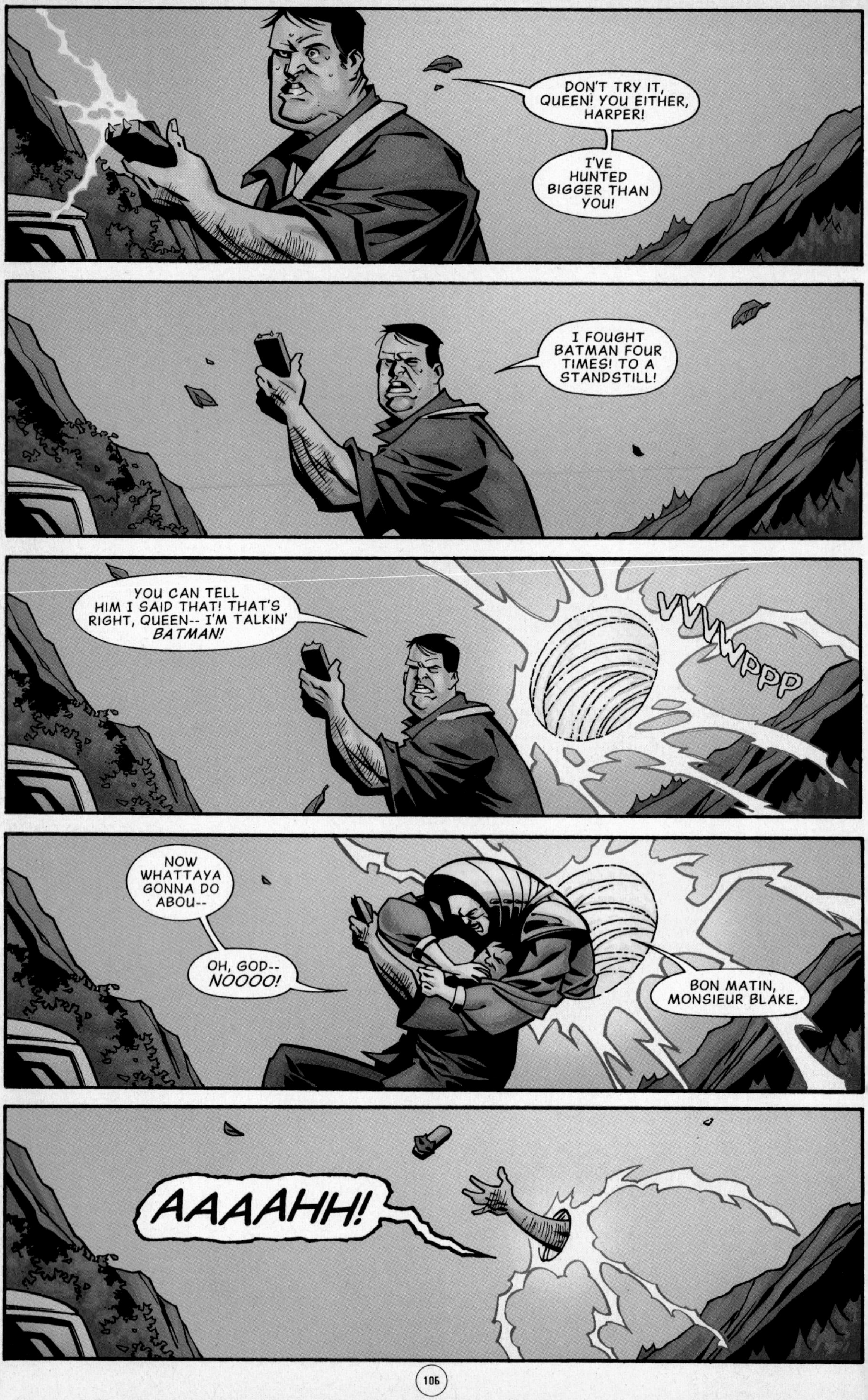
DON'T TRY IT, QUEEN! YOU EITHER, HARPER!
I'VE HUNTED BIGGER THAN YOU!
I FOUGHT BATMAN FOUR TIMES! TO A STANDSTILL!
YOU CAN TELL HIM I SAID THAT! THAT'S RIGHT, QUEEN-- I'M TALKIN' *BATMAN!*
VVVWPPP
NOW WHATTAYA GONNA DO ABOU--
OH, GOD-- *NOOOO!*
BON MATIN, MONSIEUR BLAKE.
AAAAHH!

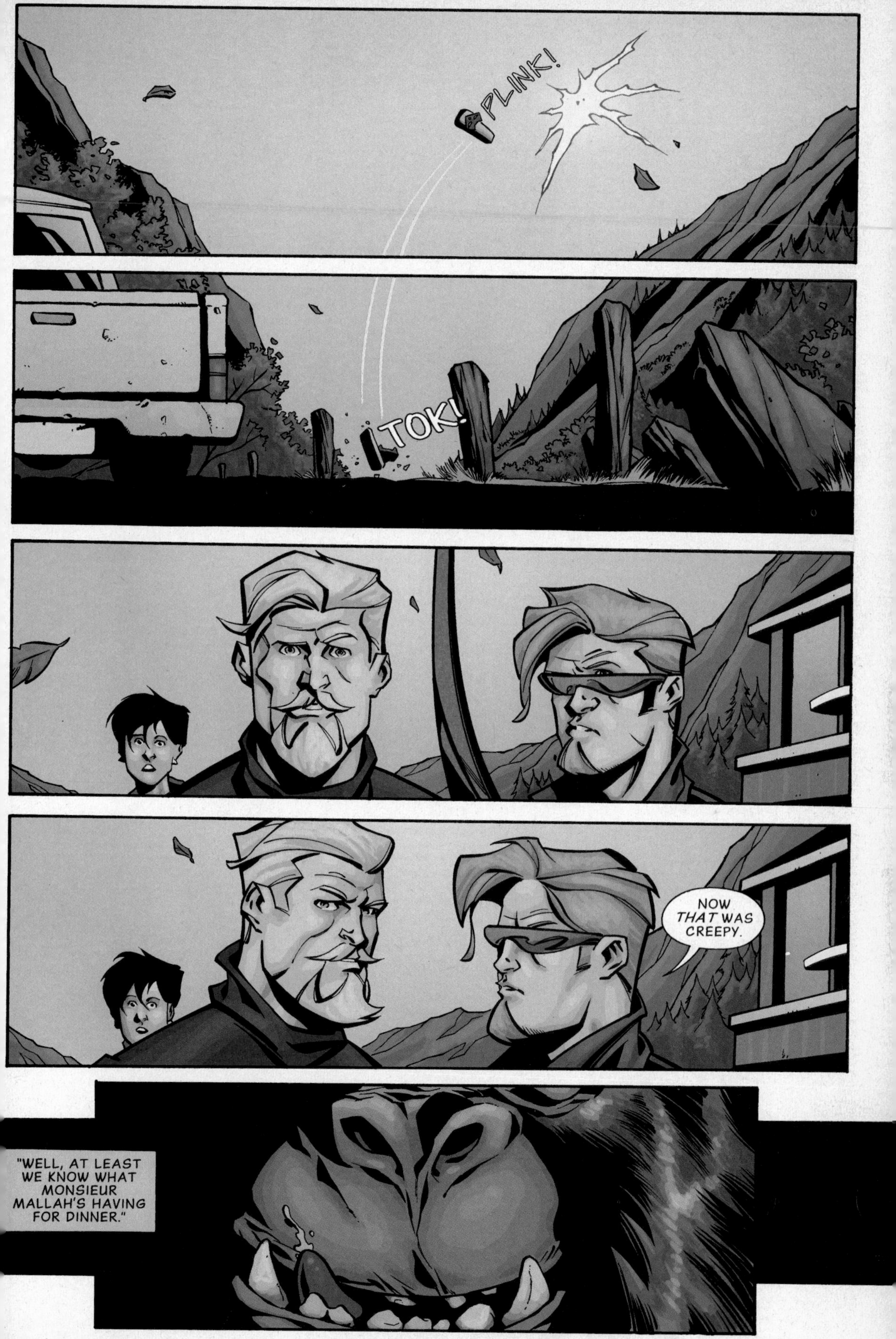
PLINK!
TOK!
NOW THAT WAS CREEPY.
"WELL, AT LEAST WE KNOW WHAT MONSIEUR MALLAH'S HAVING FOR DINNER."

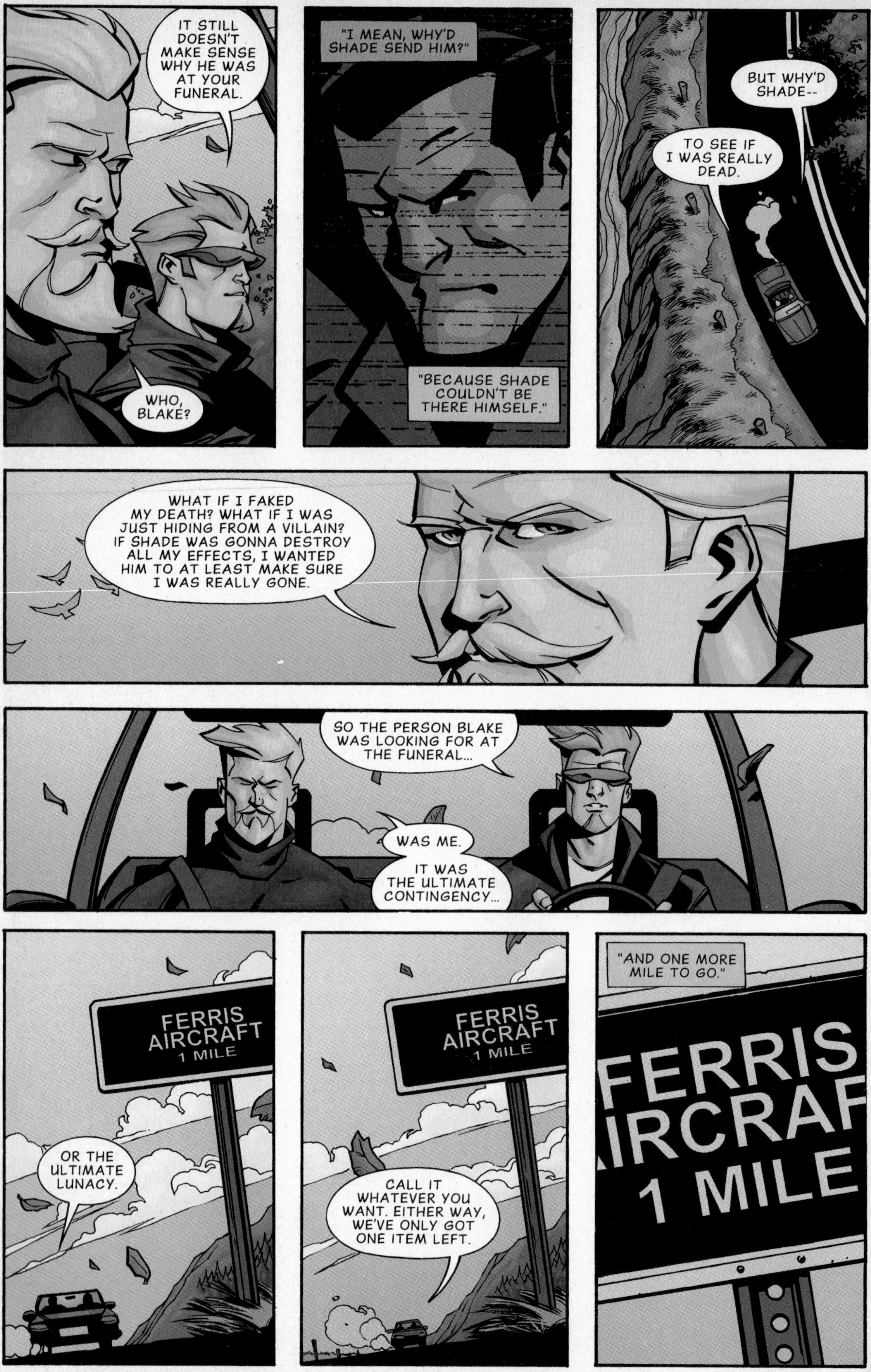
IT STILL DOESN'T MAKE SENSE WHY HE WAS AT YOUR FUNERAL.
WHO, BLAKE?
"I MEAN, WHY'D SHADE SEND HIM?"
"BECAUSE SHADE COULDN'T BE THERE HIMSELF."
BUT WHY'D SHADE--
TO SEE IF I WAS REALLY DEAD.
WHAT IF I FAKED MY DEATH? WHAT IF I WAS JUST HIDING FROM A VILLAIN? IF SHADE WAS GONNA DESTROY ALL MY EFFECTS, I WANTED HIM TO AT LEAST MAKE SURE I WAS REALLY GONE.
SO THE PERSON BLAKE WAS LOOKING FOR AT THE FUNERAL...
WAS ME.
IT WAS THE ULTIMATE CONTINGENCY...
FERRIS AIRCRAFT 1 MILE
OR THE ULTIMATE LUNACY.
FERRIS AIRCRAFT 1 MILE
CALL IT WHATEVER YOU WANT. EITHER WAY, WE'VE ONLY GOT ONE ITEM LEFT.
"AND ONE MORE MILE TO GO."
FERRIS AIRCRAF 1 MILE

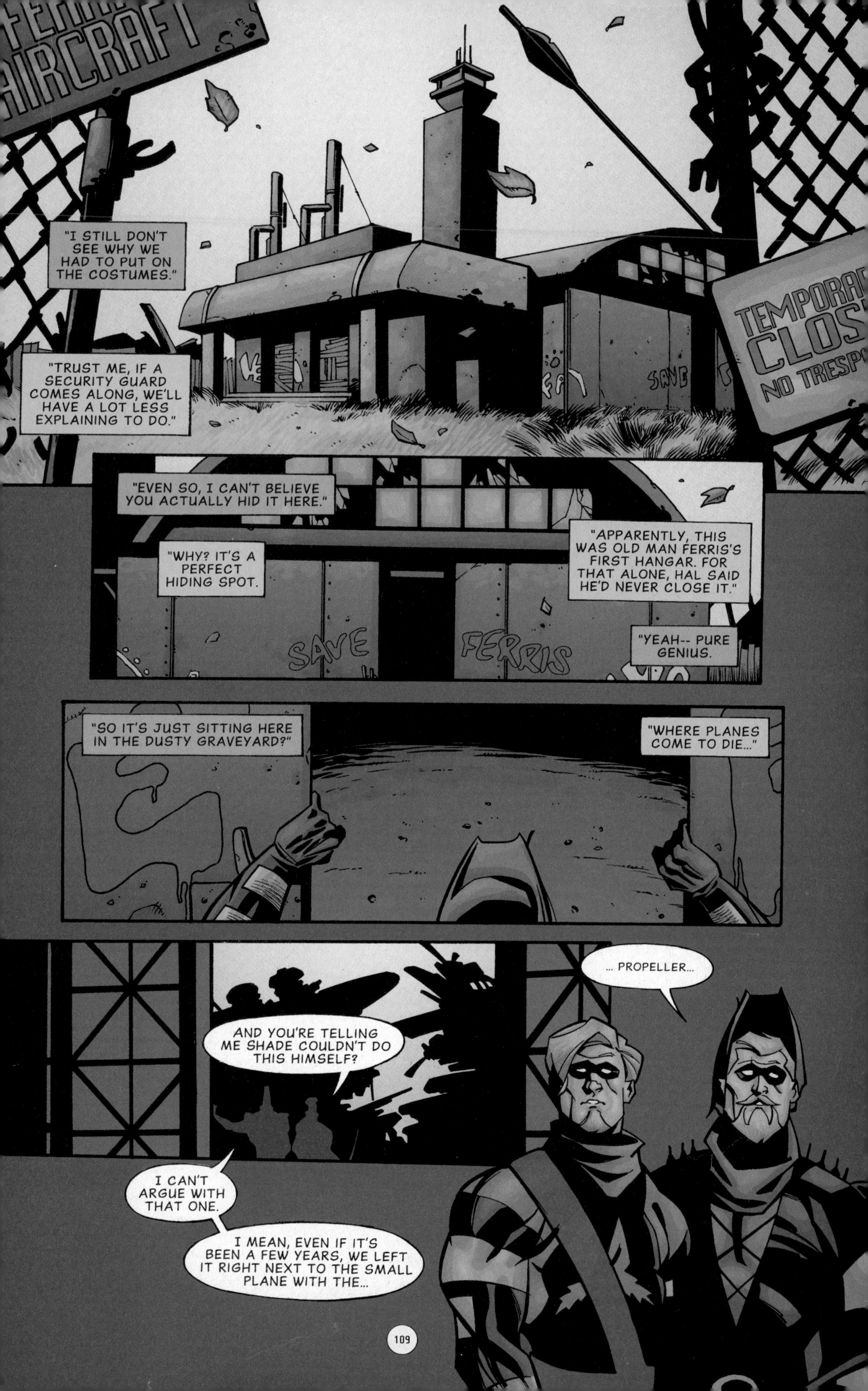
AIRCRAFT
"I STILL DON'T SEE WHY WE HAD TO PUT ON THE COSTUMES."
"TRUST ME, IF A SECURITY GUARD COMES ALONG, WE'LL HAVE A LOT LESS EXPLAINING TO DO."
SAVE
TEMPORAR CLOS NO TRESP
"EVEN SO, I CAN'T BELIEVE YOU ACTUALLY HID IT HERE."
"WHY? IT'S A PERFECT HIDING SPOT.
"APPARENTLY, THIS WAS OLD MAN FERRIS'S FIRST HANGAR. FOR THAT ALONE, HAL SAID HE'D NEVER CLOSE IT."
"YEAH-- PURE GENIUS.
SAVE FERRIS
"SO IT'S JUST SITTING HERE IN THE DUSTY GRAVEYARD?"
"WHERE PLANES COME TO DIE..."
AND YOU'RE TELLING ME SHADE COULDN'T DO THIS HIMSELF?
I CAN'T ARGUE WITH THAT ONE.
I MEAN, EVEN IF IT'S BEEN A FEW YEARS, WE LEFT IT RIGHT NEXT TO THE SMALL PLANE WITH THE...
... PROPELLER...

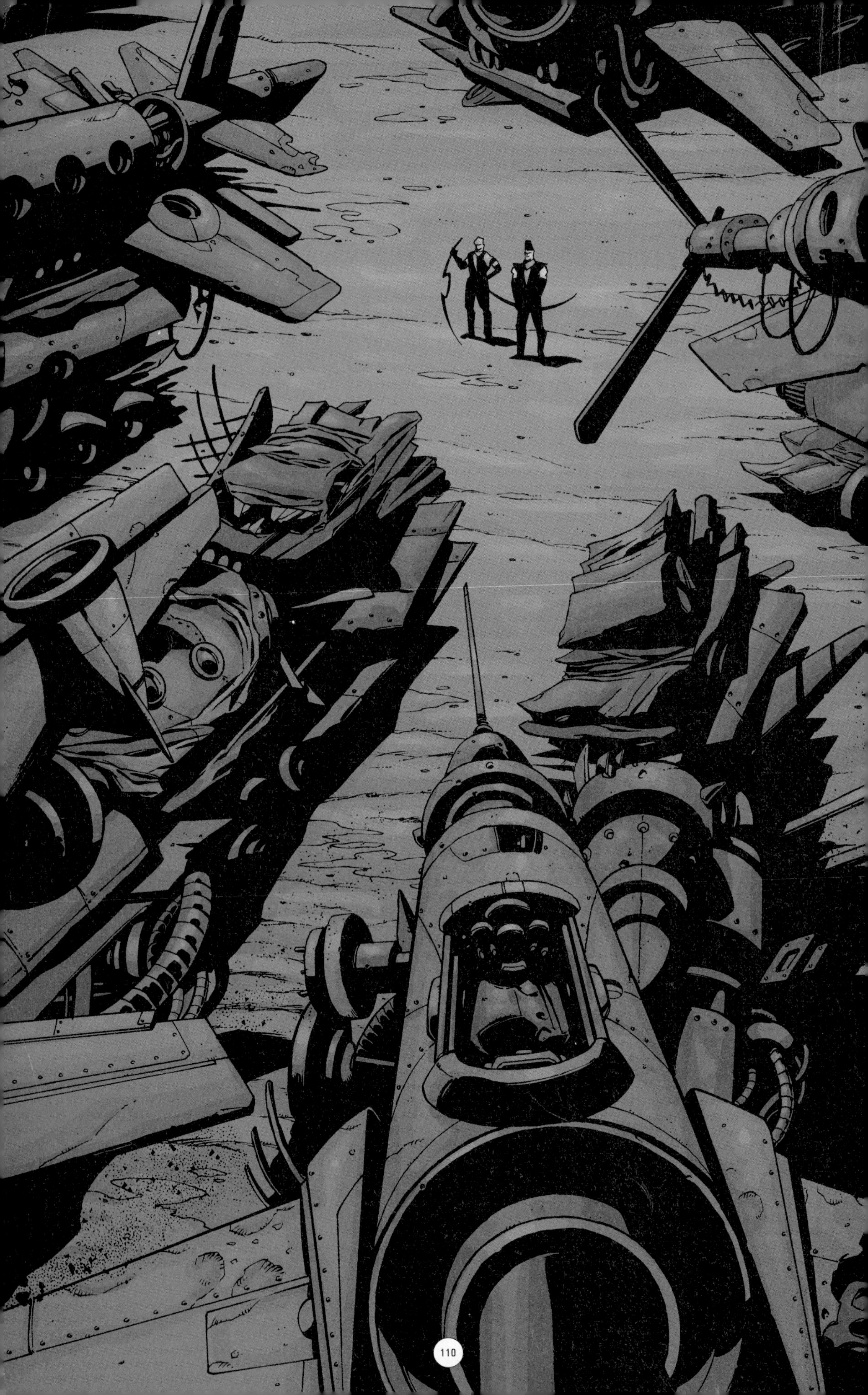

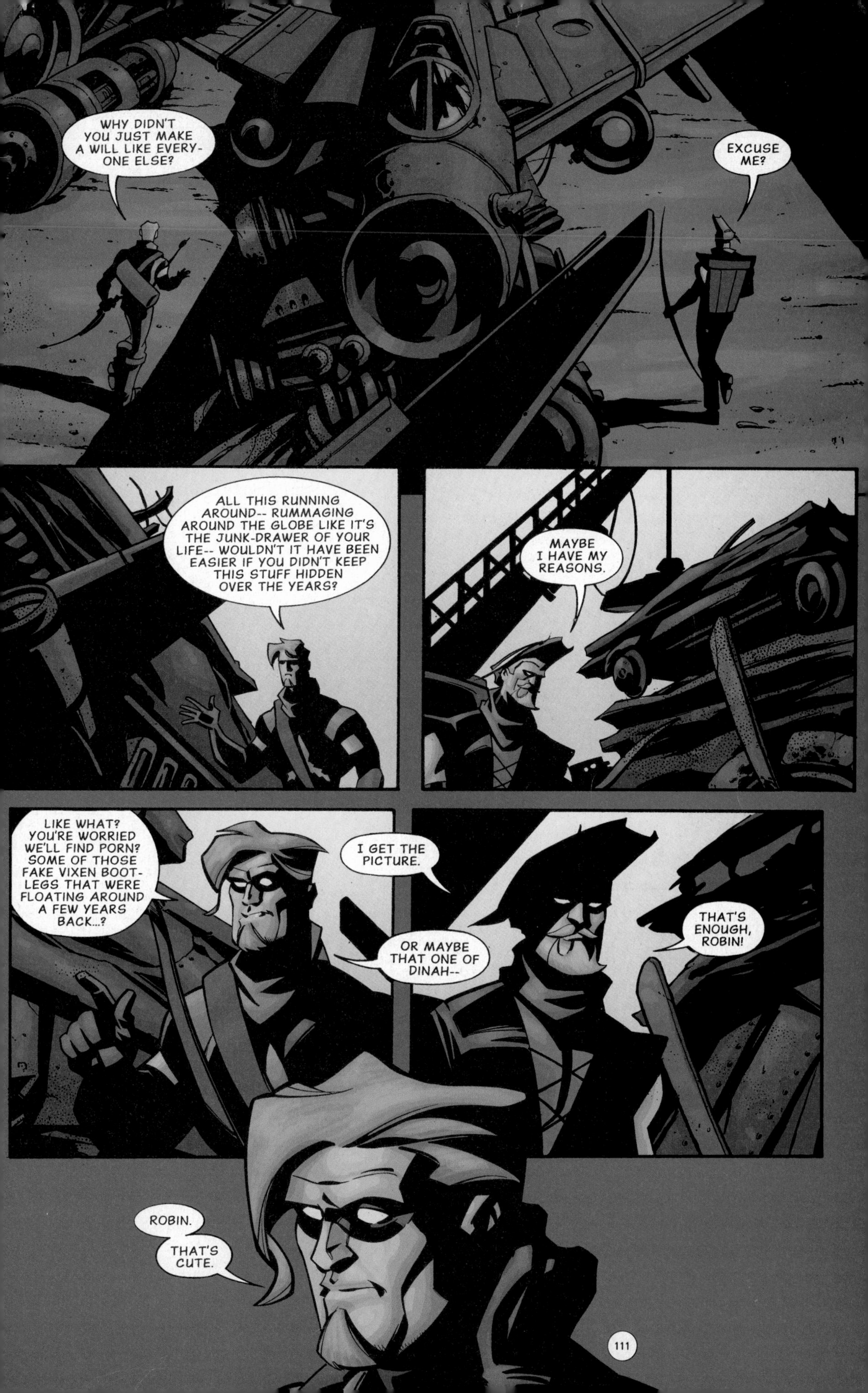
WHY DIDN'T YOU JUST MAKE A WILL LIKE EVERY-ONE ELSE?
EXCUSE ME?
ALL THIS RUNNING AROUND-- RUMMAGING AROUND THE GLOBE LIKE IT'S THE JUNK-DRAWER OF YOUR LIFE-- WOULDN'T IT HAVE BEEN EASIER IF YOU DIDN'T KEEP THIS STUFF HIDDEN OVER THE YEARS?
MAYBE I HAVE MY REASONS.
LIKE WHAT? YOU'RE WORRIED WE'LL FIND PORN? SOME OF THOSE FAKE VIXEN BOOT-LEGS THAT WERE FLOATING AROUND A FEW YEARS BACK...?
I GET THE PICTURE.
OR MAYBE THAT ONE OF DINAH--
THAT'S ENOUGH, ROBIN!
ROBIN.
THAT'S CUTE.

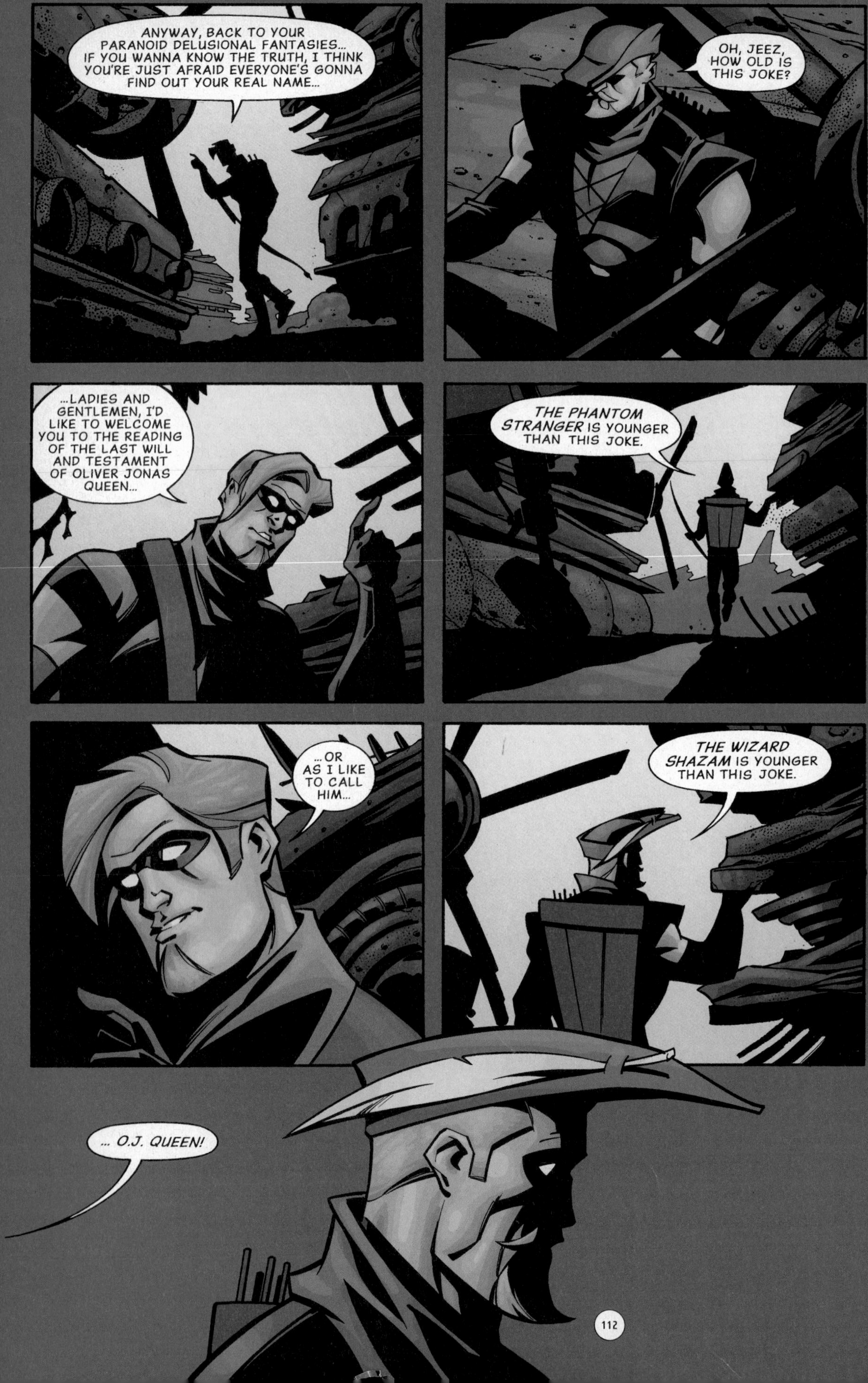

ANYWAY, BACK TO YOUR PARANOID DELUSIONAL FANTASIES... IF YOU WANNA KNOW THE TRUTH, I THINK YOU'RE JUST AFRAID EVERYONE'S GONNA FIND OUT YOUR REAL NAME...
OH, JEEZ, HOW OLD IS THIS JOKE?
...LADIES AND GENTLEMEN, I'D LIKE TO WELCOME YOU TO THE READING OF THE LAST WILL AND TESTAMENT OF OLIVER JONAS QUEEN...
THE PHANTOM STRANGER IS YOUNGER THAN THIS JOKE.
...OR AS I LIKE TO CALL HIM...
THE WIZARD SHAZAM IS YOUNGER THAN THIS JOKE.
... O.J. QUEEN!

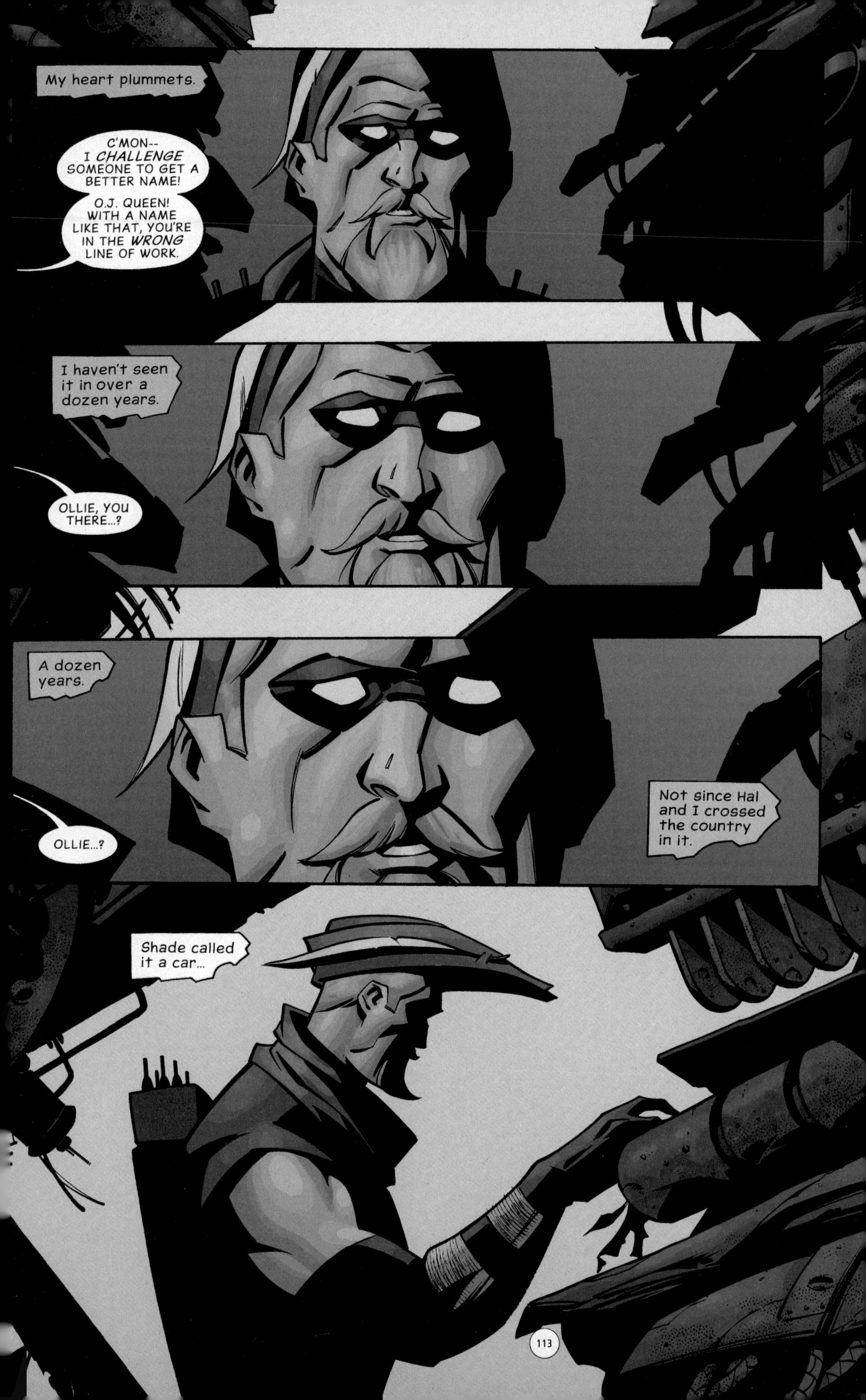
My heart plummets.
C'MON-- I *CHALLENGE* SOMEONE TO GET A BETTER NAME!
O.J. QUEEN! WITH A NAME LIKE THAT, YOU'RE IN THE *WRONG* LINE OF WORK.
I haven't seen it in over a dozen years.
OLLIE, YOU THERE...?
A dozen years.
OLLIE...?
Not since Hal and I crossed the country in it.
Shade called it a car...

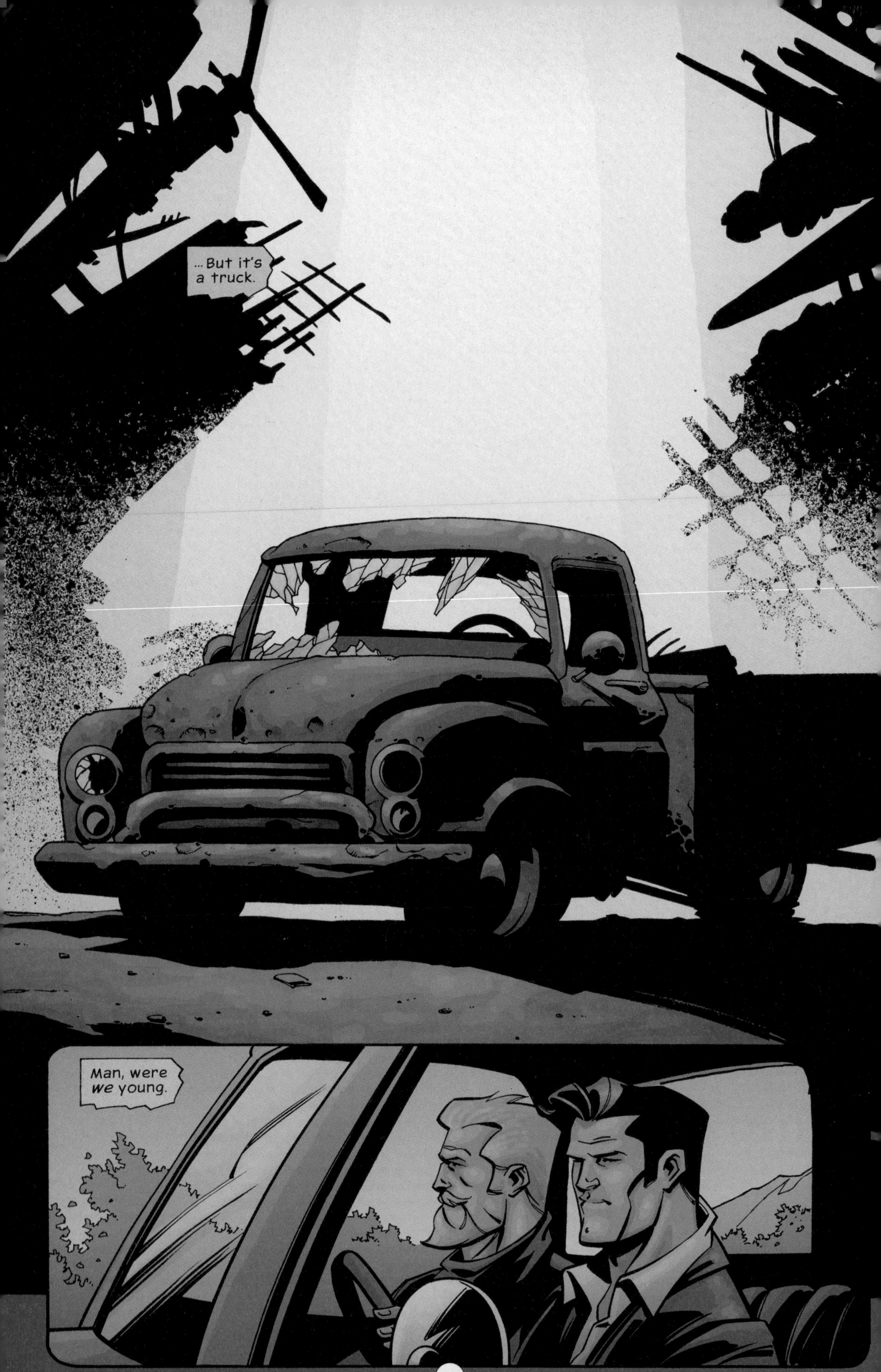
...But it's a truck.
Man, were *we* young.

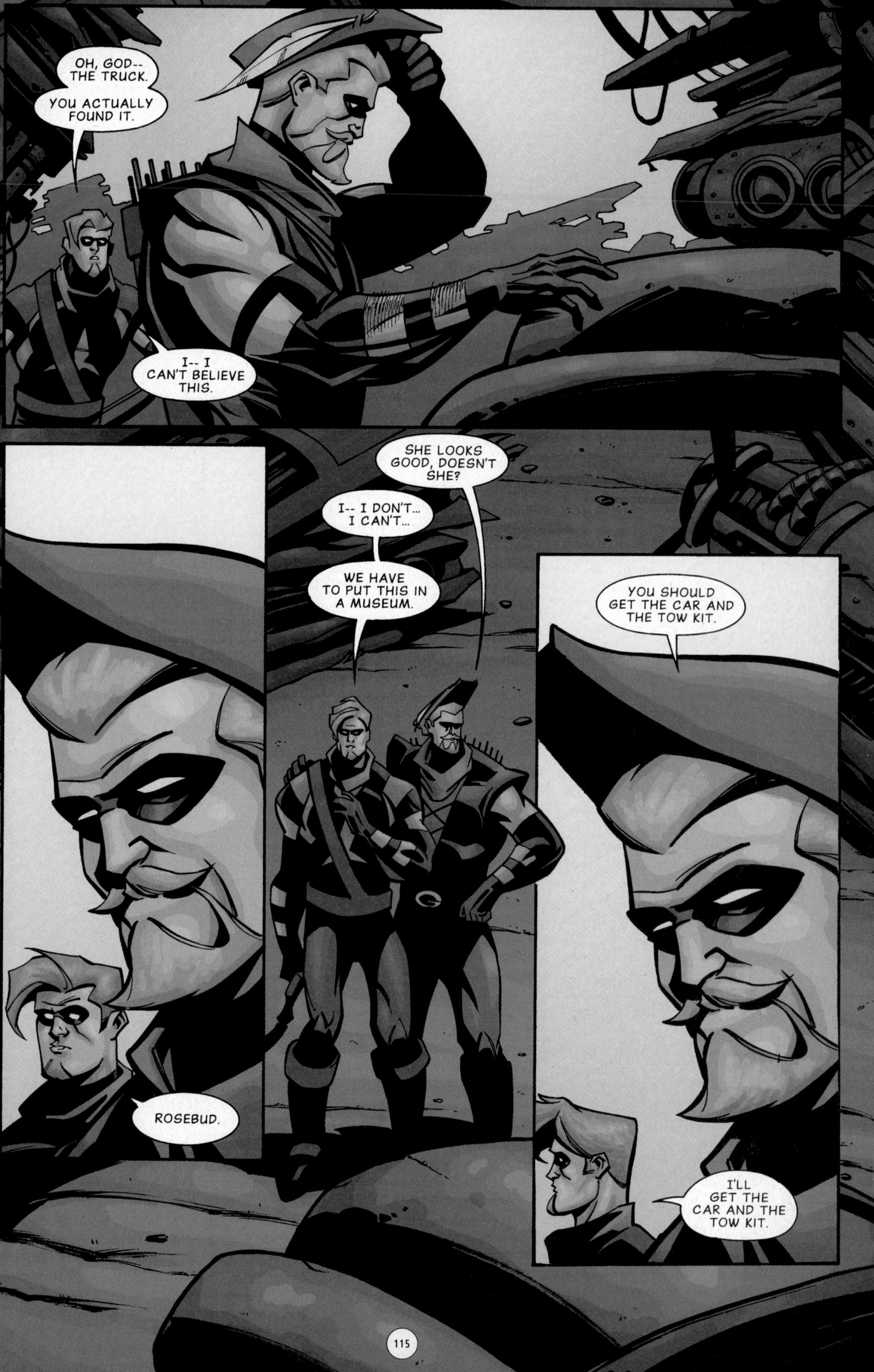
OH, GOD-- THE TRUCK.
YOU ACTUALLY FOUND IT.
I-- I CAN'T BELIEVE THIS.
ROSEBUD.
SHE LOOKS GOOD, DOESN'T SHE?
I-- I DON'T... I CAN'T...
WE HAVE TO PUT THIS IN A MUSEUM.
YOU SHOULD GET THE CAR AND THE TOW KIT.
I'LL GET THE CAR AND THE TOW KIT.

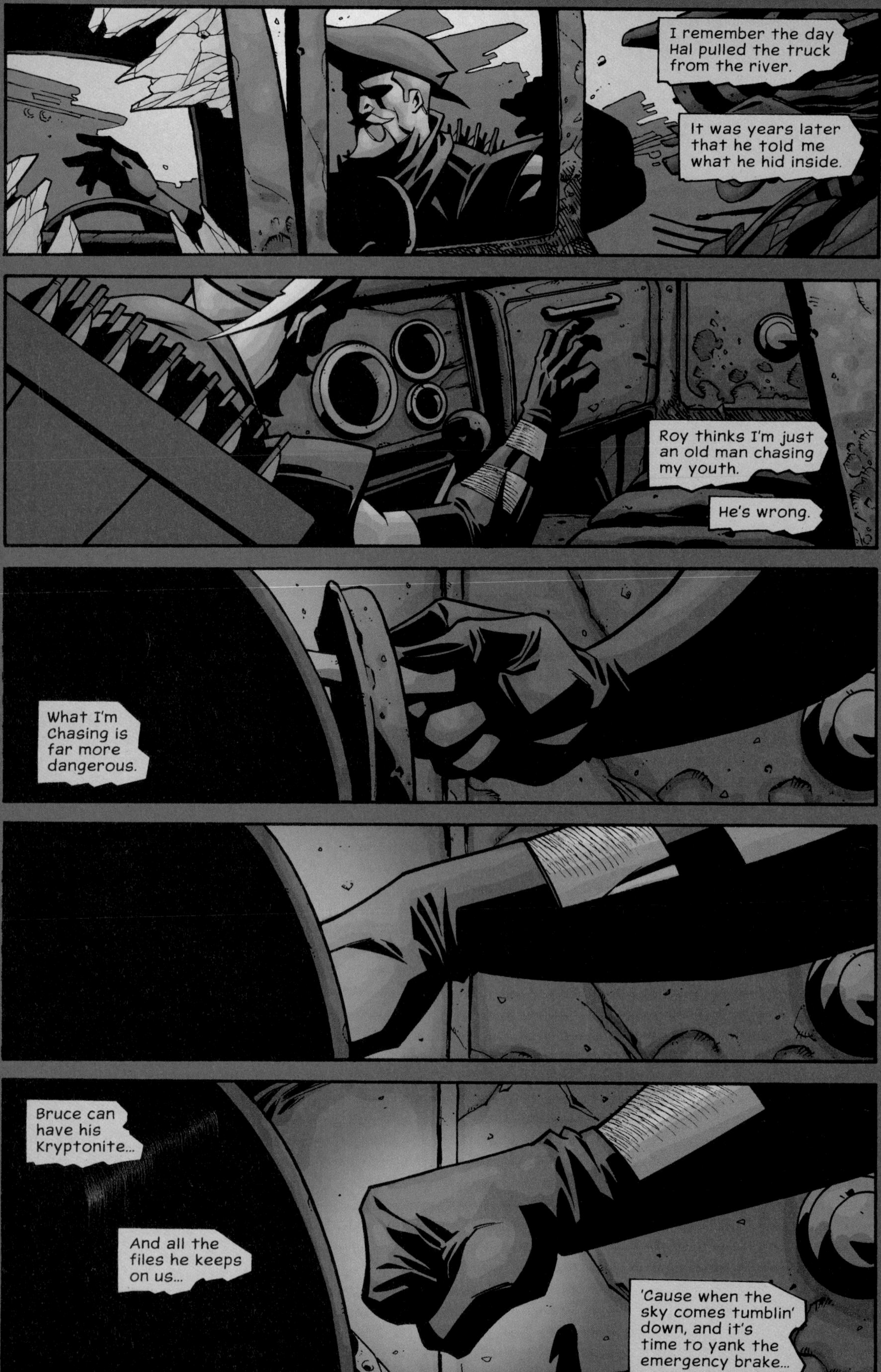
I remember the day Hal pulled the truck from the river.
It was years later that he told me what he hid inside.
Roy thinks I'm just an old man chasing my youth.
He's wrong.
What I'm Chasing is far more dangerous.
Bruce can have his Kryptonite...
And all the files he keeps on us...
'Cause when the sky comes tumblin' down, and it's time to yank the emergency brake...

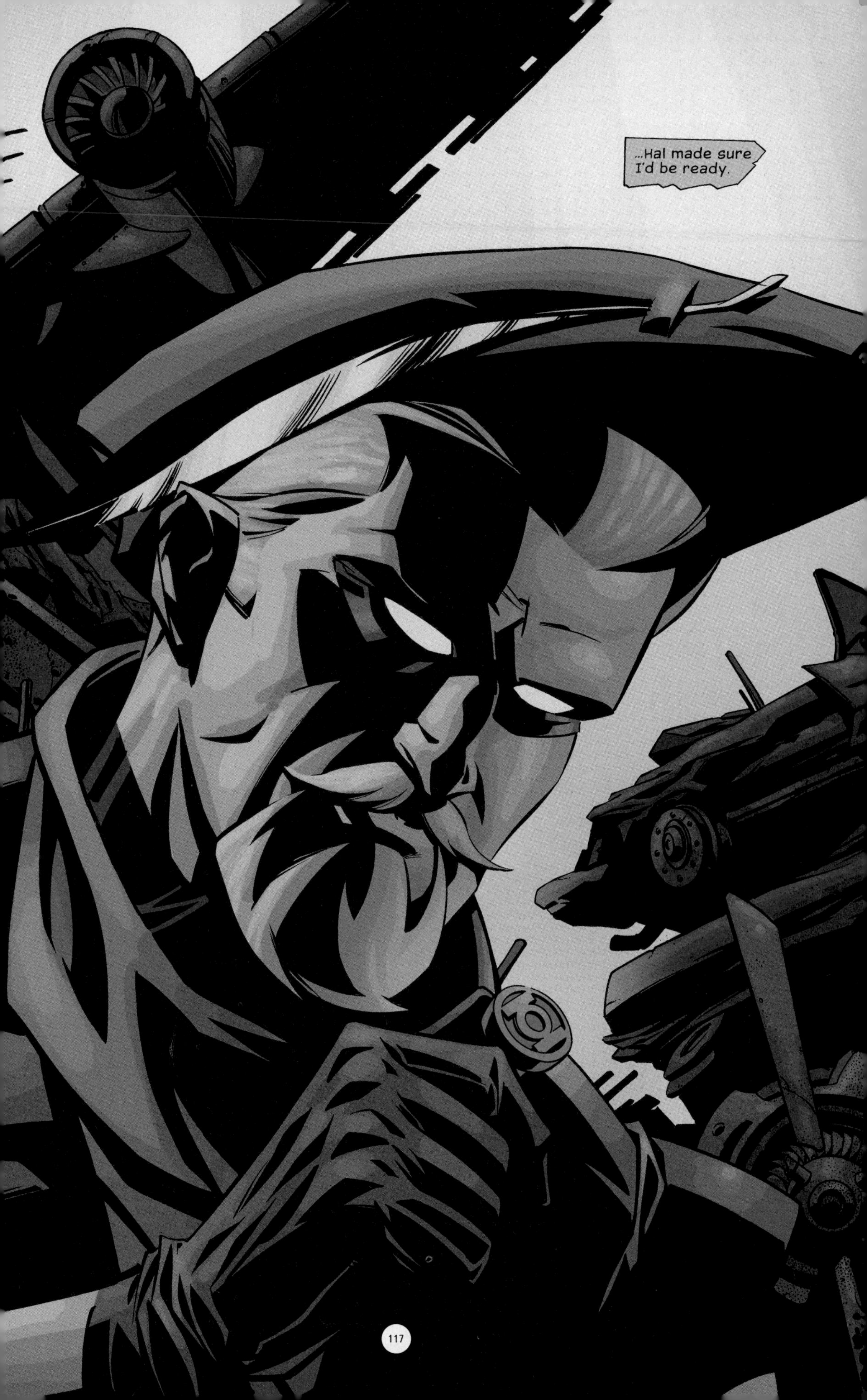
...Hal made sure I'd be ready.

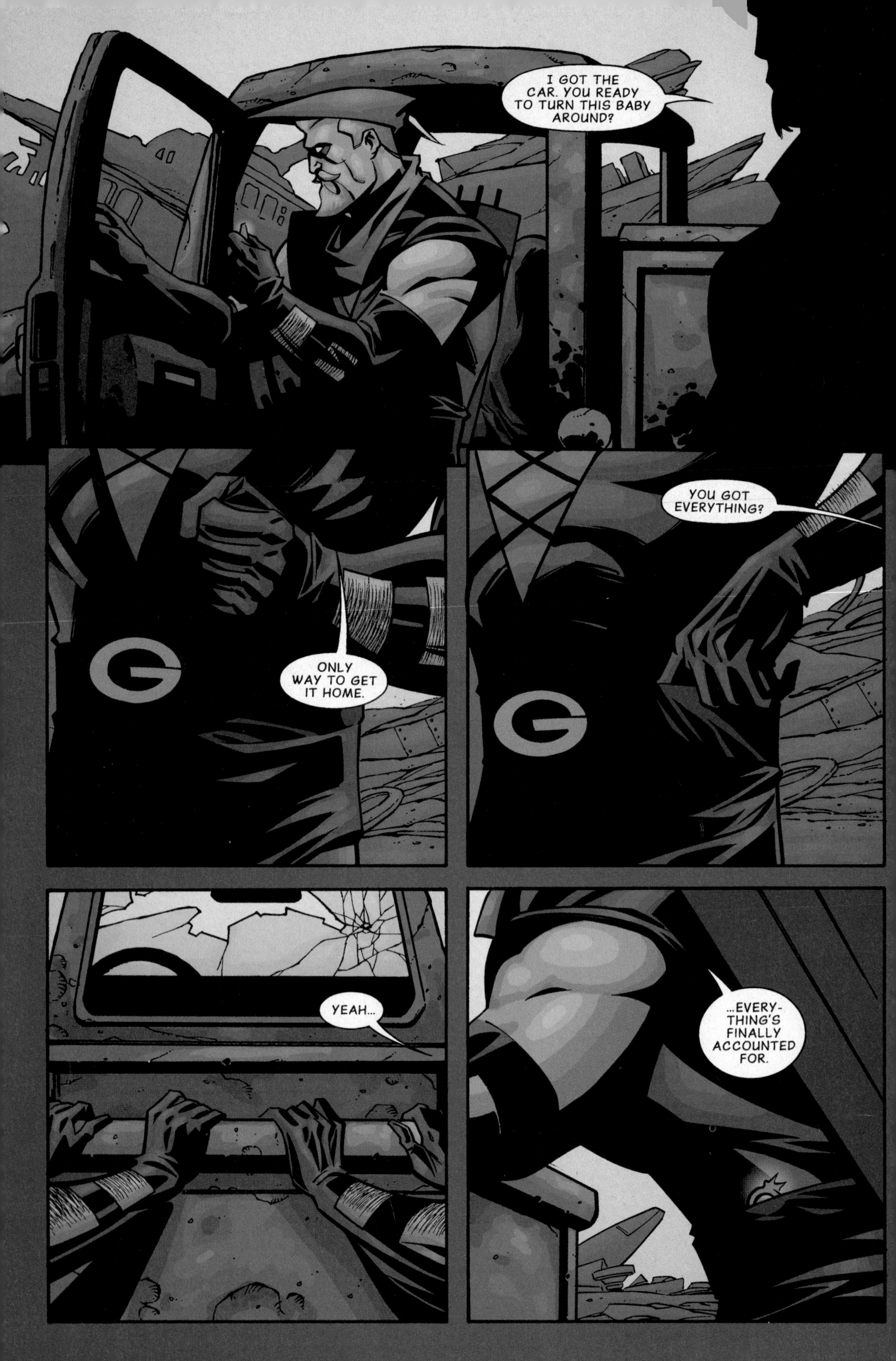

I GOT THE CAR. YOU READY TO TURN THIS BABY AROUND?
ONLY WAY TO GET IT HOME.
YOU GOT EVERYTHING?
YEAH...
...EVERY-THING'S FINALLY ACCOUNTED FOR.

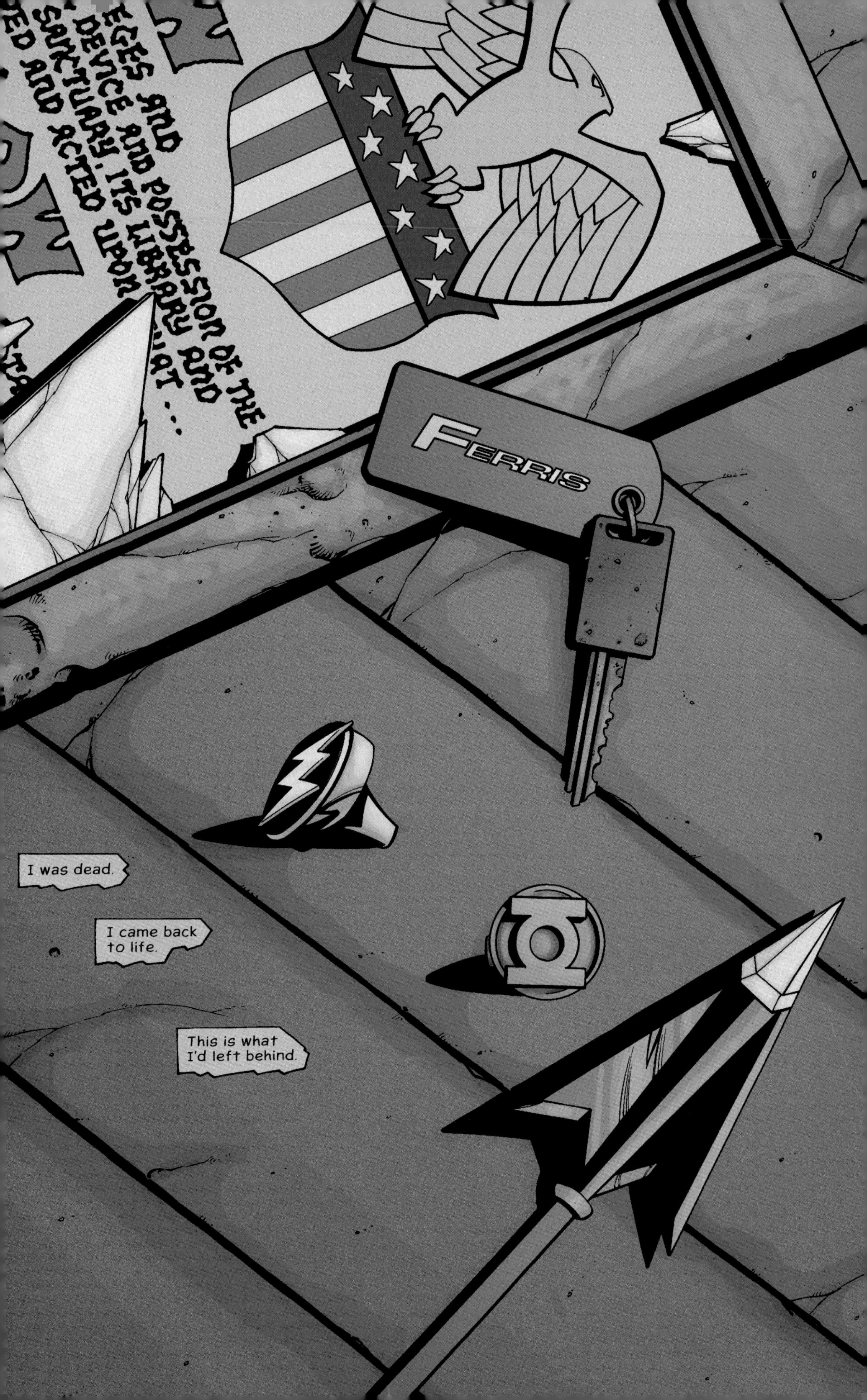
EGES AND
DEVICE AND POSSESSION OF THE
SANCTUARY. ITS LIBRARY AND
ED AND ACTED UPON
FERRIS
I was dead.
I came back to life.
This is what I'd left behind.

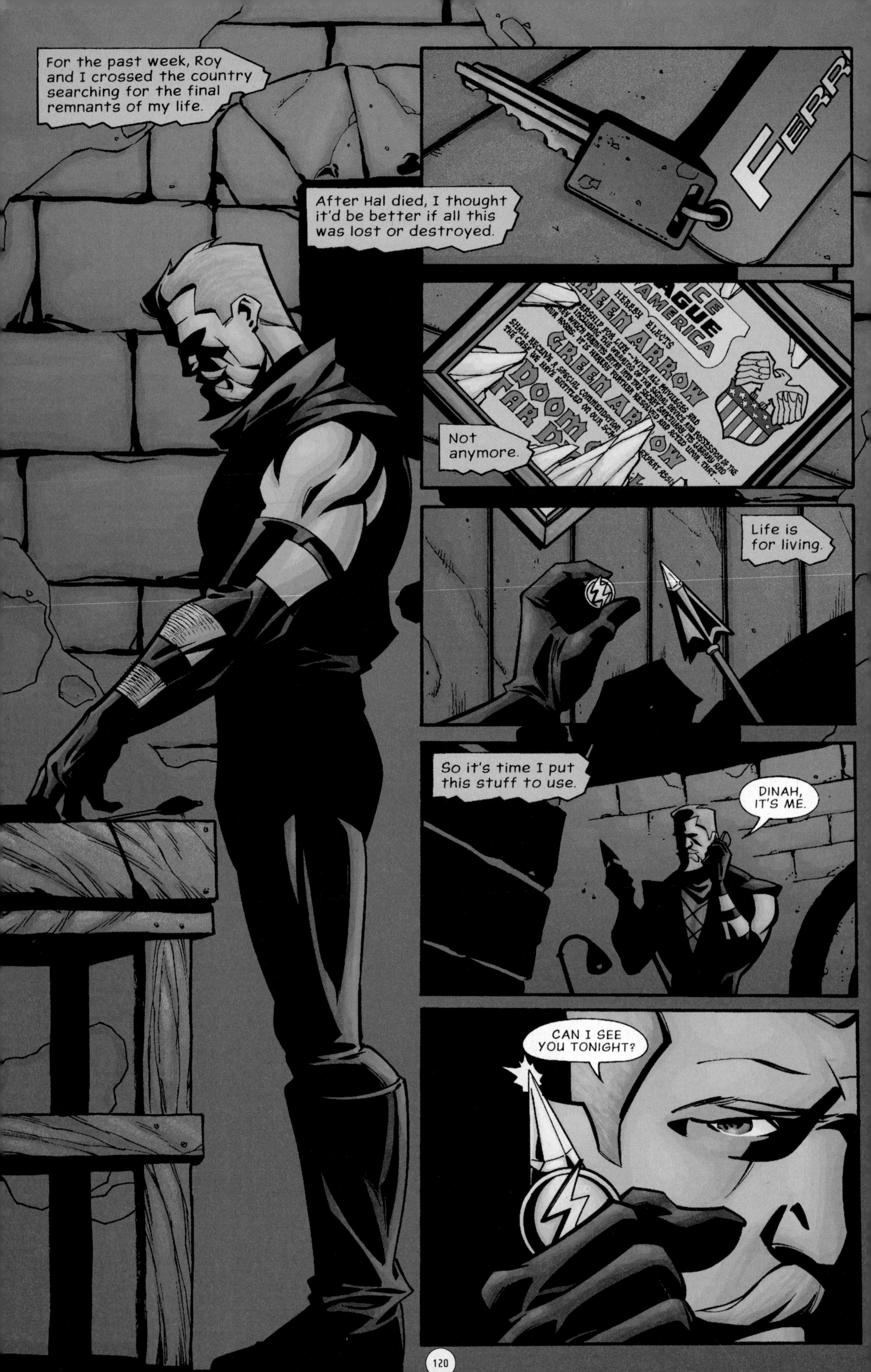
For the past week, Roy and I crossed the country searching for the final remnants of my life.
After Hal died, I thought it'd be better if all this was lost or destroyed.
Not anymore.
Life is for living.
So it's time I put this stuff to use.
DINAH, IT'S ME.
CAN I SEE YOU TONIGHT?

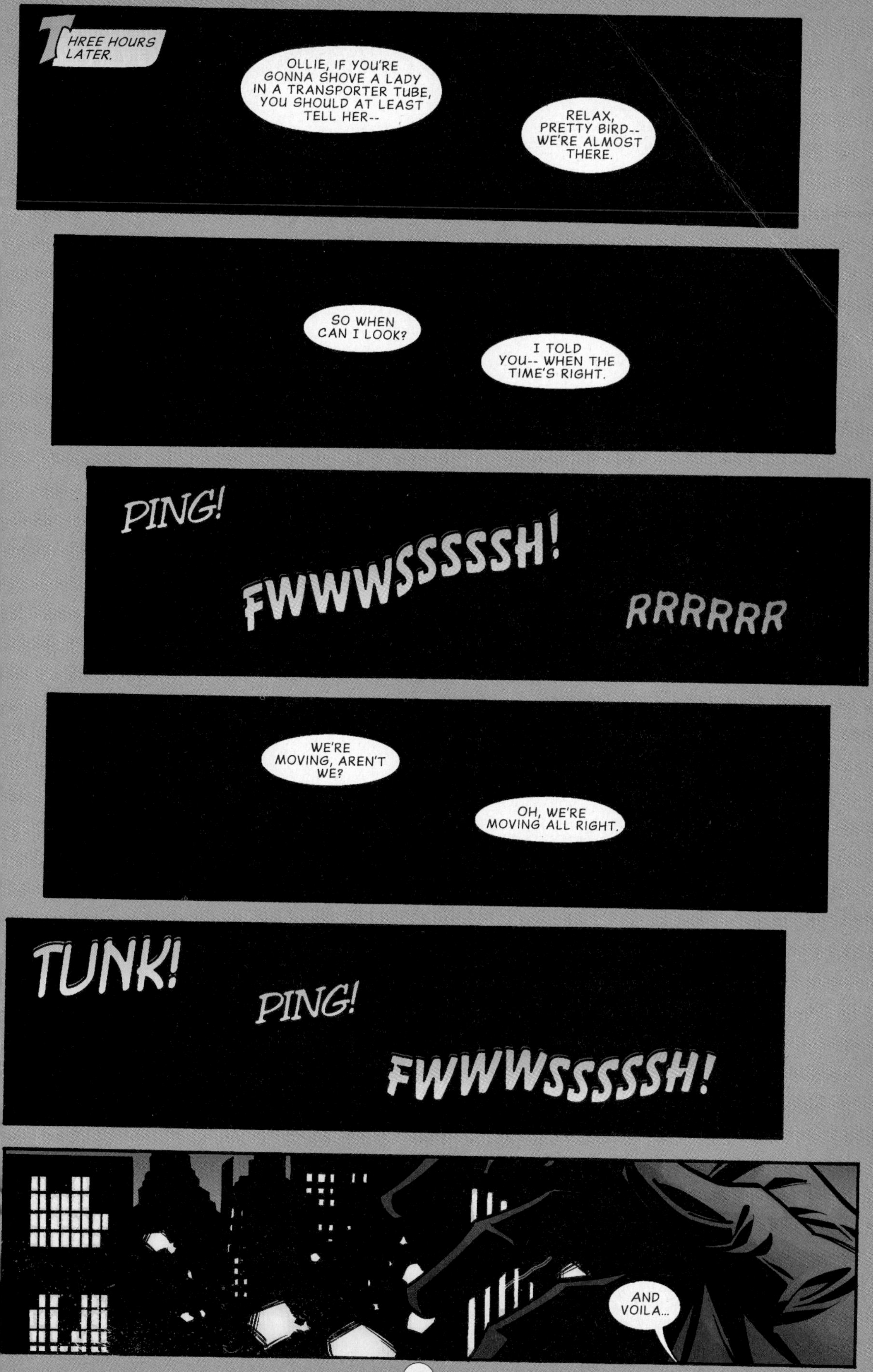
THREE HOURS LATER.
OLLIE, IF YOU'RE GONNA SHOVE A LADY IN A TRANSPORTER TUBE, YOU SHOULD AT LEAST TELL HER--
RELAX, PRETTY BIRD-- WE'RE ALMOST THERE.
SO WHEN CAN I LOOK?
I TOLD YOU-- WHEN THE TIME'S RIGHT.
PING!
FWWWSSSSSH!
RRRRRR
WE'RE MOVING, AREN'T WE?
OH, WE'RE MOVING ALL RIGHT.
TUNK!
PING!
FWWWSSSSSH!
AND VOILA...

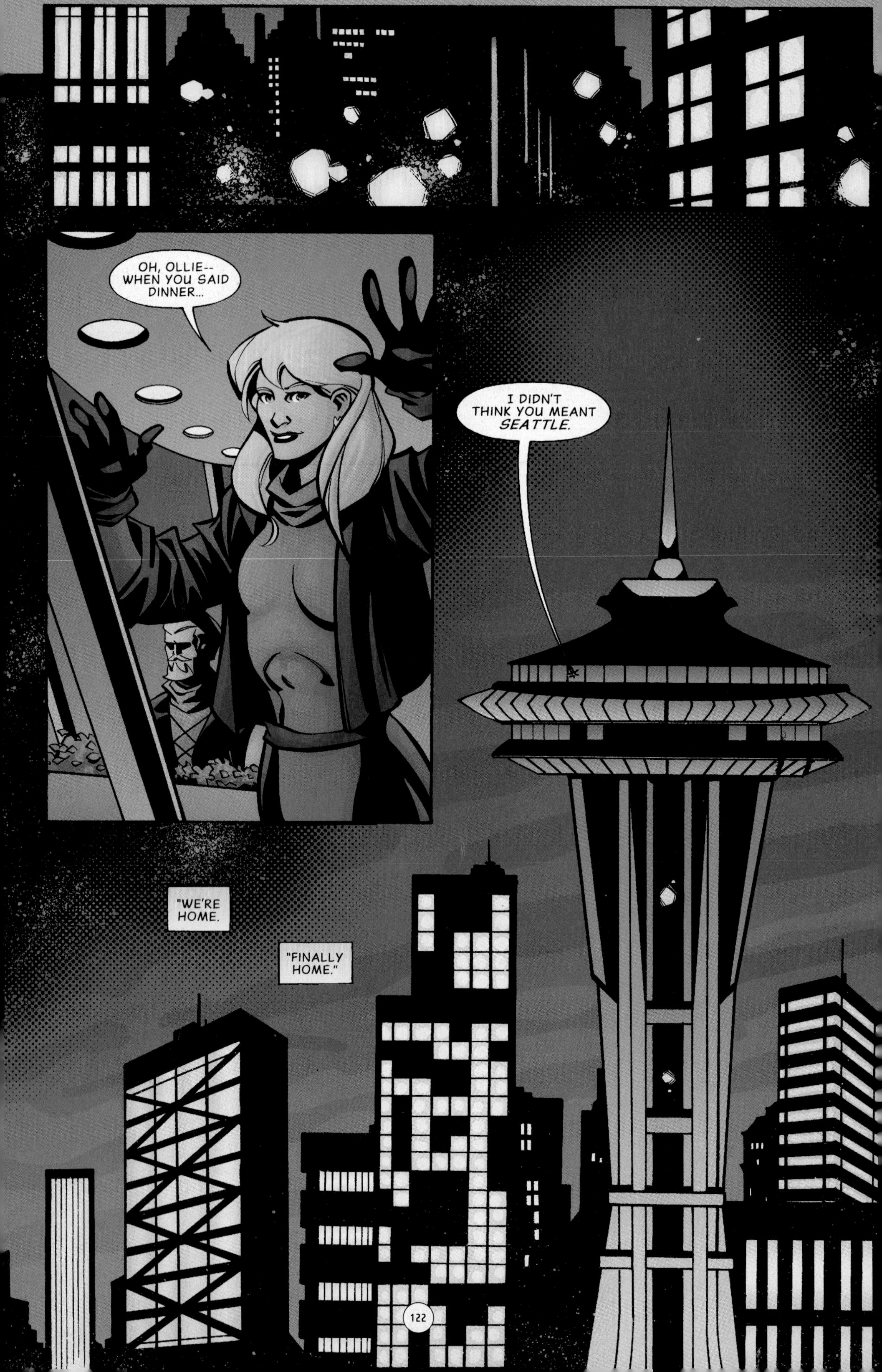

OH, OLLIE--
WHEN YOU SAID
DINNER...
I DIDN'T
THINK YOU MEANT
SEATTLE.
"WE'RE
HOME.
"FINALLY
HOME."

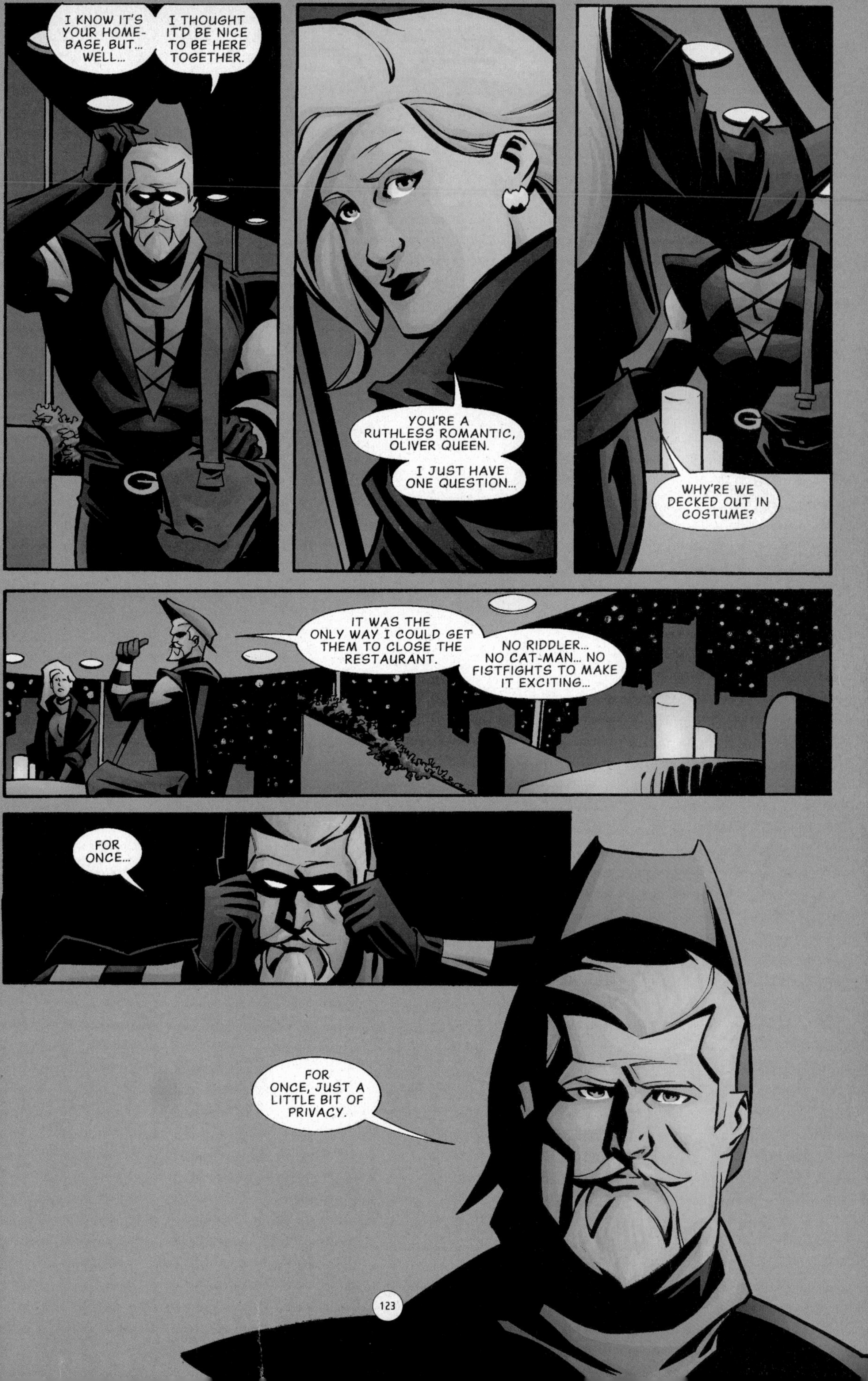
I KNOW IT'S YOUR HOME-BASE, BUT... WELL...
I THOUGHT IT'D BE NICE TO BE HERE TOGETHER.
YOU'RE A RUTHLESS ROMANTIC, OLIVER QUEEN.
I JUST HAVE ONE QUESTION...
WHY'RE WE DECKED OUT IN COSTUME?
IT WAS THE ONLY WAY I COULD GET THEM TO CLOSE THE RESTAURANT.
NO RIDDLER... NO CAT-MAN... NO FISTFIGHTS TO MAKE IT EXCITING...
FOR ONCE...
FOR ONCE, JUST A LITTLE BIT OF PRIVACY.

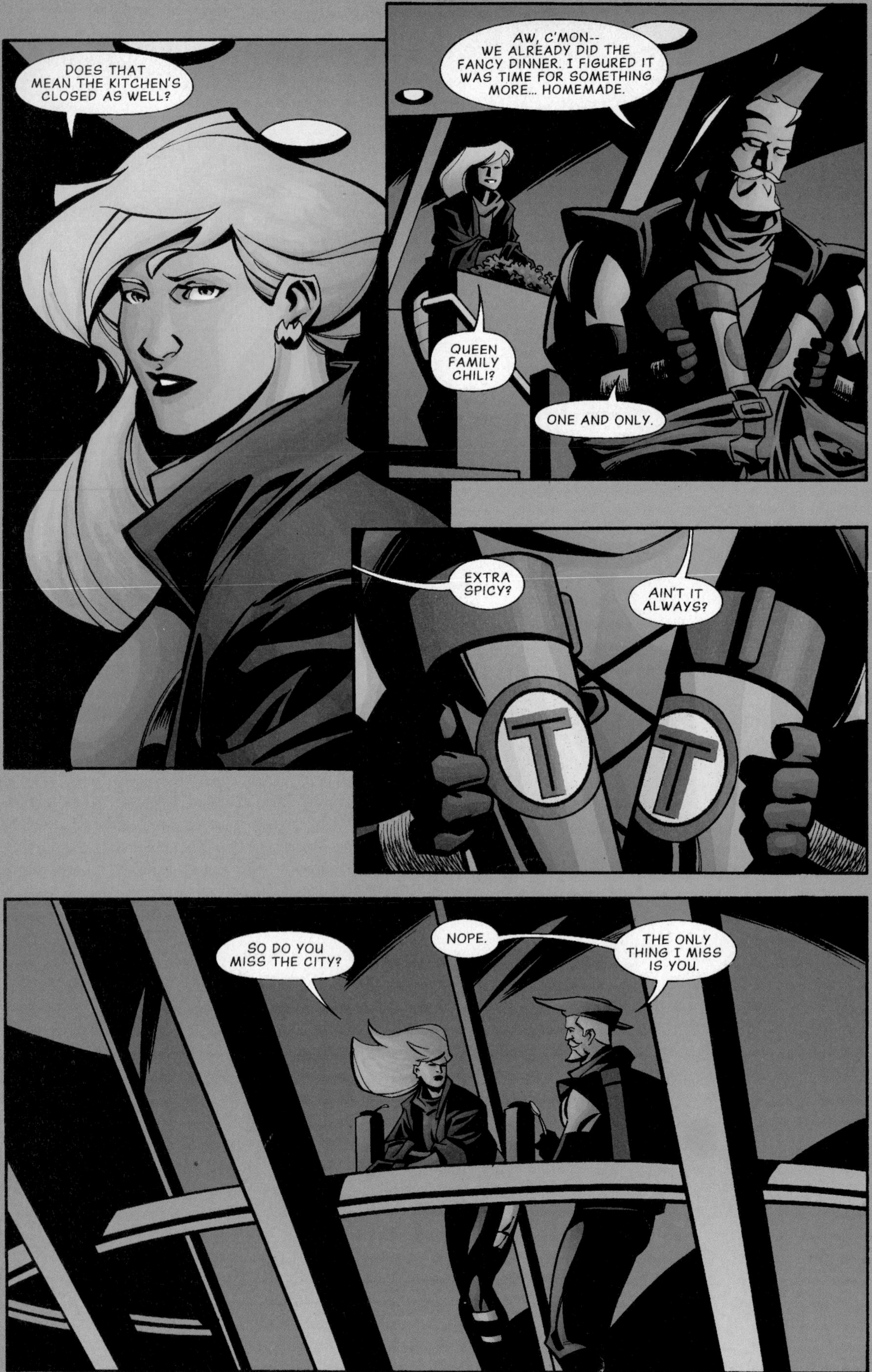
DOES THAT MEAN THE KITCHEN'S CLOSED AS WELL?
AW, C'MON-- WE ALREADY DID THE FANCY DINNER. I FIGURED IT WAS TIME FOR SOMETHING MORE... HOMEMADE.
QUEEN FAMILY CHILI?
ONE AND ONLY.
EXTRA SPICY?
AIN'T IT ALWAYS?
SO DO YOU MISS THE CITY?
NOPE.
THE ONLY THING I MISS IS YOU.

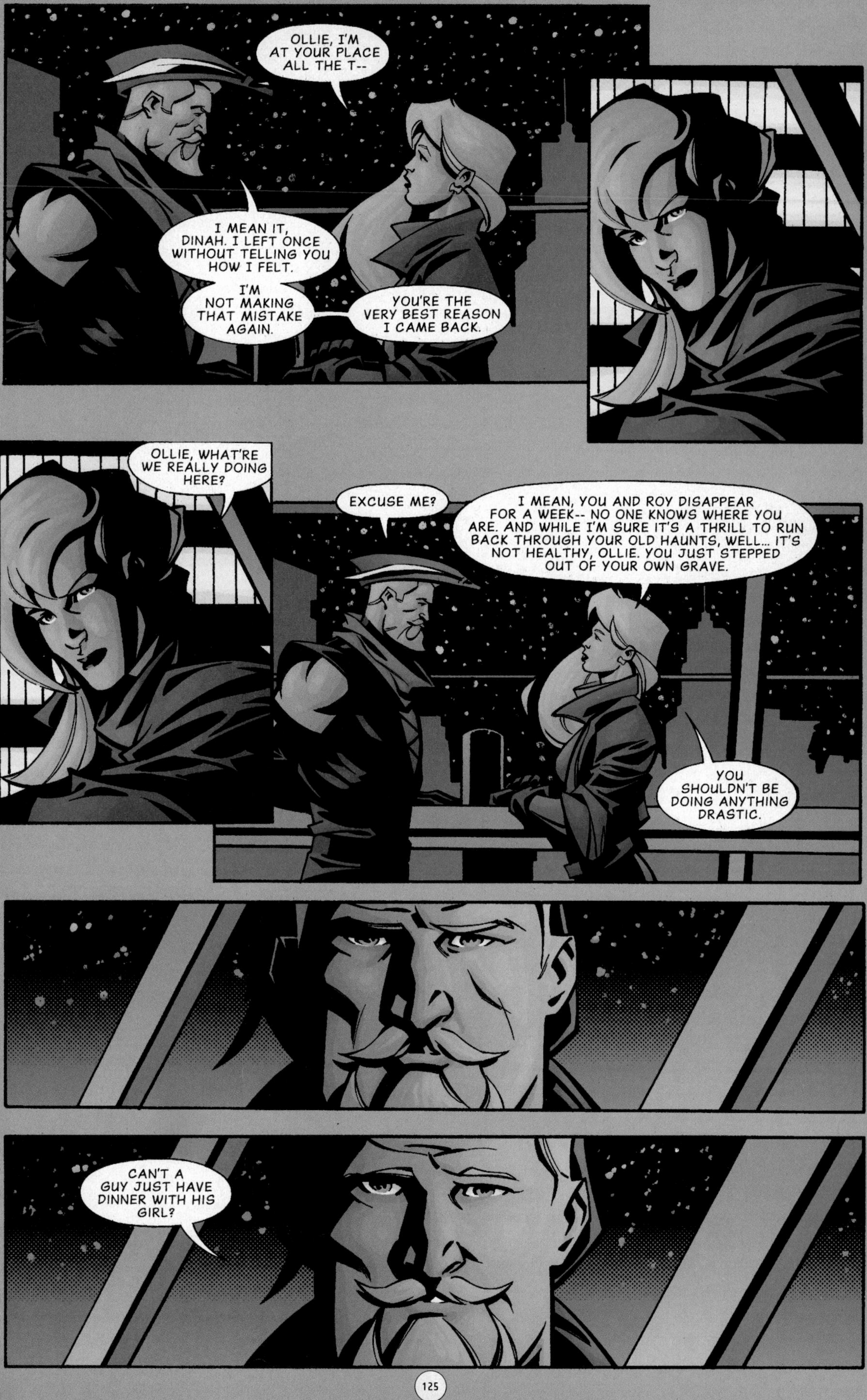
OLLIE, I'M AT YOUR PLACE ALL THE T--
I MEAN IT, DINAH. I LEFT ONCE WITHOUT TELLING YOU HOW I FELT.
I'M NOT MAKING THAT MISTAKE AGAIN.
YOU'RE THE VERY BEST REASON I CAME BACK.
OLLIE, WHAT'RE WE REALLY DOING HERE?
EXCUSE ME?
I MEAN, YOU AND ROY DISAPPEAR FOR A WEEK-- NO ONE KNOWS WHERE YOU ARE. AND WHILE I'M SURE IT'S A THRILL TO RUN BACK THROUGH YOUR OLD HAUNTS, WELL... IT'S NOT HEALTHY, OLLIE. YOU JUST STEPPED OUT OF YOUR OWN GRAVE.
YOU SHOULDN'T BE DOING ANYTHING DRASTIC.
CAN'T A GUY JUST HAVE DINNER WITH HIS GIRL?

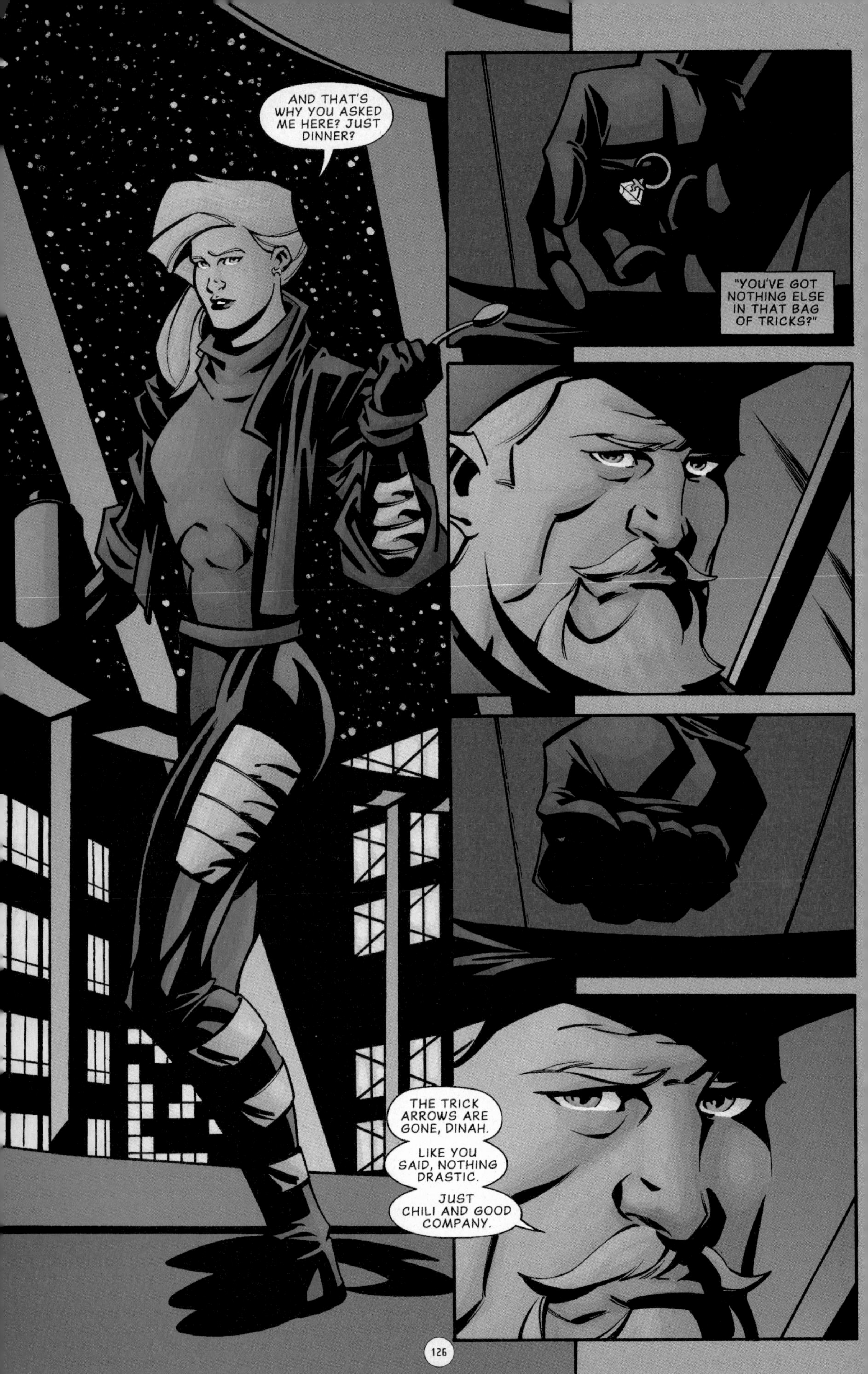
AND THAT'S WHY YOU ASKED ME HERE? JUST DINNER?
"YOU'VE GOT NOTHING ELSE IN THAT BAG OF TRICKS?"
THE TRICK ARROWS ARE GONE, DINAH.
LIKE YOU SAID, NOTHING DRASTIC.
JUST CHILI AND GOOD COMPANY.

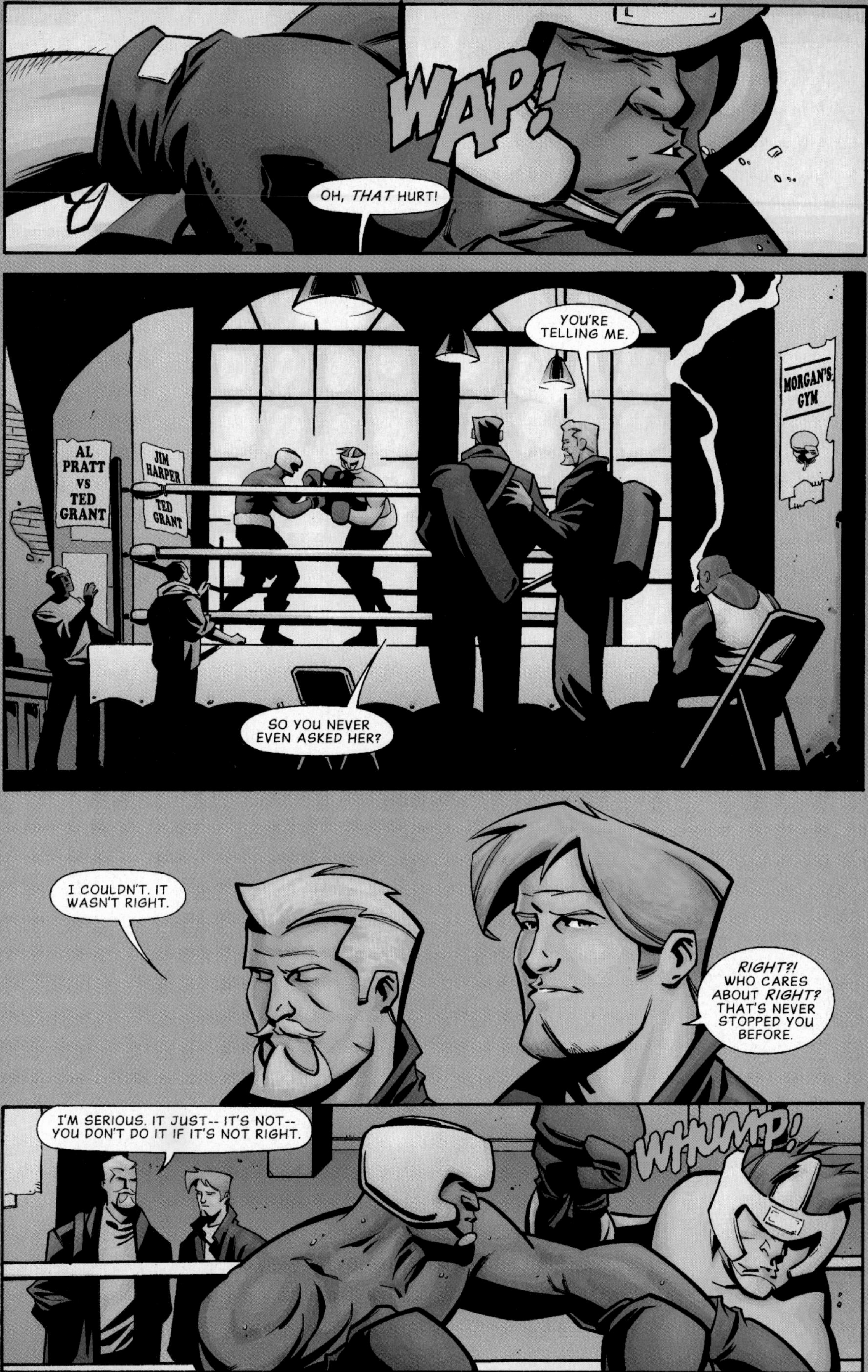
WAP!
OH, THAT HURT!
YOU'RE TELLING ME.
MORGAN'S GYM
AL PRATT VS TED GRANT
JIM HARPER TED GRANT
SO YOU NEVER EVEN ASKED HER?
I COULDN'T. IT WASN'T RIGHT.
RIGHT?! WHO CARES ABOUT RIGHT? THAT'S NEVER STOPPED YOU BEFORE.
I'M SERIOUS. IT JUST-- IT'S NOT-- YOU DON'T DO IT IF IT'S NOT RIGHT.
WHUMP!

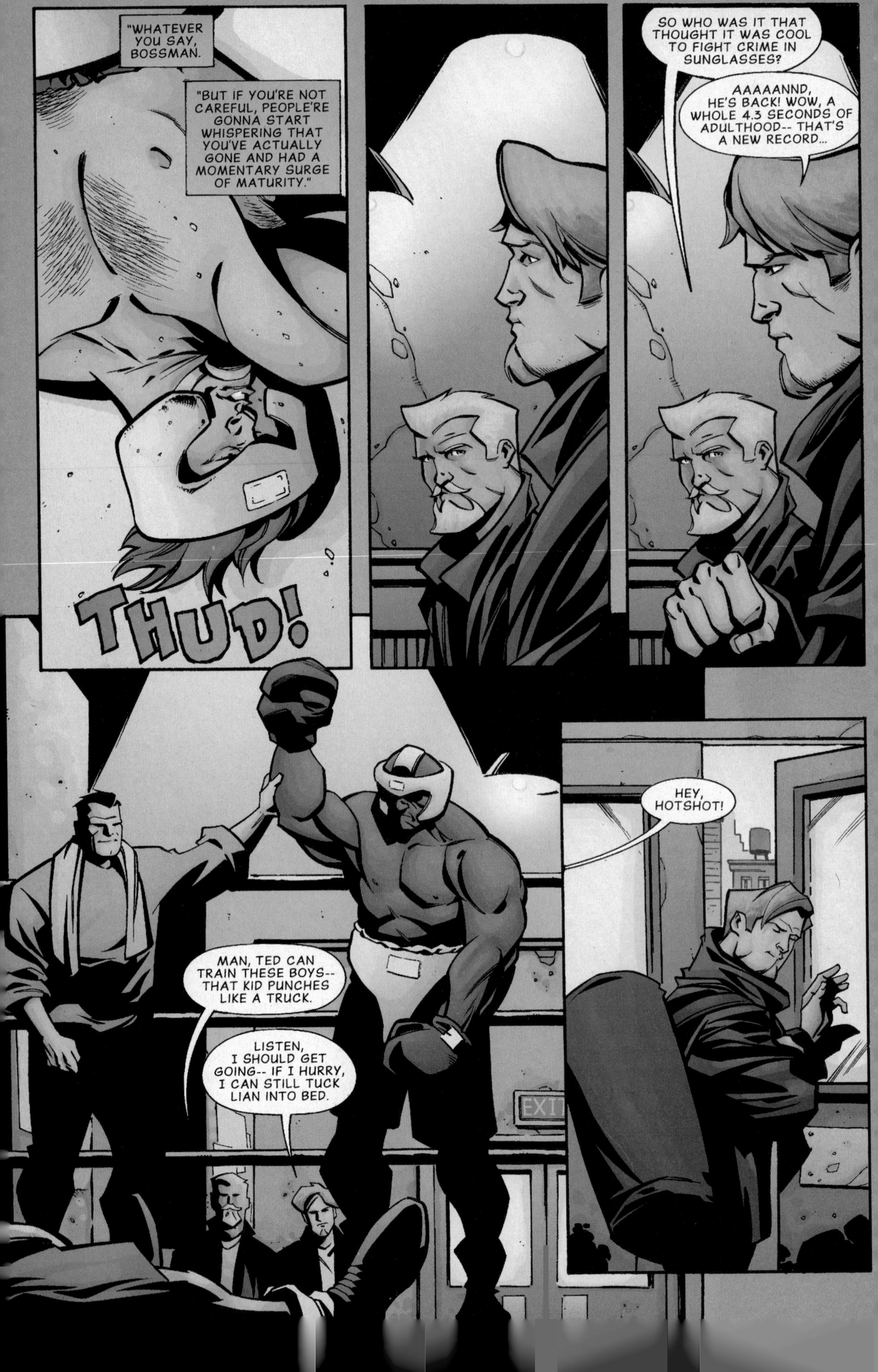
"WHATEVER YOU SAY, BOSSMAN.
"BUT IF YOU'RE NOT CAREFUL, PEOPLE'RE GONNA START WHISPERING THAT YOU'VE ACTUALLY GONE AND HAD A MOMENTARY SURGE OF MATURITY."
THUD!
SO WHO WAS IT THAT THOUGHT IT WAS COOL TO FIGHT CRIME IN SUNGLASSES?
AAAAANND, HE'S BACK! WOW, A WHOLE 4.3 SECONDS OF ADULTHOOD-- THAT'S A NEW RECORD...
MAN, TED CAN TRAIN THESE BOYS-- THAT KID PUNCHES LIKE A TRUCK.
LISTEN, I SHOULD GET GOING-- IF I HURRY, I CAN STILL TUCK LIAN INTO BED.
EXIT
HEY, HOTSHOT!

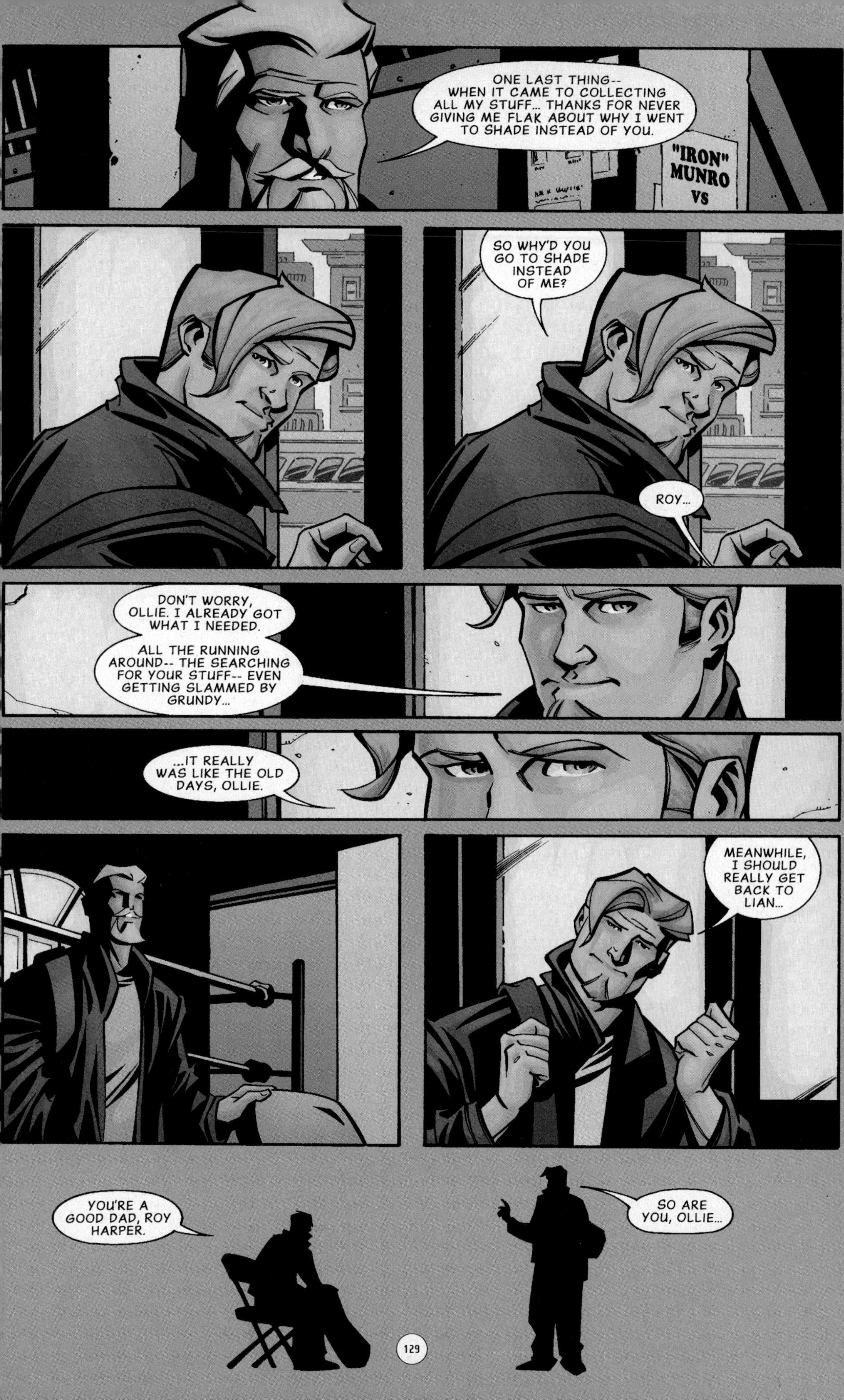
ONE LAST THING-- WHEN IT CAME TO COLLECTING ALL MY STUFF... THANKS FOR NEVER GIVING ME FLAK ABOUT WHY I WENT TO SHADE INSTEAD OF YOU.
"IRON" MUNRO VS
SO WHY'D YOU GO TO SHADE INSTEAD OF ME?
ROY...
DON'T WORRY, OLLIE. I ALREADY GOT WHAT I NEEDED.
ALL THE RUNNING AROUND-- THE SEARCHING FOR YOUR STUFF-- EVEN GETTING SLAMMED BY GRUNDY...
...IT REALLY WAS LIKE THE OLD DAYS, OLLIE.
MEANWHILE, I SHOULD REALLY GET BACK TO LIAN...
YOU'RE A GOOD DAD, ROY HARPER.
SO ARE YOU, OLLIE...

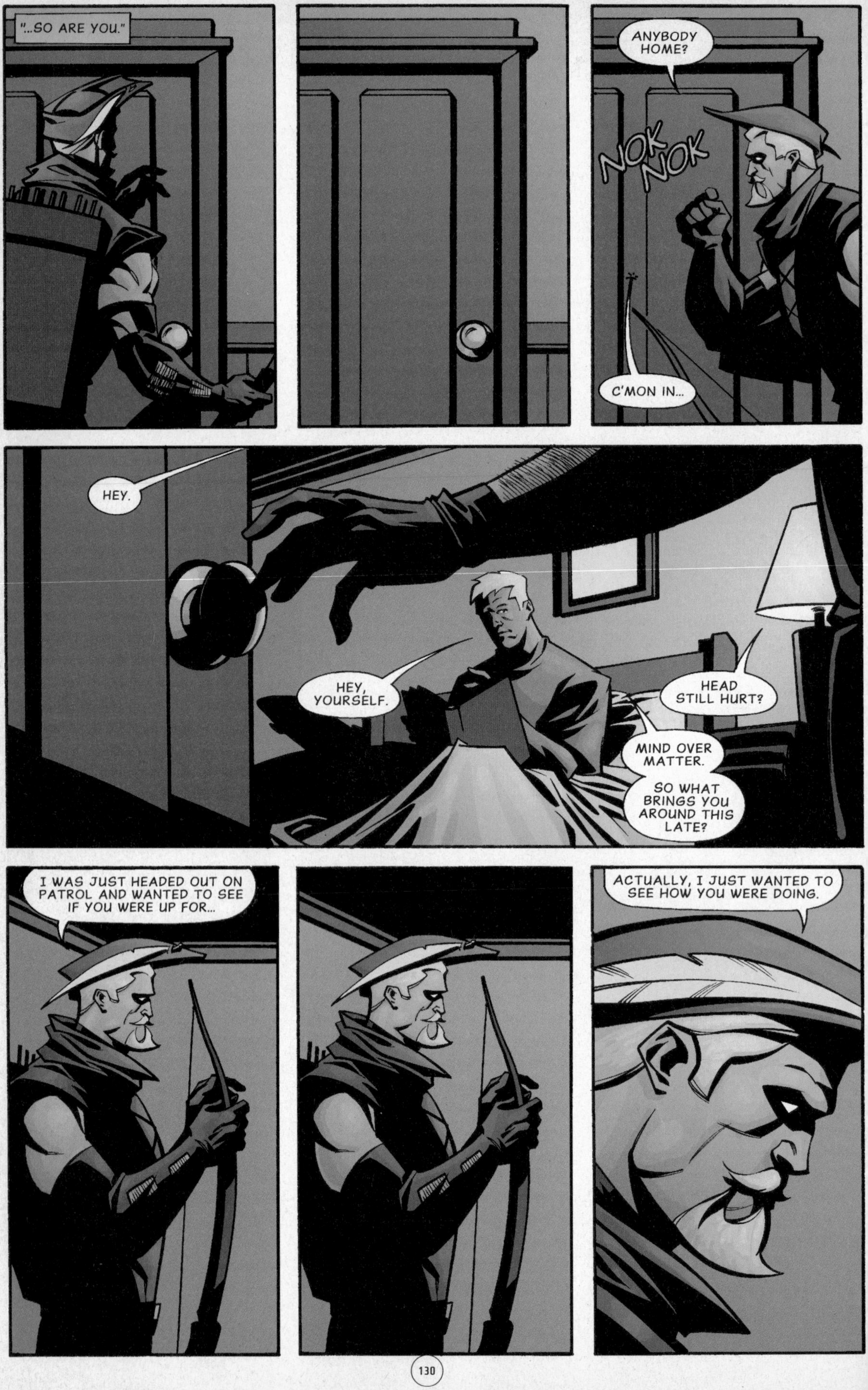
"...SO ARE YOU."
ANYBODY HOME?
NOK NOK
C'MON IN...
HEY.
HEY, YOURSELF.
HEAD STILL HURT?
MIND OVER MATTER.
SO WHAT BRINGS YOU AROUND THIS LATE?
I WAS JUST HEADED OUT ON PATROL AND WANTED TO SEE IF YOU WERE UP FOR...
ACTUALLY, I JUST WANTED TO SEE HOW YOU WERE DOING.

I'M FINE, DAD. I PROMISE.

YEAH... NO...

I KNOW.

When Roy was growing up, I didn't know the first thing about being a father.

I still don't.

SO... UH...

But I'm trying.

SO WHAT'CHA READING THERE?

YOUR SCRAPBOOK. ALL THE OLD ARTICLES AND STORIES.

SPEEDY LOWERS THE BOOM ON PSYCHO-PIRATE!

"The only face he made for me was scared," boy bowman says.

OY TO RL?!
ide her
ding
eases.

ARROWS TRUMP DARTS
Red Dart Captured by Green Arrow
"Just a no-good villain," G.A. says.

THAT'S IMPOSSIBLE.

THEY WERE ALL DESTROYED...

W-WHERE'D YOU...?

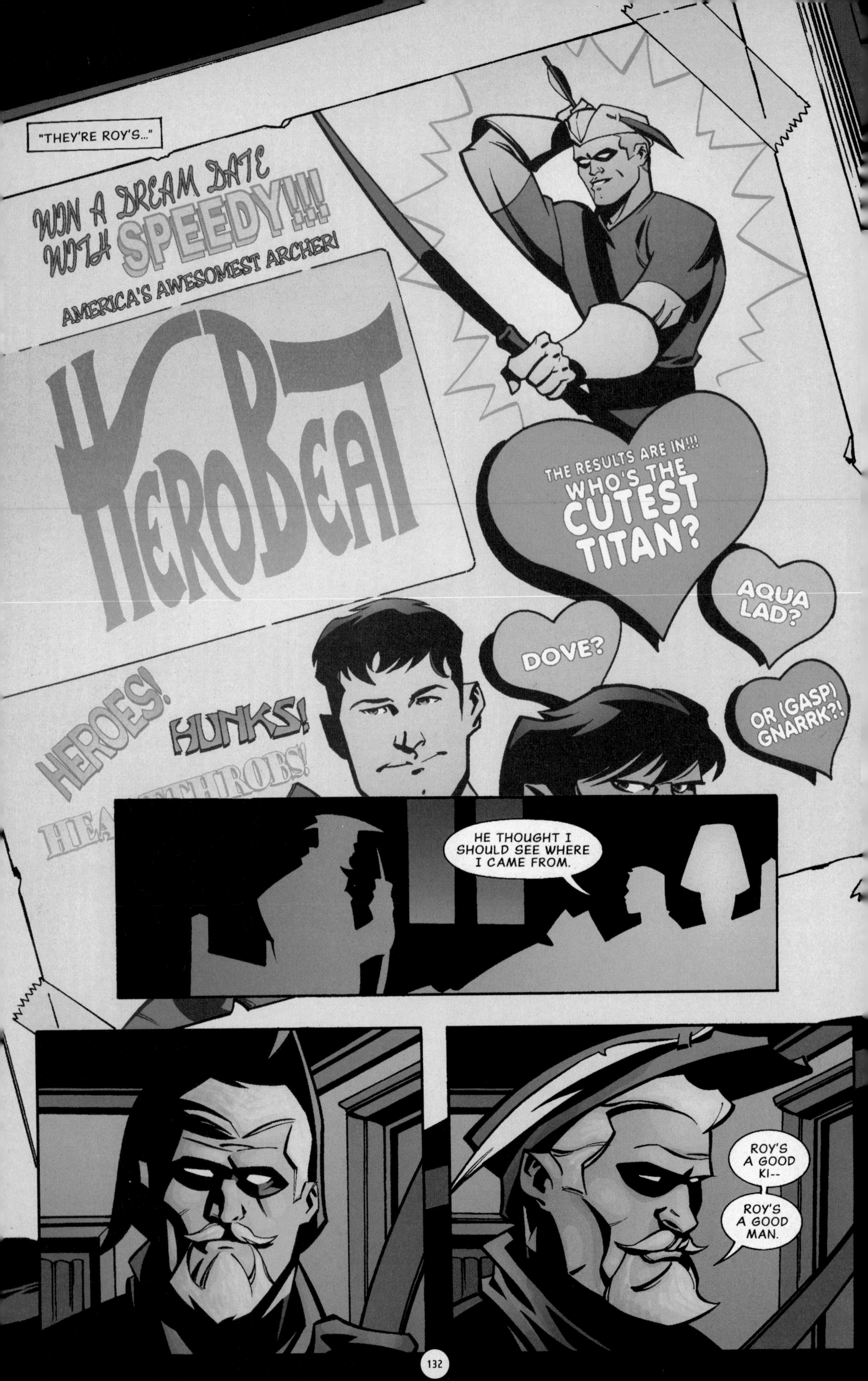
"THEY'RE ROY'S..."
WIN A DREAM DATE WITH SPEEDY!!!
AMERICA'S AWESOMEST ARCHER!
HEROBEAT
THE RESULTS ARE IN!!! WHO'S THE CUTEST TITAN?
AQUA LAD?
DOVE?
OR (GASP) GNARRK?!
HEROES!
HUNKS!
HE THOUGHT I SHOULD SEE WHERE I CAME FROM.
ROY'S A GOOD KI--
ROY'S A GOOD MAN.

I STILL CAN'T BELIEVE HE LIKED BEING CALLED "SPEEDY."

YOU KIDDING? YOU SHOULD'VE HEARD HIS FIRST CHOICE.

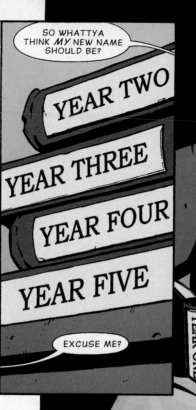

SO WHATTYA THINK *MY* NEW NAME SHOULD BE?

YEAR TWO

YEAR THREE

YEAR FOUR

YEAR FIVE

EXCUSE ME?

MY NEW CODE NAME...

"GREEN ARROW" IS ALREADY TAKEN, SO WHO SHOULD I BE?

RED ARROW? LONGSHOT? SHAFT?

YEAR ONE

HOW 'BOUT WE STICK WITH "GREEN ARROW"?

BUT THEN THERE'LL BE TWO OF US.

ACTUALLY, CONNOR, THAT'S WHAT I'M HOPING FOR.

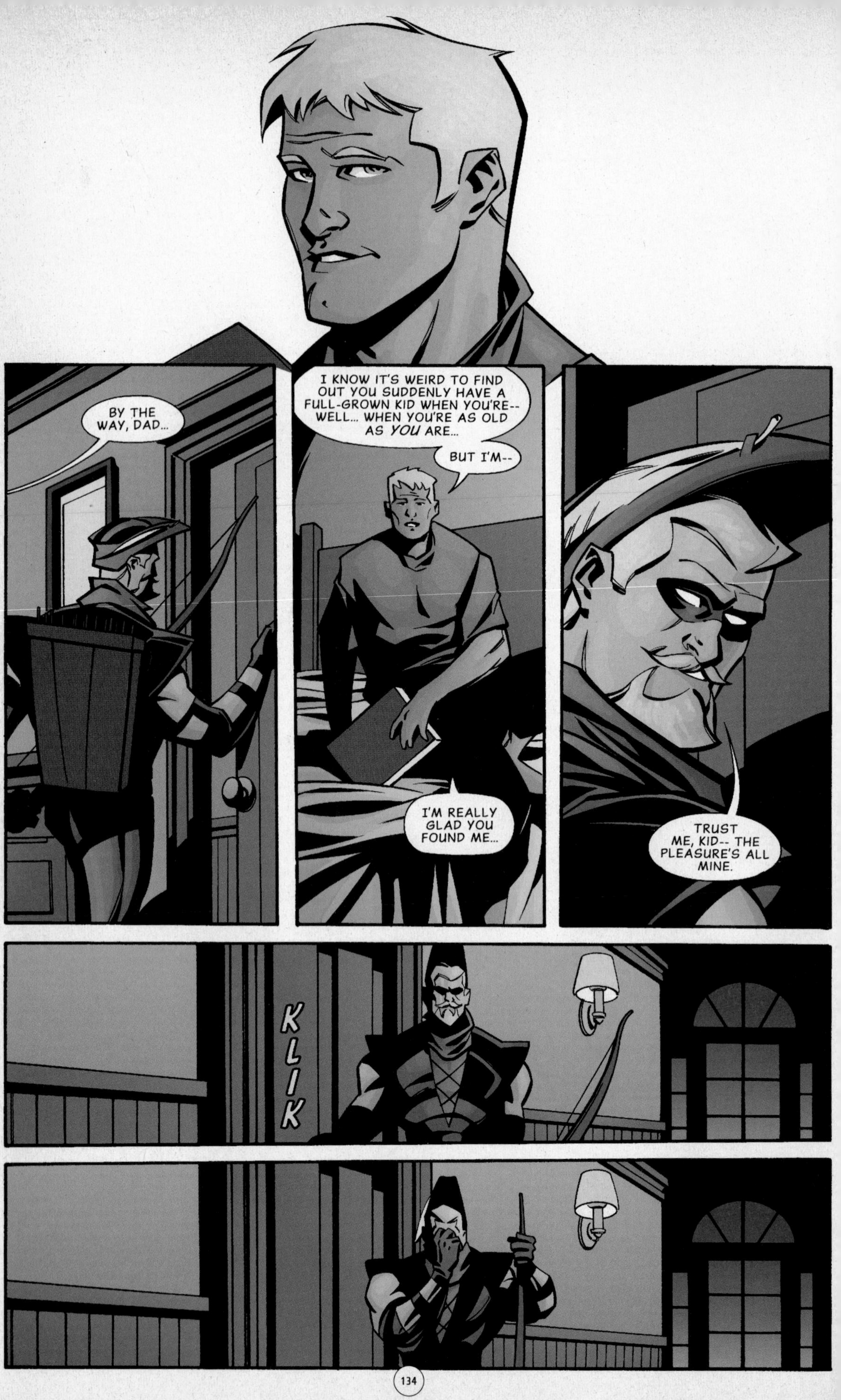

BY THE WAY, DAD...
I KNOW IT'S WEIRD TO FIND OUT YOU SUDDENLY HAVE A FULL-GROWN KID WHEN YOU'RE-- WELL... WHEN YOU'RE AS OLD AS *YOU* ARE...
BUT I'M--
I'M REALLY GLAD YOU FOUND ME...
TRUST ME, KID-- THE PLEASURE'S ALL MINE.
KLIK

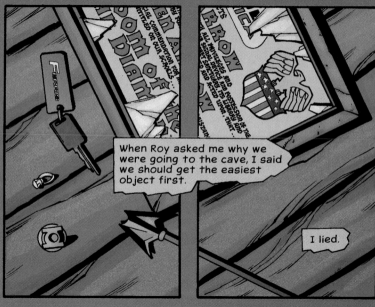

When Roy asked me why we were going to the cave, I said we should get the easiest object first.

I lied.

You start with what's most *important*.

When you're chasing something personal, you never start with what's *easiest*.

So why do people lie?

Some do it to protect...

Others do it to control...

And a few of us...

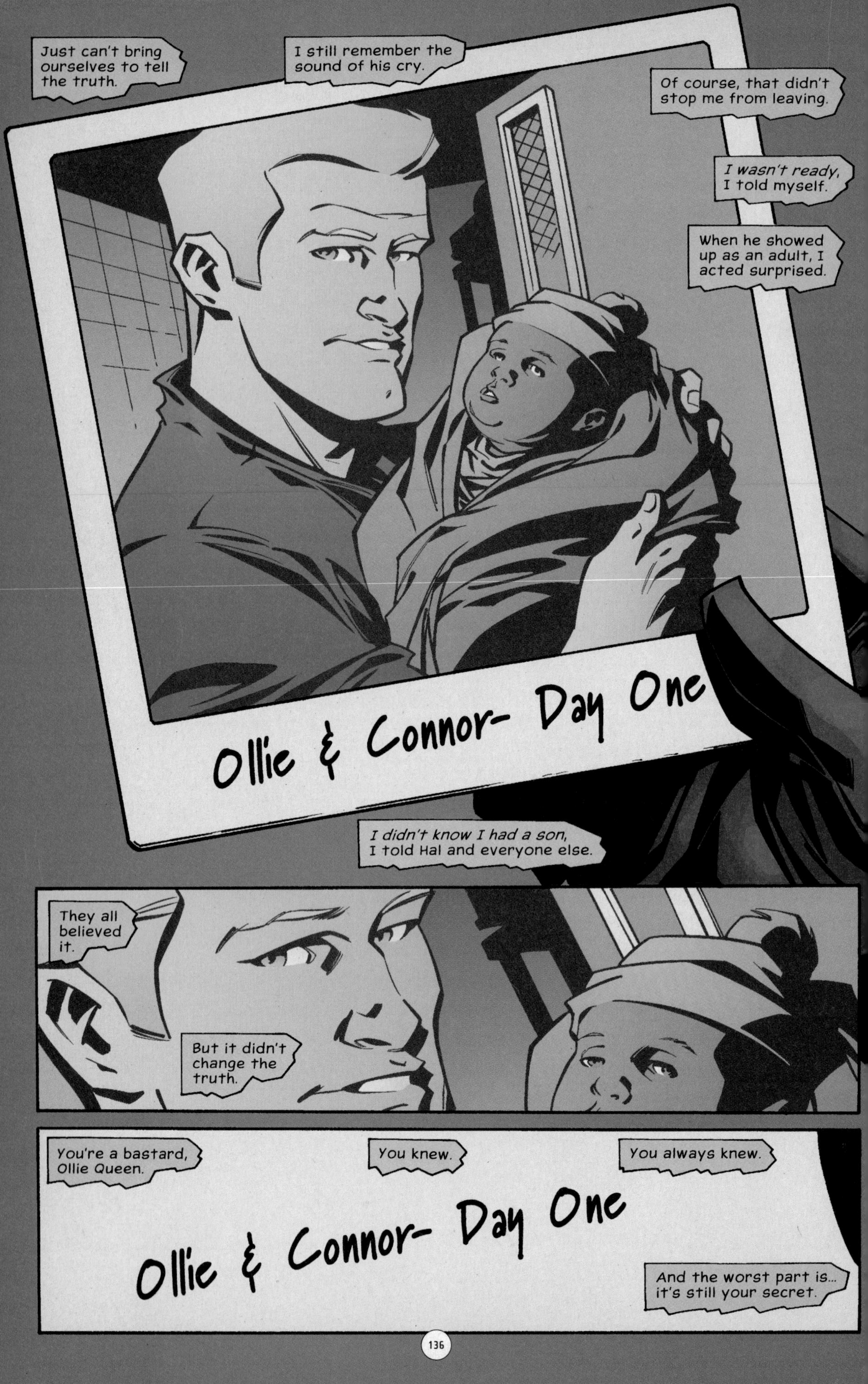

Just can't bring ourselves to tell the truth.
I still remember the sound of his cry.
Of course, that didn't stop me from leaving.
I wasn't ready, I told myself.
When he showed up as an adult, I acted surprised.
Ollie & Connor- Day One
I didn't know I had a son, I told Hal and everyone else.
They all believed it.
But it didn't change the truth.
You're a bastard, Ollie Queen.
You knew.
You always knew.
Ollie & Connor- Day One
And the worst part is... it's still your secret.

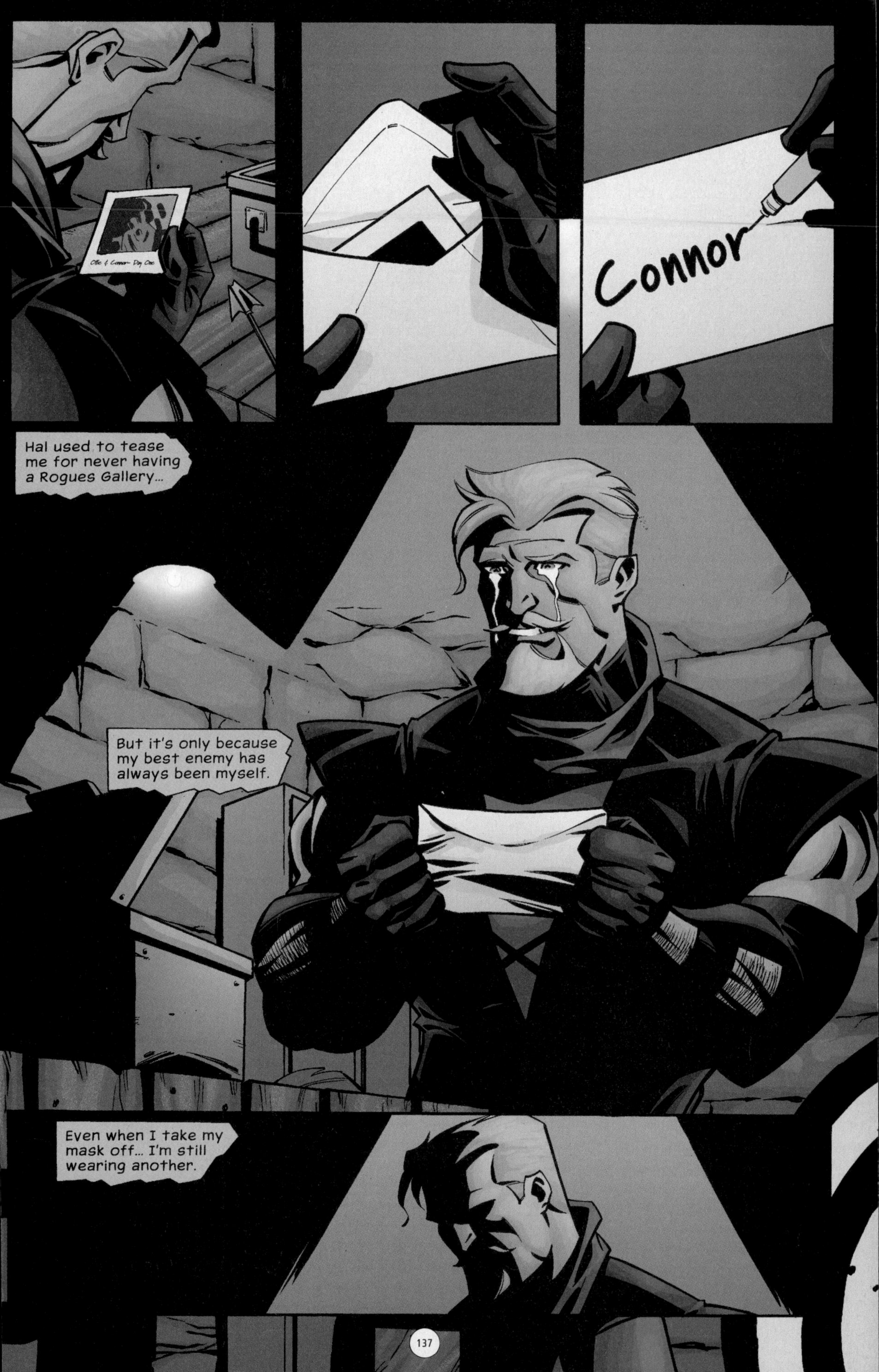
Ollie & Connor Day One
Connor
Hal used to tease me for never having a Rogues Gallery...
But it's only because my best enemy has always been myself.
Even when I take my mask off... I'm still wearing another.

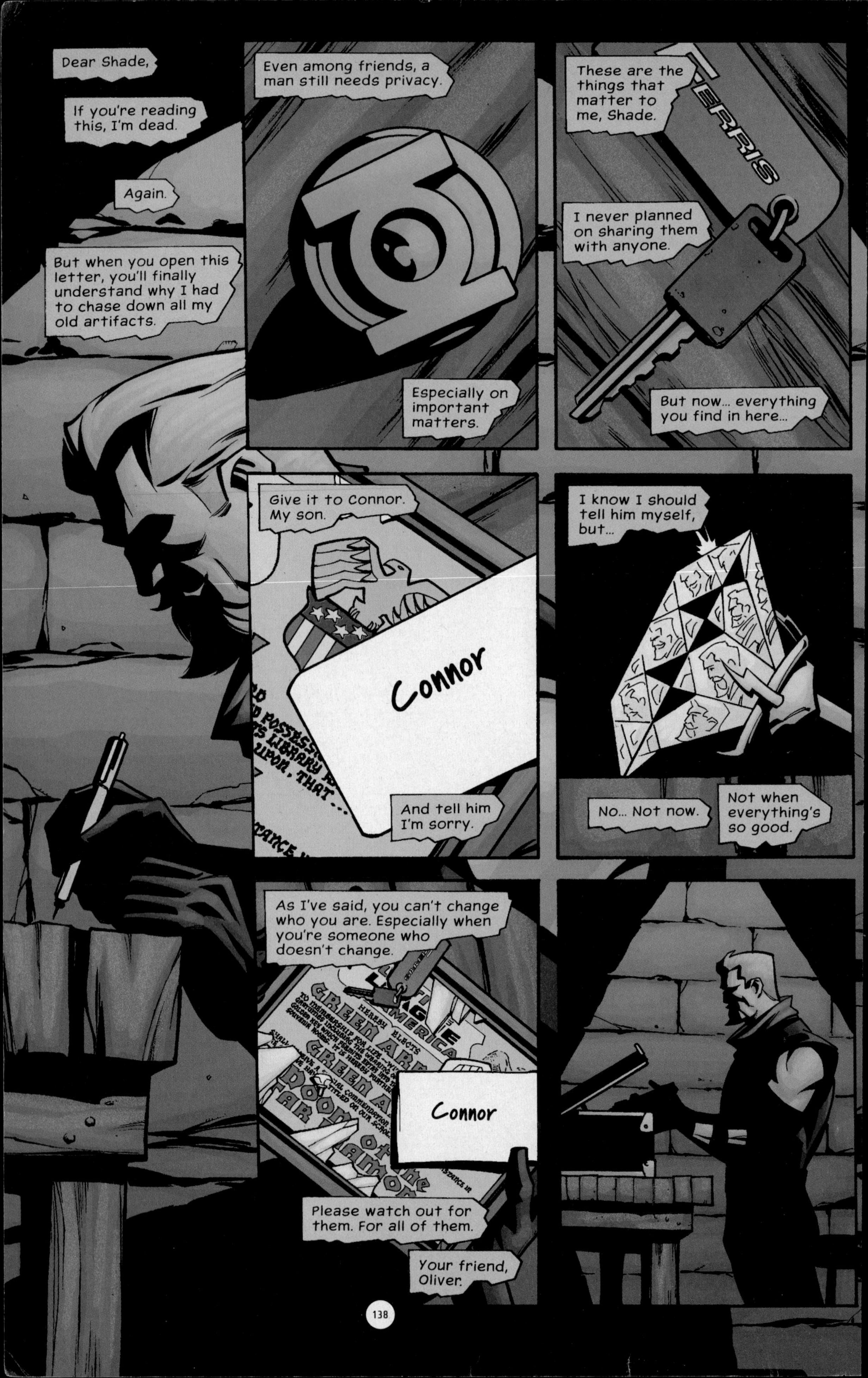

Dear Shade,
If you're reading this, I'm dead.
Again.
But when you open this letter, you'll finally understand why I had to chase down all my old artifacts.
Even among friends, a man still needs privacy.
Especially on important matters.
These are the things that matter to me, Shade.
FERRIS
I never planned on sharing them with anyone.
But now... everything you find in here...
Give it to Connor. My son.
Connor
And tell him I'm sorry.
I know I should tell him myself, but...
No... Not now.
Not when everything's so good.
As I've said, you can't change who you are. Especially when you're someone who doesn't change.
Connor
Please watch out for them. For all of them.
Your friend, Oliver.

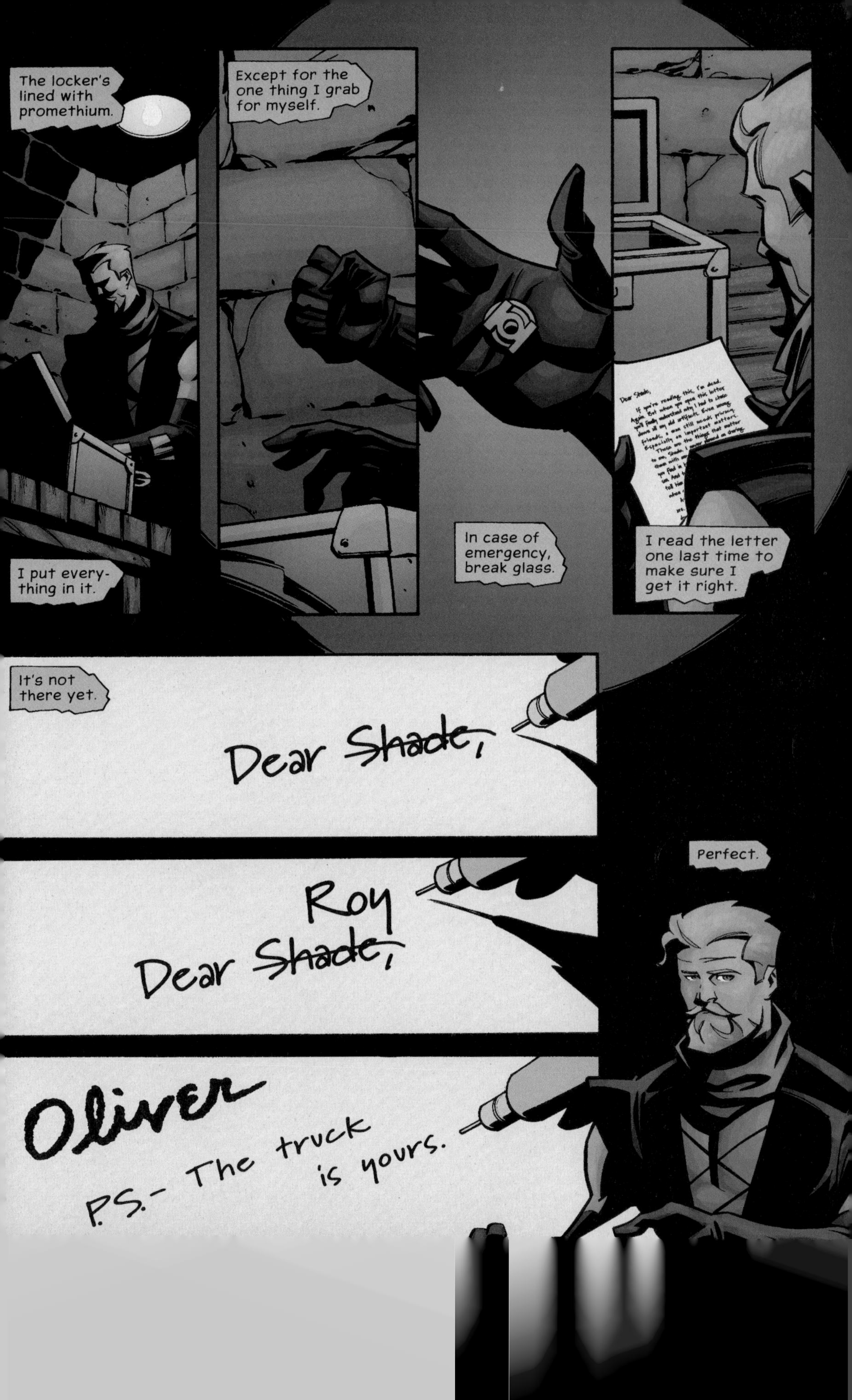
The locker's lined with promethium.
I put every-thing in it.
Except for the one thing I grab for myself.
In case of emergency, break glass.
I read the letter one last time to make sure I get it right.
It's not there yet.
Dear Shade,
Perfect.
Roy
Dear Shade,
Oliver
P.S.- The truck is yours.

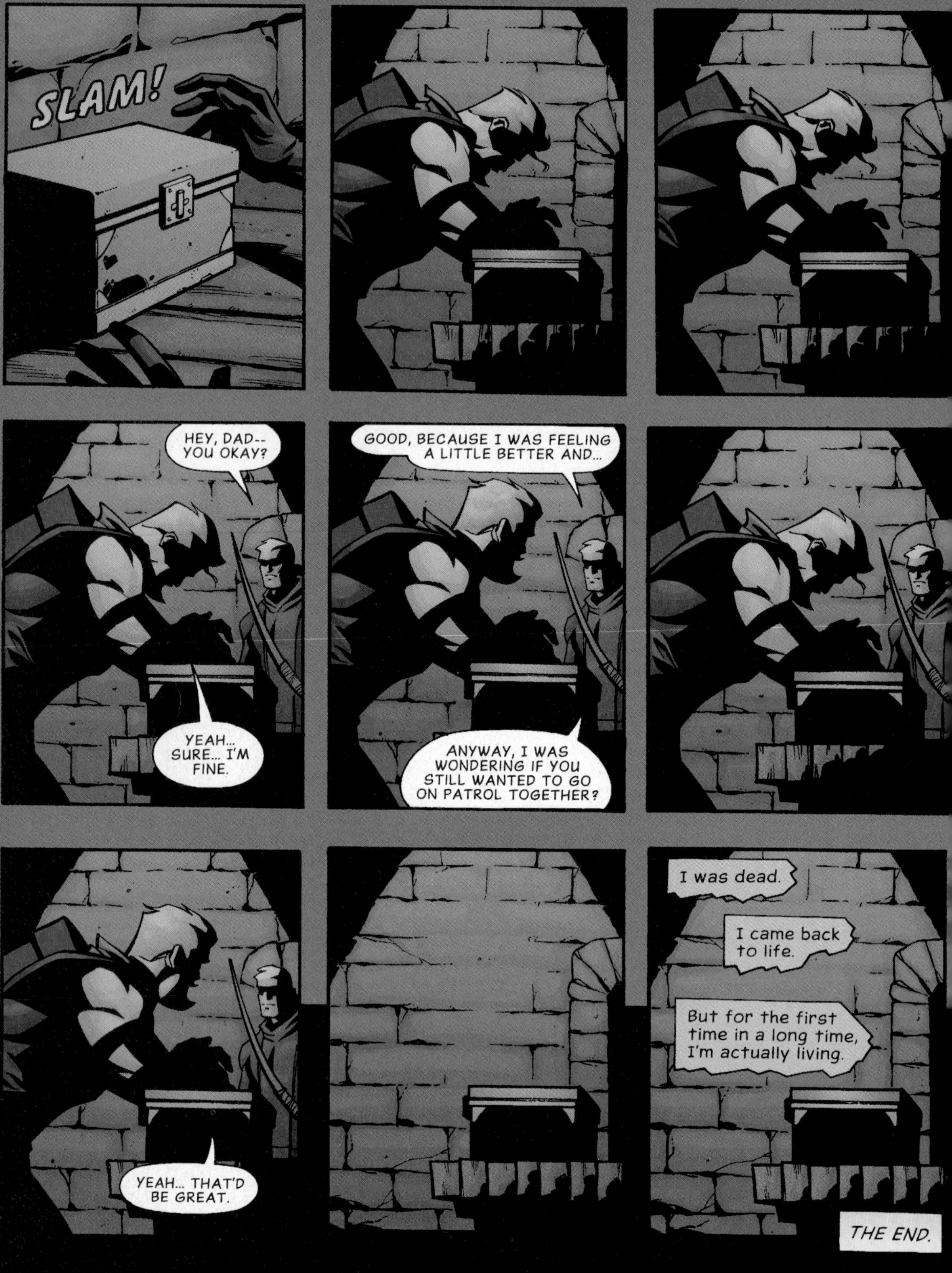
SLAM!
HEY, DAD-- YOU OKAY?
YEAH... SURE... I'M FINE.
GOOD, BECAUSE I WAS FEELING A LITTLE BETTER AND...
ANYWAY, I WAS WONDERING IF YOU STILL WANTED TO GO ON PATROL TOGETHER?
YEAH... THAT'D BE GREAT.
I was dead.
I came back to life.
But for the first time in a long time, I'm actually living.
THE END.

THE ARCHER'S QUEST
Conclusion

FATHERHOOD

Brad Meltzer Writer
Phil Hester Penciller
Ande Parks Inker
James Sinclair Colorist
Sean Konot Letterer
Morgan Dontanville Assistant Editor
Bob Schreck Editor

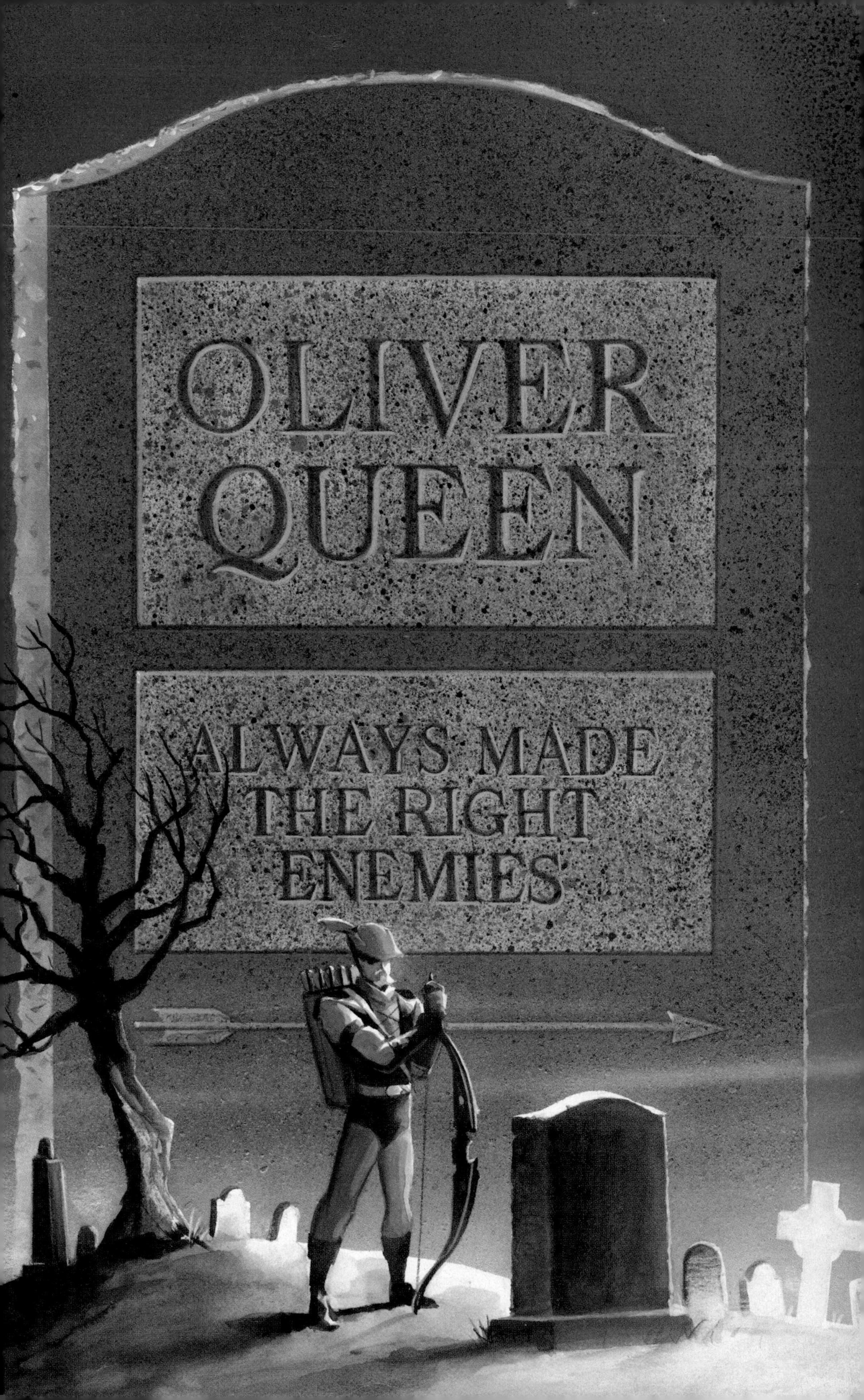
OLIVER QUEEN
ALWAYS MADE THE RIGHT ENEMIES

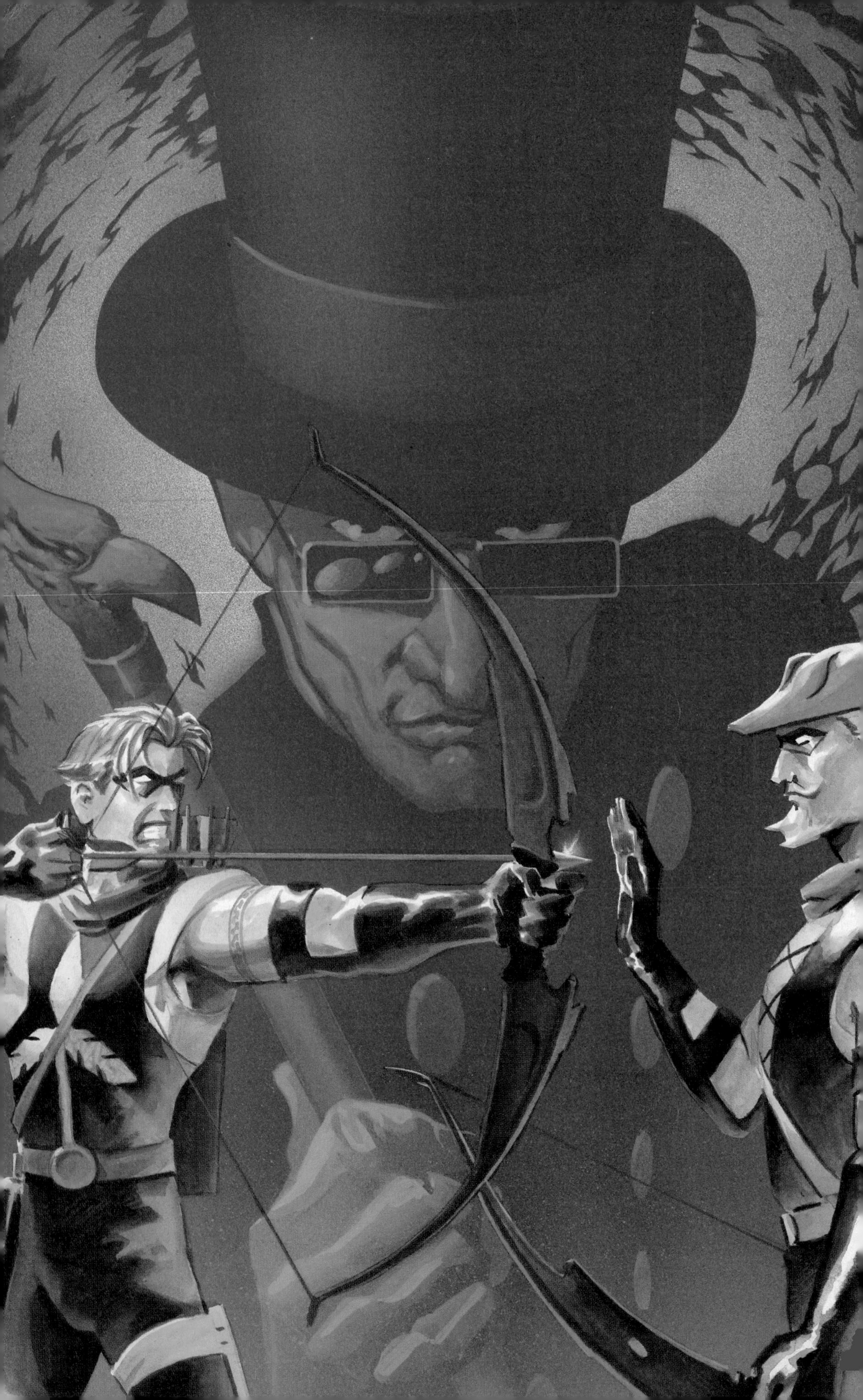

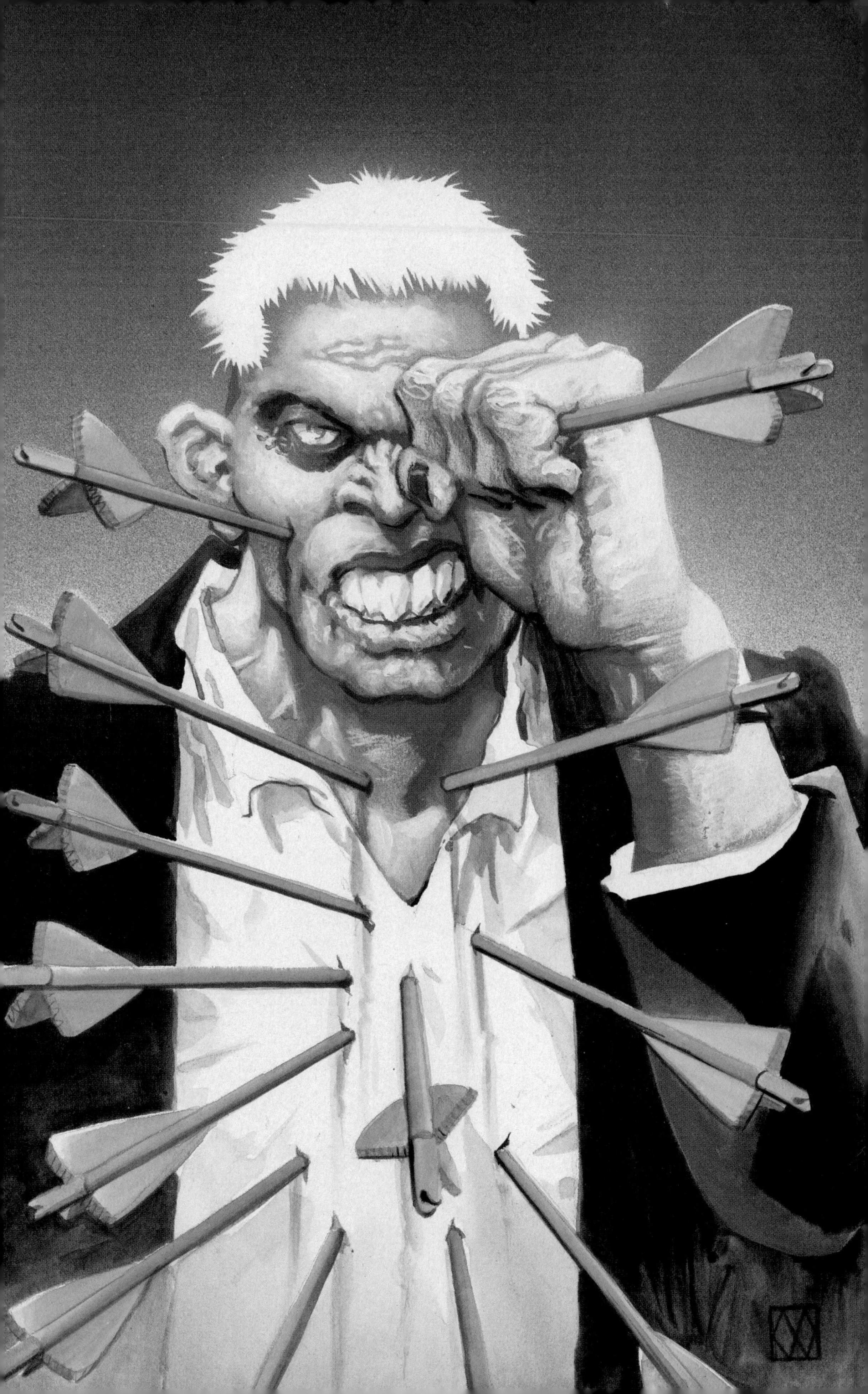

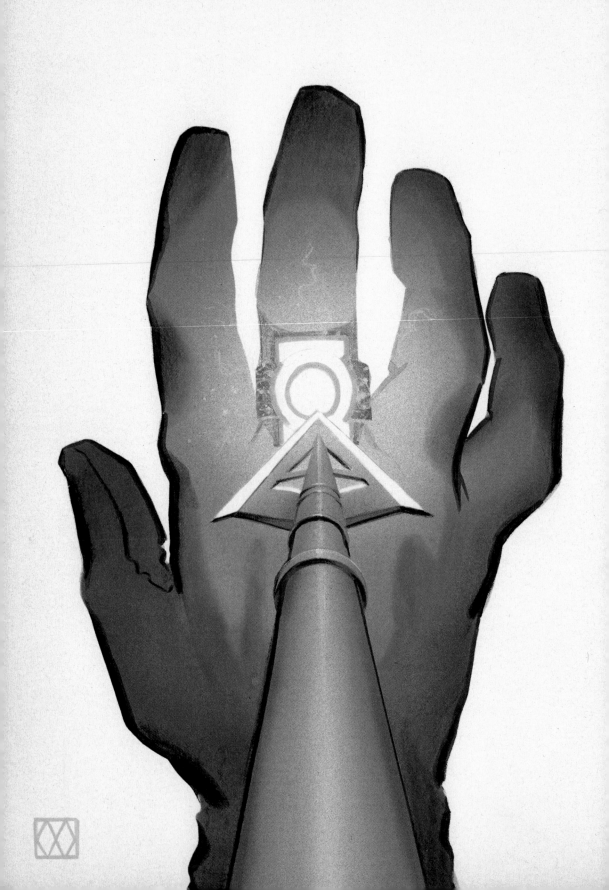

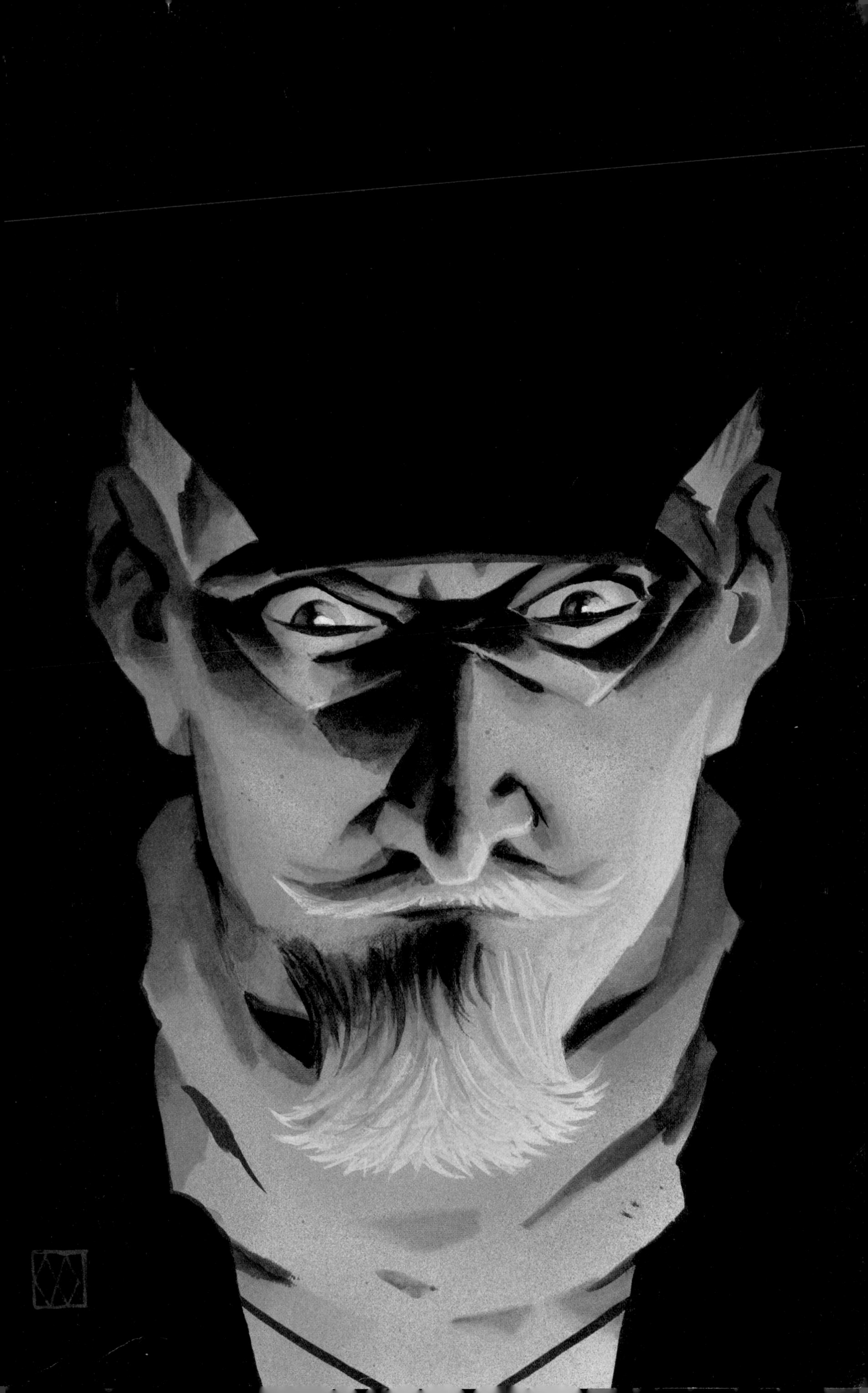

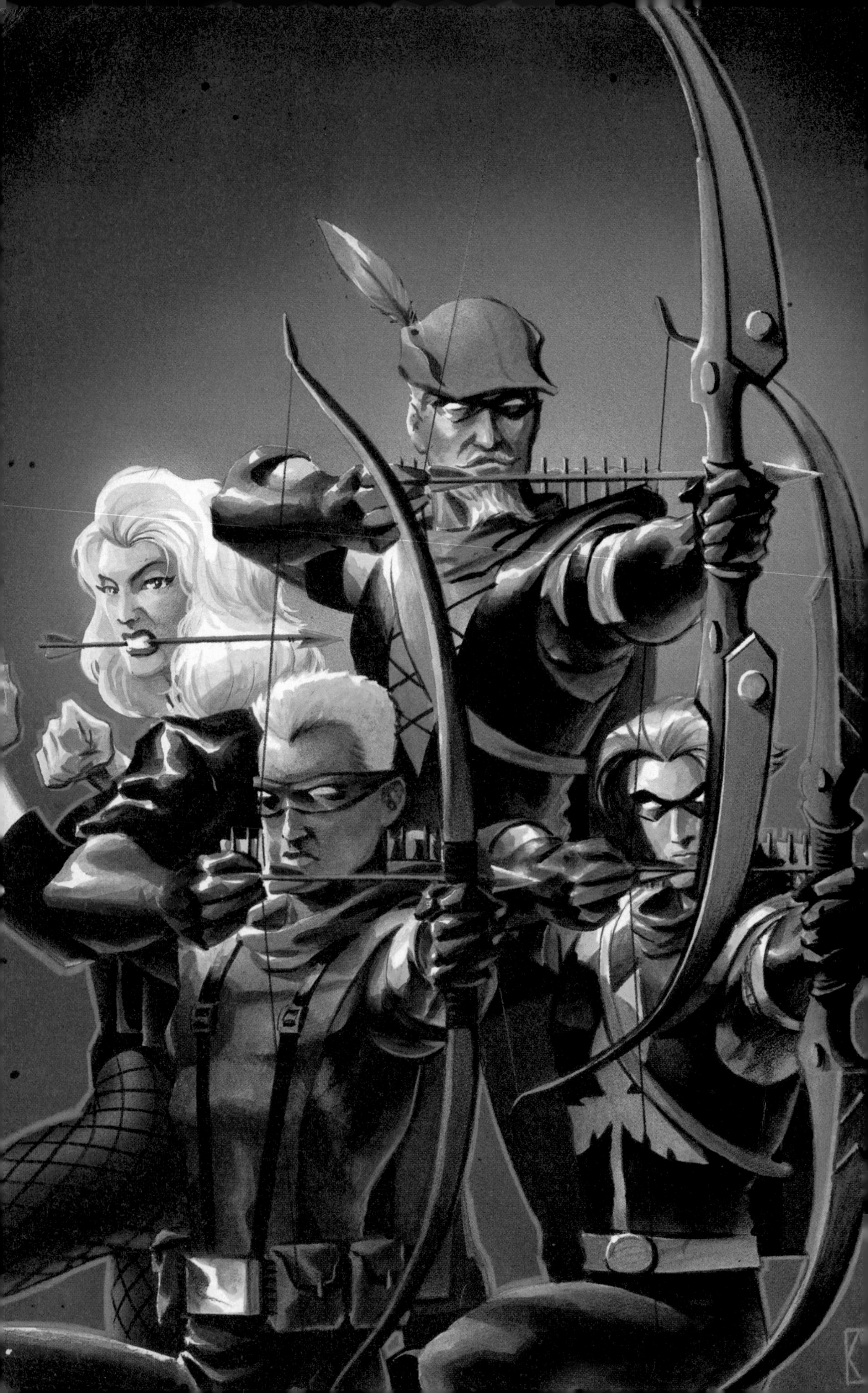

GREEN ARROW's one of the few books where you *can* judge the book by its cover. I'm not proud — I'll admit it — I begged Matt Wagner to stay on the title. Here's why:

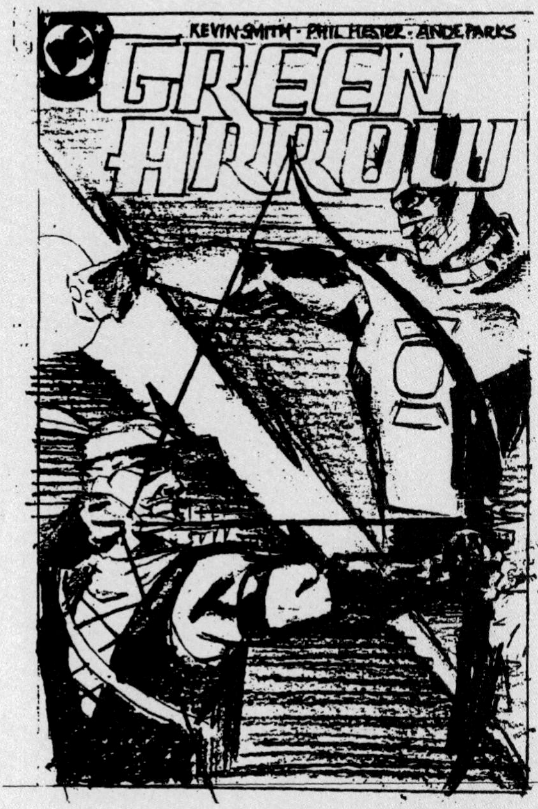
KEVIN SMITH · PHIL HESTER · ANDE PARKS
GREEN ARROW

For the Green Arrow/Green Lantern issue, we talked about Ollie and Kyle going head-to-head, as they do in the issue. I said I'd love it if we just saw the tip of the arrow hitting the ring. We didn't need to see Ollie and Kyle. Only the icons needed to collide. Readers are smart — they'll get it. Matt tried it four different ways before we finally went with the minimalist action of Kyle's hand flat against a white background.

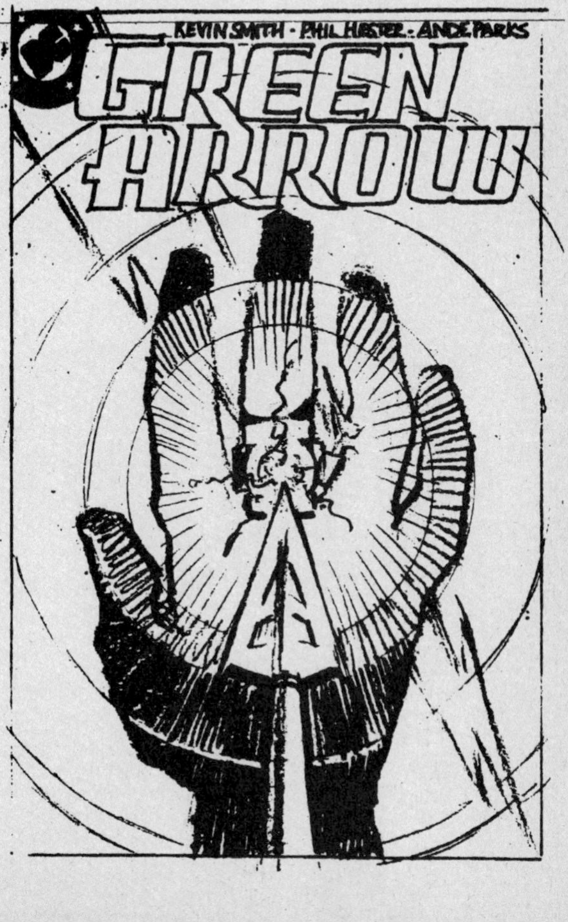
KEVIN SMITH · PHIL HESTER · ANDE PARKS
GREEN ARROW

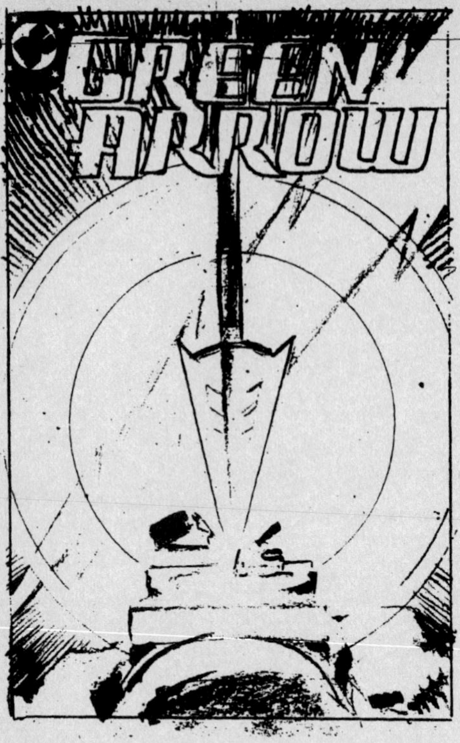
GREEN
ARROW

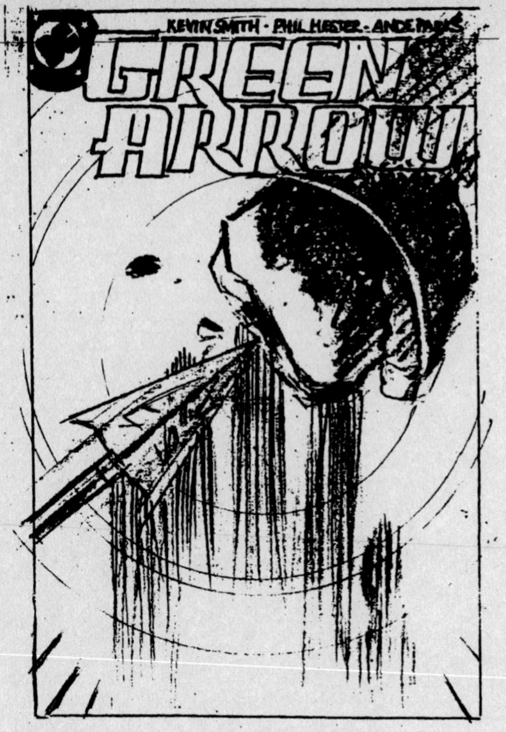
KEVIN SMITH · PHIL HESTER · ANDE PARKS
GREEN
ARROW

I asked Matt for a family portrait. We kept debating which was right. Do we show action, or calm? The public Ollie, or the private? The one he lets us see, or the one he keeps hidden? With Wagner, you never lose.

—Brad Meltzer

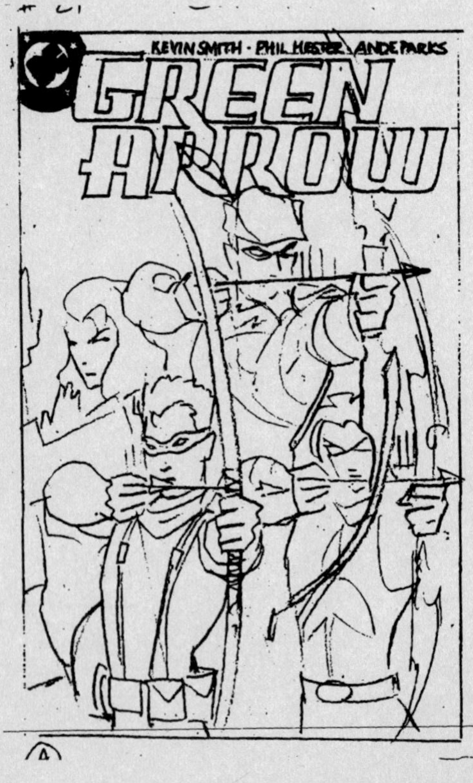
KEVIN SMITH · PHIL HESTER · ANDE PARKS
GREEN
ARROW
A

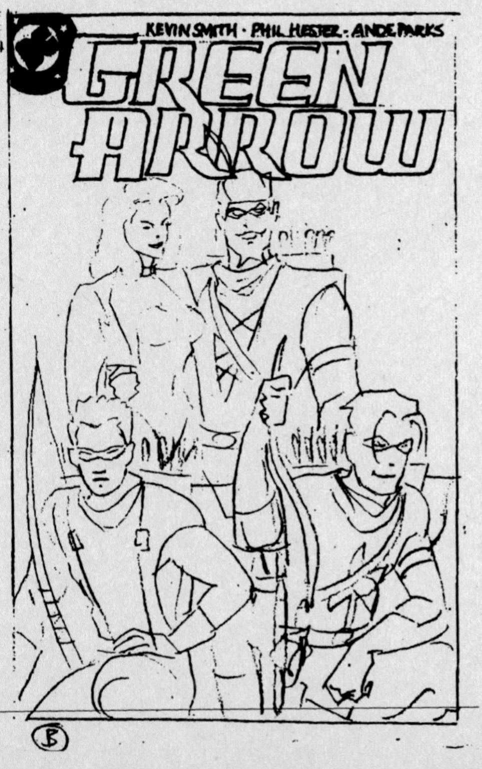
KEVIN SMITH · PHIL HESTER · ANDE PARKS
GREEN
ARROW
B

*I*t all started with porn.

In January 2002, GREEN ARROW editor Bob Schreck was looking for a new writer on the title and wanted to know if I'd be interested. I actually was about to say no. I was on a book tour and already overcommitted. My wife changed my mind. I'd been waiting my whole life for this. A few days later, on January 9th, we had the first book signing for the new novel. The last person in line was Schreck himself.

"If you're serious, I'm serious," I told him.

He nodded with a big grin.

As we walked out of the bookstore where we were talking, I told him one thing: I'd only do it if I really had something to say about the character. I wasn't interested in a villain-of-the-week story. I wanted to leave Oliver Queen different than I found him — not just change for change's sake, but in a way that would pull something central out of the character.

Bob again nodded, putting up with my pretentious ramblings.

I said I'd think about Ollie for the next few weeks and let him know if I found anything good.

On January 19, 2002, I was stuck in the airport and yammering with my friend Noah, who told me about this concept called *porn-buddies* he'd seen on BBC television. As Noah explained it (and trust me, Noah knows his porn), a porn-buddy is a contingency plan. When you die, your porn-buddy is the friend who goes to your house (before all your loved ones get there) and destroys all your porn so no one finds it. *That* is a beautiful idea. Not that I have porn, but still... It's so ruthlessly brilliant. It works with any secret. And that's when it hit me. If anyone needs a "porn-buddy," it's someone with a secret identity. Wouldn't Batman want someone to shut down the Batcave? Wouldn't Superman want someone to hide all the capes so no one would come after Lois? It was all built from there. Thank you, Noah, for your keen knowledge of British porn. What follows is the result. We applied the concept of porn-buddies to the recently revived Oliver Queen. He made plans for his death. Now he had to see if they were followed through.

Armed with my notes, I pitched Bob Schreck on the idea. Ollie didn't have porn, but he did have a few secrets of his own. That's all that mattered to me. To be clear, *The Archer's Quest* was never about a single item, or even a clever BBC trick. It was about what Ollie found within himself — and for his son.

As you'll see in the next few pages, the pitch was for four issues. When I made a complete list of items Ollie would've cared about, and added that to the character pieces I wanted to do with the Flash and Green Lantern, and then combined that with the facets of Ollie's forever-complex personality I wanted to highlight... well... as always, Ollie took over, and the story grew.

In the end, *The Archer's Quest* will be judged by others more qualified than myself, but let me say that it definitely wouldn't have been possible without a great deal of help and hard work. For that reason, I owe a huge amount of thanks to the following people: To my love Cori, who was the only reason I said yes to doing this. Worried about the pressures of work, I almost let the offer pass me by. Cori reminded me that if I did, I'd regret it for the rest of my life. I love her for far more than that. To my son Jonas, who inspired all the love Ollie feels for Connor and Roy. To my parents and Bari, who taught me the importance of family. To Noah Kuttler, my Speedy, for brainstorming every issue, and for working through all the details. And to Judd Winick, who truly provided the opportunity for me to pick up the bow and arrow in the first place.

Finally, let me say that after reading comics for over twenty years, I still never appreciated how much collaboration goes into the process. Novels are far more solitary — you leap off the trapeze by yourself. On that note, let me say thank you to the other people who were leaping off the trapeze with me issue after issue: First, GREEN ARROW editor Bob Schreck, whose friendship I treasure. The only reason I was on GA was because of Bob. He took the chance with what was then DC's number two book, and he's the one who had the faith. From there, Phil Hester and Ande Parks are the ones who brought it to life. Take a look at the last two panels on page 7 of the final issue. In the script, it said we should see Ollie dying inside. This is Ollie's entire decision. Sure, they can draw the battle as good as anyone, but only true artists can get that change in emotion. Not only are they two of the nicest guys around, they've redefined Ollie in this day and age, and I was just lucky enough to work with them. Matt Wagner, one of the most intellectually consistent people I know, for his art and his friendship. Mike Carlin, for coming to our aid in the fight. Scott McCullar, who helped me track down the items once I had my final list. Sean Konot, Morgan Dontanville, and James Sinclair, who month after month put up with my nonsense ("The JLA certificate has to be a perfect re-creation..." "Can we get a HeroBeat logo that looks just right?"). Finally, I'd like to thank Kevin Smith. He's not only a great creator in his own right, but he's the reason Ollie lives (literally and figuratively) and continues to fight the good fight. In an industry filled with petty slap-fights, Kevin passed the baton with more graciousness than I've ever seen. Thank you, sir.

And finally, thank you to everyone who is now reading this. It's been an honor to add even a single arrow to the quiver. From here on in, I'm back to watching from the other side of the four-color cover. So thanks for jumping in the Arrowcar and being part of the family.

— Brad Meltzer
Washington, D.C.
July 27, 2003

Issue One

Ollie sees a two-bit villain (Signalman/Cat-Man?) in a photo at his funeral. Now someone knows his secret — or worse, that they can harm his loved ones/Supes/etc. When he was dead, his I.D. wasn't an issue... but now that he's alive, it's a problem.

Ollie visits the villain, pins him with an arrow, and asks him who hired him.

The villain tells Ollie he was hired by him. Oliver Queen.

Confused, Ollie turns around to see the Shade standing in the doorway.
"Welcome back, Oliver."

End of issue one

Issue Two (potential title: "Grays of Shade")

We learn that Ollie had been planning on events in case he was to die without warning. He wanted to make sure that all of his things were destroyed. In part because he didn't want them to be used for evil, but also because as he states it, "Not everyone wants a *Flash Museum* built for them." Ollie's obstinate and shies from such blatant hero-worship. Most important, this is his dark side. Hal and Barry died unprepared. Ollie's not letting that happen to him. He's built different than the rest. Experience shows.

He hired the Shade because he knew none of his friends/extended family would honor such a request, but more important, because the Shade is immortal — he'd be around longer than everyone else. As Ollie tells it, "Batman isn't the only one who can be sneaky."

Ollie and Shade are old friends — Ollie's complex enough that he'd be one of the few to understand Shade's issues.

Ollie's first question is if Shade got everything. They go through the checklist and he realizes that the two most important things were not gotten.

That's because things moved/shifted, but also because Shade subcontracted the job to the villain in issue one. After all, Shade is too refined a gentleman to be digging around the swamp all day for some of the things he needed to get.

Ollie now has to go get those things. It is extremely important to him and we really don't know why, but it is almost life and death for him to find them.

End of issue two

Issue Three (title could be "Grundy No Like Arrow In Face")

Ollie goes to the old Arrowcave to find one of the things (Seven Soldiers picture? Trick arrows? Flash ring? He made it for me.) and then goes to the swamp where Swamp Thing buried the truck from Hard-Traveling Heroes. Rosebud. Inside, there's a Green Lantern ring Hal left for him.

Either place we encounter Solomon Grundy. They fight and Ollie fills him with *tons* of arrows. Cover idea: Grundy from the waist up, his chest *filled* with arrows.

We see at the end of the issue that hidden inside the first item is a picture of Connor as a baby.

Ollie knew all along he had a son.

End of issue three

Issue Four ("Epilogue")

Ollie realizes that he died once and was unprepared, but he won't do that again.

He collects all the items and decides that they should be kept in the basement of the Flash Museum. He writes a letter to Shade telling him that if he dies again, this time, don't destroy the stuff — give it all to Dinah, Roy, and most important, his son.

Throughout, we see Ollie coming to understand that he always wears a mask... even when he's with Dinah. Forever the bastard.

Oliver *is* a responsible, caring person... he just doesn't know how to say it to his family. He keeps getting tripped up by his own stubbornness and his own way of doing things.

He also begins to understand he has a family... not just an extended family (Hal, Katar, Barry...). All those years, he let his work friends stand in for his family, but hadn't adjusted to building one himself. With Connor around, he realizes he now must make that effort.

When he first hires Shade, Oliver thinks he has nobody. But now, at the end of the story, he realizes he has this true family looking out for him. Journey complete. Not just back from the dead — back to life. With Roy. With Dinah. With Connor. And always... with a secret.

Many people wonder how writers prepare a comic book script, and the frustrating answer is that there are as many different ways of doing it as there are writers themselves. However, much can still be learned from examples, and so presented here is one such case — Brad Meltzer's complete script for the first chapter of this volume's story.

GREEN ARROW ISSUE 16
By Brad Meltzer

PAGE ONE

FULL PAGE:
It's the end of winter at the Ashram Monastery — the trees don't look their healthiest — the ground has no snow, and the grass is hardly inviting. It looks like a chilly day. Oliver Queen is standing at his own grave, and we see him in a full body shot from behind. His hands are stuffed in the pockets of his hunter green trench coat, but from our angle, we can still see it's him, goatee and all. He's got a square knapsack on that we know contains his folded-up bow and his quiver. He's staring down at his headstone, which has a tiny arrow insignia and reads:

Oliver Queen
Always Made the Right Enemies

The headstone isn't boring and plain — it's got a nice angled curve to the top of it — up to you what it looks like. (I just want to make sure it's not cheap and doesn't have a cross). I think you drew it in issue 1 — and I know Matt drew it for the cover, so you may want to pick up on that.

The fading sun is on Ollie's back, so his own shadow is cast along his grave. The only other thing we see is another shadow (from someone off panel), which runs beside his own.

1Cap: I was dead.

2Cap: I came back to life.

3Ollie: So who was there?

PAGE TWO

Panel One: Closer up on Ollie (his waist and up), from the off-panel person's point of view. He's looking at Ollie from behind, so we still don't know who it is.

1Clark: C'mon, Ollie, it's not important who was there.

Panel Two: Still from the off-panel-person's POV. Ollie turns and glances over his shoulder. He's wearing a black turtleneck under his overcoat. He's got a wry grin on.

2Ollie: Really, Clark? So you're telling me you didn't ask who was at yours?

Panel Three: We see Clark Kent from the waist up, complete in suit and trench coat, with an understated, but dumbfounded look on his face.

Panel Four: Ollie's now completely facing him (and us).

3Ollie: That's what I thought.

Panel Five: It's a horizontal panel that runs across the bottom third of the page. Oliver and Clark are facing each other. We can see the trees and the grave between them.

4Cap: He was the last person I saw on this earth.

5Cap: And from the look on his face, he needs this as much as I do.

6Ollie: So who was there?

7Clark: You mean at the public memorial?

8Ollie: I don't care where the costume was buried. **I** was buried here. **Dinah** set up the service. Now who was there?

9Clark: Well... obviously, Dinah —

10Ollie: That I know. Her and Roy told me they spoke. I wanna know who else...

PAGE THREE

Panel One: Same shot as Panel Five from the previous page, but this time Clark is scratching behind his head. He's a bit uncomfortable.

1Clark: I don't know — Wally, Diana, J'onn...

2Ollie: Them I expected.

3Clark: Arthur, Ray, even Snapper... most of the League was there.

4Ollie: Do you have any photos?

Panel Two: We see Clark, this time wearing an Of-Course-Not face.

5Clark: Photos? Of course I don't have photos.

Panel Three: We see Ollie raising a quizzical eyebrow.

6Cap: He's always been a terrible liar. Doesn't have it in him.

7Ollie: I was once a well-known millionaire, Clark. You're telling me the paparazzi didn't send anyone?

Panel Four: Clark looks away sheepishly.

Panel Five: Ollie grins wider.

8Ollie: Hand 'em over — I can take it.

Panel Six: Clark reaches into his coat for an envelope.

9Clark: Perry bought them as a personal favor. Naturally, they never ran.

10Clark: I've been through this, Ollie — it's harder than you think.

Panel Seven: From Clark's POV. We see his hand reaching out as he hands Ollie the envelope. Ollie's starting to look a bit nervous, though he's trying to hide it. Even he's not that tough.

11Ollie: Trust me...

PAGE FOUR

Panel One:

1Cap: "... I'll be fine."

2Cap: It's the biggest lie I've told since I've been back.

The panel is from Ollie's POV — a close-up of a black-and-white photo from his funeral. We can see his thumb in the top right corner, holding the photo. The photo itself (and the next few photos) were supposed to be taken by someone who was hiding at another location, so it's like they're looking down on this sad crowd scene. Each photo will have a few people in it — all of them out of their costumes and instead in dark suit and tie. Obviously, they look sad.

THE KEY is that there will be six photos on this page. PHIL — if you want, I thought it'd be interesting if the photos were all separate, with their white borders on the edges, but that they almost fit together to form a huge shot of the people at Oliver's grave on his funeral day. The grave can be in the center of the page, so that we have crowds on the right and left side of the grave. Up to you if you think it'll work visually. Also, if you do the big photos, please make sure there're other people whose heads we can't see, or are cut off, since obviously this isn't EVERYONE who was there.

In this first photo, we see Dinah (in short black hair) crying on Roy's shoulder. We can barely see her from behind. Behind Roy is Connor, Wally West (Flash), Dick Grayson consoling Donna Troy, and next to them is Garth (Tempest).

THESE NEXT THREE CAPTIONS SHOULD RUN TOWARD THE BOTTOM OF THE FIRST PHOTO:

3Cap: Just the **sight** of Dinah crying claws through my heart.

4Cap: Thank God Roy was there for **her**.

5Cap: And that Dick, Donna, and Wally were there for **him**.

Panel Two:

Grave-site photo of Clark, Diana (Wonder Woman), Arthur (Aquaman), Ray Palmer (Atom), J'onn (in his private detective look), and Hawkman (in his old Katar Hawkworld uniform). In the corners we also see other minor heroes if you want to include them like Tim Drake and Impulse.

6Cap: Diana, Arthur, Ray, J'onn... and of course Carter.

7Cap: Seeing them together makes me miss Hal and Barry.

Panel Three:

Grave-site photo of Ralph Dibny (Elongated Man), his wife Sue, Vic Sage (the Question), Mari (Vixen), and Zatanna.

8Cap: Ralph, Sue, Vic, Mari, even Zee showed up...

Panel Four: Grave-site photo of Carol Ferris, Pieface, John Stewart, Maxwell Stein (the old guy from the Green Arrow first miniseries — he looks like how Frank Miller drew Alfred in Dark Knight), and Northwind (from Infinity Inc. with a mohawk).

9Cap: Carol, Pieface, John, Max — bless him — and Northwind, representing his godmother...

Panel Five: Grave-site photo of Jefferson Pierce (Black Lightning — yes, Black Lightning), Pat Dugan (Stripesy), Lucius Fox (from Batman). There're less people in this one to make room for the word balloons below:

10Cap: Jeff, Pat, Lucius...

11Ollie (off panel): So Bats didn't come?

12Clark (off panel): He was there.

13Ollie: But he's not in the—

14Clark: Trust me — I looked. He was there.

15Cap: I was hoping it'd give me closure. It does.

16Cap: There's something about knowing your friends were there for you.

Panel Six: Grave-site photo of Ted Knight (Starman I), Alan Scott, Jay Garrick, Eddie Fyers, and Thomas Blake (Cat-Man), who is looking around, away from the funeral. (See Blake physical description later in the script). Blake wears a dark suit, but it's poorly fitted. He stands back and apart from the crowd.

Note: the next two captions (17 & 18) should run toward the top of this panel.

17Cap: Seeing Ted, Alan, and Jay actually makes me proud.

18Cap: And seeing Eddie brings back the memories.

19Cap (this cap should run toward the bottom): Of course, that's not half as weird as seeing someone I don't recognize.

PAGE FIVE

Panel One: A tighter shot of panel six from the previous page. Now we see only Thomas Blake. He's clearly not mourning. He doesn't look dangerous — just like he's searching for someone.

1Clark (off panel): What's wrong?

Panel Two: We see Ollie holding up the photo and pointing to Blake.

1Ollie: Any idea who this is?

Panel Three: Ollie watches as Clark examines the photo.

2Clark: You don't know him?

3Ollie: Not a chance.

4Clark: You sure?

5Ollie: This was a private ceremony, Clark. I know every single person there. Except this guy.

Panel Four: We see Clark again looking down at the photo.

6Cap: He knows I'm getting agitated. Naturally, he doesn't break a sweat.

7Cap: I don't even know if he **can** sweat.

8Clark: Maybe he's a former employee. Someone from the old Queen Fund?

9Ollie: C'mon, look at the guy's reaction. Does he look like someone who's mourning?

Panel Five: Even closer up on the black and white photo of Thomas Blake. He's clearly looking away, searching...

Panel Six: A thin long, rectangular panel. Clark looks to his right.

Panel Seven: A thin long, rectangular panel. Clark looks to his left.

Panel Eight: Same shot as the other two (but a bit taller panel) as Clark looks at us.

10Clark: If it makes you feel better, he's nowhere in a twenty-mile radius.

PAGE SIX

Panel One: Ollie stares at Clark, his jaw off-center.

1Ollie: Sometimes you're real creepy, y'know that?

Panel Two: Clark looks diagonally upward, like he's startled by a noise. Ollie's confused.

2Clark: Shhh...

3Clark: Did you hear that?

4Ollie: Hear what?

Panel Three: Thin long panel of Clark and Ollie again facing each other, but we no longer see the grave in the shot. Now, Clark is in full Superman costume.

5Clark: 27.3 miles away, a 147-pound woman tripped on a red plastic squeaky toy and smashed her head on the corner of an antique glass coffee-table.

6Ollie: Really?

Panel Four: Pull in a little more on Superman and Ollie facing each other.

7Clark: Actually, no.

8Clark: But there is an earthquake in Ecuador.

Panel Five: Close-up head shot of Supes. He's got on a full grin, no teeth showing, but clearly pleased with his joke.

Panel Six: Superman is taking off, and all we see are the tops of his boots next to Ollie's head as Ollie refuses to look up.

9Cap: I wanna hate him, but he doesn't make it easy.

10Superman: I should fly...

11Superman: But just so you know, it really is great to have you back, Ollie.

12Ollie: Yeah, yeah — get outta my face.

13Superman: Listen, if you need any help with the —

14Ollie: I'll be fine, Big Blue. Go save the world.

Panel Seven: Same shot, but now all we see are the toes of Superman's boots and Ollie is looking down at the photo.

14Cap: Of course, some things never change.

15Superman: Just do me a favor, Ollie.

16Superman: When you track this guy down...

17Superman: Keep it clean.

PAGE SEVEN

For this scene, we're in Oliver Queen's apartment, more specifically, his bedroom. The place is already a bit of a mess. The bed is undone. The nightstand is next to it. In the background, there's a window that looks out into an alley and the sky. It's day, but the sun is fading into night. Not dark yet, but getting there.

Panel One: Tight close-up on Green Arrow's pointer and thumb (he's in full costume, minus the mask) as he picks up a yellow (?) round earring from the nightstand. It's Black Canary's — the one she talks to Oracle on.

1Cap: I've always said, you don't need heat-vision to fight your battles.

2Cap: All it takes is stubbornness... and a few friends in the right places.

Panel Two: Full body shot of GA standing next to the bed, and the window is on our left, on the left side of the page. He's holding the earring to his lips (like he's talking into it), and he's turned toward the window. In his other hand, he's got the photo with Thomas Blake in it. Note: I wrote this as Ollie and Oracle but leave it to you whether you want to draw Oracle or not.

3Ollie: Hello, hello — anyone there?

4Oracle: This is Oracle.

5Ollie: Oracle, it's Ollie.

6Oracle: Ollie? *Ollie*, Ollie?

Panel Three: Same shot of Ollie talking to the earring, but with a grin on his face.

7Ollie: The one and only. Ain't you surprised?

8Oracle: I find info for a living, old man. I knew you were back fifteen minutes after you first hit the streets. Now what're you doing on Dinah's line?

Panel Four: Ollie looks down at his unmade and messy bed anxiously.

9Ollie: She left her earrings on my... uh... on my kitchen table.

10Oracle: Don't lie, Oliver. That microphone was on all night. I heard everything. **Everything**.

11Oracle: Trick arrows, my rear end.

Panel Five: Same shot as Ollie blushes red.

12Ollie: You serious?

13Oracle: Jeez, Ollie — Clark was right — you **have** gotten gullible in your old age.

Panel Six: Same shot, but Ollie looks mad.

14Ollie: Listen, you gonna help me or not?

15Oracle: Just tell me what you need.

PAGE EIGHT

Panel One: Ollie holds up the Blake photo from his funeral and examines it.

16Ollie: I'm lookin' for a positive I.D. on a guy in a photo.

17Oracle: Now you're singing my song. Just hold it up to the window — and don't block it with your fingers. I'll have one of my satellites scan it from space.

Panel Two: Same shot, but Ollie holds it up to the window.

18Ollie: You can do that?

19Oracle: Oh, Ollie — such a sucker. *"Don't block it with your fingers."* God, you're worse than Firestorm.

Panel Three: Similar shot as Ollie quickly pulls the photo down.

20Ollie: I knew you were joking on that one...

21Oracle: Sure you did.

22Oracle: Just send me a scan. I'll walk you through it. Now how fast do you need the I.D.?

Panel Four: Same shot, but pull in closer on Ollie. He's nervous.

23Ollie: Lightspeed.

Panel Five: There a contemplative shot of Barbara. (Phil, please show her here). We see she's worried about him. And she knows something's up.

Panel Six: Same shot, but pull in closer on Barbara.

24Oracle: It's that important to you?

Panel Seven: Close-up shot of just Blake in the photo.

25Ollie: No games. This one's personal.

26Oracle: I'm on it — don't even sweat.

28Oracle: I'll call you as soon as I know something.

PAGE NINE

These next 6 panels should all be the same size (they're all of Ollie out on the streets and rooftops, making INCREDIBLE shots with the bow and arrow). They have the word "Nothing" at the bottom of each to show how unimpressed Ollie is — all of this pales to him getting the info from Oracle. Feel free to places obstacles (i.e., telephone lines, traffic lights, other cars) in the way as the shots get harder.

[Sean — Note: I think all the captions should be at the bottom of the panels for this page.]

Panel One: We see Ollie from behind just as he's fired a shot that is now through the hand of a mugger who's holding a purse. The old woman who owns the purse is still on the ground.

1Cap: Nothing.

Panel Two: Again, Ollie from behind, but this time the shot/arrow is through a glass window in an apartment — and inside the apartment, the arrow has a guy in a wife-beater shirt pinned to the wall by his arm, which is still raised in the air holding an iron. The woman he's beating is cowering on the floor.

2Cap: Nothing.

Panel Three: From the ground, we're looking up at a burning building. Ollie has fired an arrow with a rope tied to it up to the fourth floor and a black man and his wife are now climbing down the rope. Note: This is NOT an arrowline. In fact, we see it's makeshift — Ollie has tied the rope to his arrow for the shot.

3Cap: Nothing.

Panel Four: This is Ollie stopping Angleman with a single shot. The shot went through the side window of a car, out the other side window, and pinned Angleman's triangular weapon to the wall. The weapon is shattered, with computer wires dangling out of the weapon. And a second arrow has pinned Angleman as well, straight through his hand. He's screaming toward the air and clenching both fists, though we see no sound balloons. Up the street, two policemen are frozen in place — hands at their sides, feet locked together — just coming out of the immobilized state Angleman had them in.

4Cap: Nothing.

Panel Five: This is the best shot of all — we see a white man in mid-fall toward the sidewalk. Two arrows are in his legs — one in each of his Achilles' heels. In mid-air a few feet in front of him is a swaddled black baby, pinned to the wall by an arrow, so he doesn't fall. The baby's African American parents are racing up the block, chasing the man.

5Cap: Nothing.

Panel Six: We see Ollie from behind, standing on the edge of a gargoyle, overlooking the city. He holds a bow in one hand, but no arrows nocked.

6Oracle (as just a radio-voice): Ollie, it's Barbara. I got the I.D.

7Cap: Gratification.

Panel One: Similar shot of Ollie on the gargoyle as he's sharpening an arrow against a small piece of grindstone. Again, this will be a conversation with Oracle, so we see Dinah's yellow earring pinned to GA's lapel. Phil, I think it's better here if we don't see Oracle in the scene (just because there's lots of talking), but I leave that up to you.

1Ollie: Talk to me.

2Oracle (off-panel): The guy's name is Thomas Blake.

3Ollie: Should that ring a bell?

Panel Two: Close-up of the arrow being sharpened.

4SFX (in tiny letters by the arrow): Skrrrch

Panel Three: Closer-up of Ollie on the gargoyle.

5Oracle (off-panel): What's that noise?

6Ollie: Just sharpening arrows. These things don't grow on trees, y'know.

7Oracle (off-panel): For a rich guy, Queen — you're a cheap $!#%.

Panel Four: Closer-up of the arrow being sharpened.

8Ollie: Just tell me who Blake is.

9SFX: Skrrrch.

Panel Five: Same shot, closer-up on Ollie's hands.

10Oracle (off-panel): Pathetic scrub villain. Used to put on a cape. Called himself Cat-Man.

11Ollie: Cat-Man?

Panel Six: Even closer-up on Ollie's hands as he sharpens the arrow. His finger slices across the point and he's bleeding.

12Ollie: Aaaaa — damn!

13Oracle (off-panel): What's wrong?

Panel Seven: From the POV of the arrow, we see Oliver staring down at us. He's holding his exposed finger and we still see some blood run down his other still-gloved hands.

14Ollie: Nothing — I'm fine.

15Ollie: So, Cat-Man...

PAGE ELEVEN

Panel One: We see just the black and white photo of Blake, as it's held by Ollie's thumb.

1Oracle (off-panel): I'm not sure who he's ripping off — Catwoman or Bats — but either way, he gets an F for originality.

2Oracle (off-panel): His background is just as clichéd. Used to be rich... a big-game hunter type. Too bad he's also a compulsive gambler. When he lost all his money, he set out to rob banks **and** get his rear-end handed to him by our favorite Dark Knight on a regular basis.

Panel Two: Same shot of the photo, but now there's a drop of Ollie's blood on it, next to Blake's face.

3Ollie: I still don't get it... *Cat-Man*?

4Oracle (off-panel): Oh, it's worse than that. He went whole hog: Made a Cat-A-Rang... a Cat-Line... even a Cat-Mobile. How pathetic is that?

Panel Three: Ollie, stone-cold as he stares down at the photo. He's not laughing.

Panel Four: Same shot of the photo in Panel Three, but now closer-up on the drop of Ollie's blood, next to Blake's face.

5Oracle (off-panel): Ollie, you okay there?

6Ollie: He was at my funeral.

7Oracle (off-panel): What?

Panel Five: Ollie lowers his head, as if he's almost embarrassed.

8Ollie: That's where the picture's from. Blake was at my **funeral**. Even if he's a laughingstock... a villain... a **villain** was at my funeral.

Panel Six: The blood is still dripping from Ollie's exposed finger.

9Oracle: What was Cat-Man doing at your funeral?

10Ollie: That's what I'm trying to find out.

11Oracle: Ollie, this isn't funny.

Panel One: Shot of the side of Ollie's head. We see the first drop of sweat running down his temple (from the blood on his finger in the last panel, we now transition to the sweat on his temple).

1Ollie: You think I don't realize that? He saw all my family. My friends...

2Ollie: He saw Dinah.

3Oracle (off-panel): Ollie, he saw Clark.

Panel Two: Tight, tight, tight close-up of Blake in the black and white photo — so close it almost looks sinister.

Panel Three: Pull in tighter on the sweat on Ollie's temple.

4Oracle: (off-panel): You have any idea what he can do with that information?

5Ollie: Just tell me how to find him.

Panel Four: Shot of only the gargoyle Ollie's standing on.

6Oracle (Off-panel): I-I can't. Cat-Man's invisible. In witness protection. Apparently, he played snitch on Monsieur Mallah.

Panel Five: Ollie on the rooftop in silhouette, staring at the city below.

7Ollie: You're telling me **you** can't find someone in witness protection?

Panel Six: Close on the sweat as it runs down Ollie's neck (or his mask — your choice).

8Oracle (Off-panel): Not this time, Ollie. Amanda Waller hid this one herself. Whatever Cat-Man had on Mallah, it was *big*.

9Oracle (Off-panel): Amanda Waller big.

10Ollie (Off-panel): Or Clark Kent big.

Panel Seven: Even closer-up on the photo of Blake with Ollie's blood. It's grainy at this point.

11Oracle (Off-panel): Ollie, we should call—

12Ollie: I can handle it.

13Oracle (Off-panel): Then you better find someone in the government. What about trying the other guy in the photo — Eddie whatshisname...?

Panel Eight: Shift a little over on the black and white photo, so we see Eddie Fyers now as well.

14Cap: No. My Eddie days are over.

15Cap: Fortunately for me, when it comes to the government... there's still one card to play...

PAGE THIRTEEN

We're in Oliver's apartment, in the foyer, right where you walk in.

Panel One: A shot of Oliver's front door as a manila envelope comes sliding under it.

1Cap: Three hours later, an envelope comes sliding under my door.

2Cap: The boy — as always — comes through.

Panel Two: Ollie, dressed as GA, but without the mask or hat, opens the flap of the folder and inside is a sheet of paper with the following words written in cursive handwriting on it:

3Words on the paper: Open the door, genius.

4Cap: Aw, no.

Panel Three: Ollie opens the door and we see Roy (Arsenal) in jeans, a black T-shirt that says the words "Great Frog" (which is Roy's old band), and a three-quarter length black leather jacket. His Arsenal sunglasses are up on his head. He's holding a thin army duffelbag at his side, which holds the bow and arrows. In his other hand, he's holding a blue file folder, with a red file folder peeking out of it.

5Ollie: What're you doing? I told you not to come.

Panel Four: Roy walking into the house.

6Roy: Yeah, well... you also called me up in the middle of the night, yelled me out of bed, then asked me to find Cat-Man by calling in every last favor I had since the day I left Checkmate.

7Roy: By the way, nice to see you too.

Panel Five: Ollie's looking nervous. He runs his hand through his hair. He's trying to play cool.

8Ollie: I'm telling you... it really is nothing.

Panel Six: Roy from the chest up. He's got his arms crossed, staring at his old mentor.

Panel Seven: Same shot, a bit closer up on Roy.

9Roy: Do I still look thirteen to you?

PAGE FOURTEEN

Panel One: Ollie laughs like it's hysterical. He heads downstairs to the basement, where all his arrows and bows are. As Roy follows, he isn't amused. They can be in silhouette going down the stairs, except for the red folder in the blue one (Phil: I also use this in panel four, so I leave it to you if you want to repeat it, or where it works better).

1Ollie: Thirteen... HA! Nice one...

2Roy: It's not funny, Ollie. This is a red file inside in a blue one. The red means *FBI*. Know what the blue means?

Panel Two: Ollie's at a worktable in the basement, where all the arrows are laid out across a table. They're all regular arrows. No trick ones.

3Ollie: I swear to you, Roy — it's just a dumb case. It's Cat-Man for chrissakes! *Cat-Man*!

Panel Three: Again, we see Roy, arms crossed, staring down his mentor.

Panel Four: Thin, long rectangular panel. Silhouette of Ollie and Roy facing each other. Roy is clearly a bit shorter. It's all black, except for the blue file folder Roy holds out between them — and inside the blue folder is a red one.

4Roy: Ollie, we all wear our masks. And the moment you start making jokes is the exact same moment you're officially nervous.

5Roy: Trust me, you need more than just what's in this file.

Panel Five: Ollie looks down at his old ward. He's scared. And he knows Roy's right.

Panel Six: Ollie lets out a timid grin.

Ollie: You bring your good sneakers?

Panel Seven: Shot of just Roy's chest as he lifts up his Great Frog shirt and reveals his red costume underneath.

Roy: And my lucky underwear.

[BOB: Can we make sure that this page (15) is a right-hand page, so the reader can't see the next page (16) until they turn the page?]

Panel One: We're at Roy's POV — staring at Ollie, who's standing behind the worktable. We see Ollie reach down into a small drawer of the worktable.

1Ollie: Good — then do me one last favor...

Panel Two: Ollie hands Roy a thin rectangular box with a green bow on it.

2Ollie: I was saving this for a later date, but... well, here you go...

Panel Three: Roy lifts the lid off and we see — from Roy's POV — what's inside: a red mask, *a la* his Speedy days.

Panel Four: Roy looks up at Oliver, holding the mask.

3Roy: A mask?

Panel Five: Ollie's already started to collect a fistful of arrows in preparation for their outing. He's proud about the gift.

4Ollie: Keep your voice down. If Mia even sees it, she'll jump in the bathtub and start calling herself Aqualad.

5Roy: Why do I need a mask?

Panel Six: Close-up on Ollie as he puts on his own mask.

6Ollie: Trust me. You need it.

Panel Seven: Roy pulls the sunglasses on his head down across his face.

7Roy: You saying you don't like my sunglasses?

Panel Eight: Closer up on Ollie, who's putting on his Robin Hood hat and now wearing a wicked grin.

8Ollie: The eighties are over, Speedy. Welcome to the future.

9Roy: Did you just call me "Speedy"?

Panel Nine: All we see is the mask in Roy's hands. We're not sure what he's going to do.

10Ollie (off-panel): C'mon, it's not like I'm asking you to wear the hat.

11Ollie (off-panel): Do your old man a favor and put it on. It'll make you feel young again...

PAGE SIXTEEN

Panel One: Big splash page of Green Arrow and Arsenal (though with the red mask on, he looks more like an older Speedy). In fact, Phil, the more Speedy and less Arsenal he looks, the better. GA has his green longbow, while Arsenal has his red compound bow. Forget that crossbow nonsense he sometimes carries. This is Arsenal with a bow and a quiver full of red arrows.

1CAP: "... younger than you've felt in a long time."

Panel Two: Rectangular panel at the bottom of the page. Cat-Man's house in San Francisco. We look up at a gorgeous house on the corner of one of San Francisco's most expensive neighborhoods. It's big, imposing, and instantly conveys serious cash. Not a cheesy mansion with columns, but a big, beautiful "home." Phil, think of the house from Mrs. Doubtfire, or Pacific Heights — a huge Victorian with big bay windows. The house sits on the corner of the block. (What's sadder — me referencing Pacific Heights or Mrs. Doubtfire?)

2Cap: San Francisco, California

3Cap: According to Roy's file, the home of Thomas Blake.

PAGE SEVENTEEN

Panel One: We pull out some more and see the backs of GA and Arsenal in full costumes as they look up at the beautiful house.

1Roy: This may be the one time when the term "fat-cat" is actually appropriate.

2Ollie: It's not funny, Roy. Blake was at my funeral.

3Ollie: He saw you. And Dinah. And Connor.

4Ollie: Everyone I care about.

Panel Two: They're heading up the front paved path toward the front steps of the house. The shrubs and lawn are perfectly trimmed.

5Roy: That doesn't mean he knows who we are.

6Roy: Besides, it's **Cat-Man**. He had a Catamaran!

Panel Three: POV through the keyhole from inside the house. GA and Arsenal are stepping up the front steps, toward the front porch.

7Ollie: That doesn't mean he's a joke.

8Roy: You're defending his Catamaran?

Panel Four: Same shot, only closer.

9Ollie: We used to have an Arrowplane and a yellow submarine.

10Roy: Now you're making fun of *our* weapons?

Panel Five: Reverse the shot, so we see what Ollie and Roy see (the front door and keyhole) as they approach.

11Ollie: Only that compound bow you're carrying.

12Roy: I told you, it gives me more power.

13Roy: Now did you bring the lockpick-arrow?

Panel Six: POV from Ollie — Ollie's foot as he's about to kick the front door open

14Ollie: Yeah, I got it right here.

15SFX: Whuump

PAGE EIGHTEEN

Panel One: POV from just inside the house. We see the door fly open and smash against the wall.

1SFX: Crash

Panel Two: Roy and Ollie rush inside, arrows and bows drawn, ready for anything.

2Ollie: Don't underestimate him.

Panel Three: Close-up on just their faces. They have a SHOCKED look on. They can't believe what they see.

3Roy: It's impossible...

Panel Four: POV of Ollie and Arsenal. Across the floor, all we see are four adorable puppies.

4SFX (placed by the dogs): Yip Yip Yip Yip

5Roy (Off-panel): He's got dogs.

6Roy (Off-panel): Cat-Man has dogs.

Panel Five: POV from the dogs. A thin rectangular panel. Arsenal is looking down, laughing at the scene. GA looks up as he hears something.

7SFX (placed in the far right corner, closer to GA): Creak

8Ollie: What was **that**?

PAGE NINTEEN

Phil, I'd love if this page could play like a movie with long rectangular boxes for all the panels (can you tell I like those?)

Panel One: Cat-Man/Thomas Blake is dressed in a midnight blue rich guy's bathrobe, with light blue boxer shorts on underneath. Under the robe, he's got his old yellow-and-red Cat-Man shirt on. Just the shirt under the robe — not the cape or anything else. The years have not been kind, though. Blake is heavier now. Five o'clock shadow, losing his hair, an extra chin, and a bit jowly. But not a bumbling moron. More like a (ahem) fat cat who can afford to let himself go a little. He's got a **Cat-A-Rang** in his hand and he's about to throw it.

1Blake: Don't move!

Panel Two: GA and Arsenal move. Fast. It's from the POV of the dogs, so we see them just as two arrows leave their two bows. Both Roy and GA have two fingers (pointer and middle) straight out as the arrows are loosed. They're twins of each other. Their bow-strings are still vibrating with movement.

2SFX (small): Twang

3SFX (small): Twang

Panel Three: Blake is pinned to the wall by the two arrows. The **red** arrow pins him by the **robe** to the wall (**just through his clothes, not his shoulder**). The green arrow pins him by the left **shoulder**. Some blood spills out of the shoulder wound.

4Blake: Uhh! Son of a—!

Panel Four: Same POV as panel two, but here, Ollie and Arsenal look at each other.

5Ollie & Arsenal (simultaneously in one balloon): You missed.

Panel Five: Blake is pinned to the wall. Now he's pissed, though. His teeth are gritted. He looks angrily at us.

6Blake: G-Get... get outta my house... Q-Queen!

Panel One: Ollie and Roy are standing in front of Blake as he's pinned to the wall. His gut hangs out a bit below his Cat-Man shirt. We can see a TV on in the background.

1Blake: M-My arm...

2Ollie: You're watching TV in your old costume? You have any idea how sad that is?

3Roy (in small tiny letters): Not half as sad as owning those dogs.

Panel Two: Closer-up on Ollie as he leans in toward Blake from Blake's left-hand side. The green arrow in Blake's shoulder is between them. Blake now looks confused — and in pain — the sweat's all over his forehead.

4Ollie: Why were you at my funeral?

5Blake: What're you talking about?

Panel Three: Closer-up on Ollie as he's about to grab the feathers on the back of the arrow in Blake's shoulder. Blake looks petrified.

7Ollie: Know what arrows are made of, Blake? Most are wood or fiberglass.

8Ollie: This one's aluminum. Wanna see why?

Panel Four: Ollie bends the arrow upwards about ten degrees. It's still in Blake's arm and the wall.

9Blake: Aaaaaaaahhh!

Panel Five: Same shot, but close-up on Blake's shoulder and the shaft of the arrow, which is now curved in a ten-degree grin.

10Ollie: That's ten degrees, Blake. Imagine the pain when we pull it out.

11Blake: You **know**! Y-You already **know**!

Panel Six: Close-up shot of just Ollie's face screaming straight at us (*a la* the old sixties shots of when he was really pissed off).

12Ollie: Last time, fat-man.

13Ollie: Why. Were. You. **There**?

Panel One: Small panel. Close-up on Blake, who's about to pass out.

1Blake: I-In my p-p-purse. T-The leather purse... coffee-table...

Panel Two: Small panel. Shot from Oliver POV, looking down at Ollie's gloved hands rummaging through the purse. There's money, a File-o-Fax, lots of papers...

2Ollie: This better not be a stall tactic...

Panel Three: Close-up on an unfolded piece of paper. We just see the top part of the page, where there's cursive handwriting across the top that's underlined and says in big letters: <u>Funeral Instructions</u>.

3Handwritten-letter (in a different cursive than Roy's — something more masculine; or maybe it's even printed, but it looks like handwritten printing, if that makes sense): <u>Funeral Instructions</u>

4CAP: I find it immediately.

Panel Four: Close-up of just Ollie's eyes (and his mask). They're wide with shock.

5Ollie: Oh, no...

Panel Five: Now we see a close-up that's similar to Panel Three, but now we can only read the signature at the bottom of the letter. It says: Sincerely, Oliver Queen.

6Signature at the bottom of the letter: Sincerely, Oliver Queen

7CAP: It's hard to miss your own handwriting.

Panel Six: (Phil, if the page is too cramped, this is the panel you can cut. I like it, but up to you.) Same shot, but, close-up real tight on the inky words: Oliver Queen.

Panel Seven: Ollie's still looking at the letter, completely shaken; Blake's completely in pain, and Roy's completely confused. In the bottom corner of the panel (closest to us), a small black cloud <u>barely</u> starts to wisp through.

8Ollie: I-I don't believe it.

9Blake: H-He said... he said you knew...

10Roy: Whattya mean? Who's *h e*? Who're you talking about?

Panel Eight: Similar shot, but now Ollie, Roy, and Blake all look up, shocked and surprised, toward us. The black cloud wisps a bit more on the edge of the panel.

11Shade (off-panel): Oh, who doesn't love a dramatic entrance?

PAGE TWENTY-TWO

Splash page. Shade (from Starman) is standing there complete in black hat, black coat, black pants. We see it from Cat-Man's POV, so we also see just the razor arrow-tips of GA's and Arsenal's arrows (one from the right side of the page, and one from the left).

1Shade: Nice to see you again, Oliver.

2Shade: It's been far too long.

Credits Box on the last page:

THE ARCHER'S QUEST
Chapter One — Photograph
Brad Meltzer: Writer
Phil Hester: Penciller
Ande, Sean, Bob, the whole family...

We're all so hard-core, now.

We're all tough-as-nails, chip-on-the-shoulder readers, screaming for things like "realism" and "maturity" in the portrayal of our super-heroes. We want our Bad Guys to be oh so very vile, and our Good Guys to be, perhaps, not so good after all. A little more of the anti-hero, if you please; a little more of the tortured, brooding vigilante plagued by neuroses, and a lot less of the hands-on-the-hips, eyes-to-the-horizon optimism of yesteryear.

There are good reasons for this, I suppose. We live in a world where Golden Age idealism and solutions just won't hold water, no matter how much we may wish it were otherwise. We live in a world where Silver Age adventures take our suspension of disbelief and bend it until it snaps into slivers. We live in a world where, it seems, every one of our real heroes has been revealed as a drug addict, or a wife beater, or a pedophile, or worse.

So comics have evolved, and super-hero comics in particular have become grittier and meaner and darker and, arguably more realistic (inasmuch as stories where the main character is, say, the sole survivor of a dying planet who can leap tall buildings in a single bound can make a claim to realism). Certainly, many super-hero books *have* become more mature, and many of those books are the better for it.

And sentimentalism has become a very dirty word.

This is, in part, why *The Archer's Quest* is so very remarkable. In an age of super-heroes suffering from everything from marital discord to blatant self-loathing, Meltzer, Hester, and Parks have together crafted a story that manages to successfully mine the purity of yesterday's super-heroism without failing the expectations of today.

The story of Ollie and Roy's road trip — deliberately evocative of Dennis O'Neil and Neal Adams's *Hard-Traveling Heroes* — could have easily become a syrupy car wreck on the road to yesteryear. But instead, guided by Brad Meltzer's able hands, it becomes at once a journey into both the past and the future. Ollie's memories of days and friends long gone, of trick arrows and bloodless fights, are gently, even delicately reinvigorated with deceptive purity and innocence.

And the neatest trick of it is that, while Meltzer crafts this trip down memory lane, Hester and Park never once allow us to forget where we are now; or more crucially, where *Ollie* is. Back from the dead, still trying to anchor himself to the living, and still grappling with all the pain that his resurrection has brought. Look to the moment when Ollie cuts himself while speaking with Oracle, the strain of the man behind the mask, and you'll see what I mean; look to the fight with Solomon Grundy, the tactile savagery of the combat, and you'll see what I mean. While Ollie talks about the fun of the old days, Hester and Park steadfastly remind us that those days are gone forever, for better or for worse.

It's hard to explain the ultimate beauty of *The Archer's Quest*, its success as both narrative and art, without betraying the ending. Suffice it to say that, in the space of six closing pages, Meltzer, Hester, and Parks execute one of the most elegant narrative turns it has ever been my pleasure to read, and they do it with the same gentle touch that has graced every page that has come before, without faltering and without fail.

And yes, it *is* sentimental. But it is a sentimentalism that is perfectly appropriate, never self-indulgent, never self-aware, and, most important, never self-loathing. It is the *right* ending, reached with inevitable purpose, absolutely proper, and emotionally true.

There is nothing so rare as the beauty of a story well told. Very few of them are, these days.

You are about to read a thing of beauty.

— Greg Rucka
Portland, Oregon
July, 2003

Like Brad Meltzer, Greg Rucka got his start writing prose, notably the Atticus Kodiak mystery novels. He then segued into comics with Oni Press's White Out and joined DC Comics in time to be a major contributor to the "No Man's Land" storyline in the Batman titles. Since then he has written for DC, Marvel, and Oni. For DC Comics, Greg has become the current writer for Wonder Woman. His newest novel is A Fistful of Rain, published in summer 2003 by Bantam Books.

THE STARS OF THE
DC UNIVERSE
CAN ALSO BE FOUND IN THESE BOOKS:

DCU0011